Sept. 16, 1993

Public Relations Review Copy —

with all good wishes!

[signature]

Fifty Years Ahead Of The News

A Lifetime of Practical Public Relations Experience

John E. Sattler

Fellow, Public Relations Society of America
Member Emeritus, International Public Relations Association

Book design by Tucker Worthington
The Studio, Mansfield, Pennsylvania 16933

A Whistlestop/SI book, published by Sattler International
2525 Waite Avenue, Kalamazoo, Michigan 49008, U.S.A.

First Edition, September 1993

Printed in the United States of America

Library of Congress Catalog Card Number 93-92750

ISBN 0-9636987-0-2

For Elinore, whose inspiration, love and encouragement helped make possible whatever I have achieved in life. This is her book as much as it is mine.

reface

Over the years I've had occasion to discuss some of the incidents and experiences described in this book with friends and colleagues, and a number of them suggested putting them in a memoir.

Dr. David Lewis, professor of business history at the University of Michigan, said the same thing a year ago when I provided personal recollections for a post-World War II history of Ford Motor Company, which the university is under contract to produce, and which Dr. Lewis is writing.

And my wife, whose advice I respect, also encouraged me to record my experiences, if only for the entertainment and enlightenment of our own family.

What follows, then, is the end result of all those words of encouragement.

I have titled what I have written, "Fifty Years Ahead Of the News," because I have spent a good part of my life providing information or creating newsworthy events and happenings for newspapers, magazines, radio stations, television services, and other news- and information-gathering outlets to report to their readers, viewers and listeners.

Few people realize as they read, watch or listen to the events reported daily, that behind the editors, reporters, and TV anchor men and women, there is a veritable army of communicators — press agents, publicists, and public relations professionals who spend much of their daily lives trying to figure out ways to focus favorable attention on their employers, clients, communities, countries, or, occasionally, themselves.

These busy people are generators, handlers, and/or distributors of ideas, story suggestions, breaking news events, and sometimes even crises and unexpected disasters They are generally very helpful to the news outlets, but there are times, unfortunately when some who are less scrupulous will try to cover up, conceal, or avoid comment when things go wrong. It then becomes the job of the journalist and reporter to get behind the inertia, stonewalling or smoke screen to find out what is actually happening and to report it.

The media have their own way of dealing with those who bring discredit to the public relations and information services field. They also recognize and appreciate the efforts of countless dedicated, honest, and hardworking public relations "support troops" all over the world who are above reproach in credibility and performance.

I'm proud to have been in the latter group for more than half a century.

About The Author

John Edward Sattler was born in Williamsburg, Brooklyn, and grew up on Long Island. He attended Public Schools 115 and 133 in the Borough of Queens, Sewanhaka Central High School in Floral Park, and New York University in Manhattan in addition to post-graduate study at schools in various other locations. He spent most of his career in the field of public relations with Ford Motor Company, in New York and Michigan, a total of almost thirty-five years. He is married to the former Elinore Evelin Richter of Mineola, New York, and they observed their fifty-second wedding anniversary in February, 1993. They have five children and ten grandchildren, three adopted, from the Philippines and Nepal. They currently live in Kalamazoo, Michigan, and Hampton Bays, New York.

John Sattler has been in the communication field since 1937 and in the field of public relations since 1940. He is seventy-four years old and has provided volunteer public relations service to a wide range of organizations throughout his life. The world's two leading public relations professional groups, the Public Relations Society of America and the International Public Relations Association, have given him their highest honors for professional achievement, the Gold Anvil and Fellow status from PRSA and Member Emeritus status and a Golden World Award from IPRA. In its thirty-eight-year existence, IPRA has given ME status to only sixteen individuals, five of them from the United States.

John Sattler taught elementary and advanced public relations courses at Bernard Baruch School of Business, City College of New York, and has lectured widely on PR subjects in the United States, Indonesia, Japan, People's Republic of China, Africa, Europe and the Middle East. In 1988, the International Executive Service Corps presented its "Service to Country

Award" to him for his work as an IESC overseas volunteer, and he has been recognized for his volunteer efforts by a wide range of social and philanthropic organizations, including the Boy Scouts, Girl Scouts, American Heart Association, Salvation Army and Goodwill Industries. In 1991, the New York Chapter of the Public Relations Society of America presented its John Wiley Hill Award to him for "Outstanding Leadership in the Public Relations Profession."

He was a public relations information specialist with the United States Air Force during World War II, and is on inactive status with the rank of Major.

Acknowledgments

While virtually all of the content of this book is based on the author's personal observations, experiences, and recollections, it has been helpful to refer to additional sources of information for verification of dates and events. A principal source has been *The Public Image of Henry Ford* by Dr. David L. Lewis, published by Wayne State University Press, Detroit, Michigan. Also consulted were the Henry Ford Museum and the Ford Archives, located in Dearborn, Michigan; Jack O'Dwyer's *Public Relations Services Report* magazine; and various photographic services.

I am indebted to Ruth Tamburello, Ronkonkoma, New York, my sister-in-law, for typing the original manuscript; Sheran Lawton, of Mansfield, Pennsylvania, who suffered my ongoing editing while she was putting the manuscript on a disk; Tucker Worthington, also of Mansfield, my son-in-law, who is an accomplished artist and who handled all design, graphics and production requirements; and the inventors of the copying machine, without which, work of this type would be infinitely more frustrating and difficult.

My wife, Elinore, gave me room to breathe and to write, and our daughter, Sandra Jones, read the first draft and provided much-needed encouragement and critical comment.

Finally, Shirley Stone, wife of Bob Stone, my long-time PR colleague and close personal friend, provided her services as editor and advisor based on her many years as a professional editor, as did Dr. Lewis, whom I regard as the academic world's foremost authority on Ford Motor Company and Ford family history.

To all of them, I express deep appreciation.

Contents

Chapter I

ublic Relations?
t's Honest Work!"

Public relations has to be one of the most misunderstood, if not maligned, terms ever created. Fifty years ago, the words were rarely heard. Today, they pop up regularly on the evening newscasts, in print media and in everyday conversations. Everyone seems to know what they mean, but sometimes you wonder if anyone really knows what they mean.

"Ladies of the evening" often tell people they are in "public relations." The President of the United States announces a program or an action and is frequently accused of adopting a public relations ploy. The vice president puts an e on the word potato while monitoring a spelling bee and is said to have made a personal public relations boner. And Boris Yeltsin, the president of Russia, addressing the Congress of the United States, says the right things and is given a standing ovation for what some people called a PR coup.

The term has become a catchall, and too often for the wrong things or for the wrong reasons. It lends itself to anything and everything, and people often nod their heads knowingly when in response to the question, "What type of work do you do?" you reply "I'm in public relations."

Do they know what you are saying? More often than not, they don't. If you said, "I'm a doctor," lawyer, dentist, automobile mechanic, pharmacist, there would be instant understanding. But public relations? . . . only occasionally.

I've always enjoyed a story the late T. J. Ross, a veteran PR counselor, told about his wife and her understanding of public relations — or lack of understanding. Tom Ross was being recognized for his many community endeavors by a group at a luncheon in the Grand Ballroom of the Waldorf Astoria Hotel. As part of his response, he said he didn't think his wife actually understood what it was he did for a living, and he told a humorous story to illustrate it.

"My wife was attending a luncheon like this some years ago," he said, "When another guest asked what I did for a living, she replied, Tommy is in public relations."

"Public relations? What's that? she was asked. She hesitated for a moment, and replied, Well, I'm not really sure, but I do know it's honest work. My Tommy would never do anything wrong!"

The story, told many times, I'm sure, brought an appreciative laugh from the audience and a smile from Mrs. Ross, who no doubt was tired of hearing it. Yet it did have a message. Public relations is not simple to explain, and it is not always fully understood, even today, when many thousands of people earn their living in the field.

The public relations professional groups have had a difficult time trying to put together any simple explanation of what the term means and what the practice of public relations is all about. The same applies to the people who write and report on the field. The Public Relations Society of America, for example, which has more than fifteen thousand members throughout the United States, has adopted what it calls an "Official Statement on Public Relations." It contains more than three hundred words. In fact, it is not a definition, per se, but a wordy attempt to explain public relations in all its ramifications. The net result is stuffy and confusing, beginning with the paragraph: "Public relations helps our complex, pluralistic society to reach decisions and function more effectively by contributing to mutual understanding among groups and institutions. It serves to bring private and public policies into harmony."

The statement attempts to explain what the PR function encompasses and what skills are required to work in the field. It concludes: "In helping to define and implement policy, the public relations practitioner uses a variety of professional communication skills and plays an integrative role both within the organization and between the organization and the external environment."

It's a noble effort but clearly over the head of the average person. It's no wonder Mrs. Ross had trouble explaining what her husband did for a living.

Denny Griswold, one of the early reporters and editors in the PR field, created her own definition of public relations, which she used to promote her trade paper, *Public Relations News*. It reads: "PUBLIC RELATIONS is the management function which evaluates public attitudes, identifies the policies and procedures of an individual or an organization with the public interest, and plans and executes a program of action to earn public understanding and acceptance."

One of the simplest explanations I've ever heard was written by Terri Thompson, business and financial editor of *U.S. News and World Report*. In her book for children eight to twelve years of age, *Biz Kids Guide to Success*, Ms. Thompson states: "Public relations is the art of getting people to understand and like something."

Frankly, after more than fifty years in and around communication and public relations, I never understood why those of us in the field made it seem and sound involved and complicated, when so often it can be reduced to the simplest form of interpersonal relationships. Public relations, it seems to me, is simply what it says — relations with the public (good, bad, or indifferent) on the part of individuals, groups, organizations, corporations, governments, or whom-ever/ whatever.

There was a time when the term was rarely used by the average person, but today it has common usage, and you read or hear it applied almost daily to world leaders like Gorbachev, Bush, Clinton, Yeltsin, Mandela or to Dow Corning, General Motors, the government of Japan.

What do people think of these individuals or entities at any given point in time? Are they regarded favorably, unfavorably, passively, antagonistically?

Samuel Johnson said: "Intentions must be judged by acts."

All attitudes and opinions are subject to changing conditions, actions and mood swings on the part of individuals as well as the public at large, and they form the basis of what public relations is all about. In the simplest of terms, it is about the ebb and flow of public opinion, public approval and disapproval.

We all would like to have "good" public relations all of the time, but that is almost impossible to achieve. The best one can hope for is a good, respectable average. If we can achieve that for ourselves and those we represent, we are doing well considering the many possible pitfalls to good performance and good behavior under constantly changing conditions.

Changing circumstances can create a crisis for anyone, particularly consumer product organizations. Look what happened when poison was placed in some Tylenol capsules that were returned to display shelves and then sold to the public. That criminal action created a tremendous problem for Johnson and Johnson, the makers of Tylenol, and its public relations department. Quick action by management on the PR front resulted in alerting the buying public to the problem. The product was taken off the market, changed to prevent further tampering, and then reintroduced with new packaging. Within a relatively short period of time, Tylenol recovered from a major image and marketing setback and regained — in fact, improved — sales levels. Johnson and Johnson and its PR department were applauded for the manner in which the problem was recognized, announced to the public, and then handled in a forthright and reassuring manner.

Other organizations with similar crises have not been as fortunate. They either tried to ignore the situation, hoping the problem would go away or resolve itself, or dragged their feet in facing up to it. In that category, I think we can include Exxon's delayed and inept handling of the Alaskan oil spill from the tanker ship Exxon Valdes. Alaskans from the governor on down, and environmentalists and concerned people all over the world were incensed, and Exxon was widely criticized for its response. It was a major public relations setback for Exxon, and the incident continues to cause major problems for the company and its reputation.

Many organizations have experienced similar unexpected emergencies or disasters that left them with serious image problems — public relations problems. Among them are Union Carbide for its handling of a situation in Bhopal, India, when tanks containing highly toxic chemicals leaked and the escaping fumes killed or disabled large numbers of people living near a Union Carbide plant.

America's automobile companies have also had their share of problems over the years. General Motors became enmeshed in a major controversy with Ralph Nader in 1965 over the publication of Nader's book *Unsafe at Any Speed,* which dealt with deaths resulting from roll-overs of GM's Corvair cars. General Motors made the mistake of hiring private eyes to shadow Nader and had to apologize when its actions became public knowledge. The decision by GM legal staff to "try to get something on Nader" was a perfect example of poor judgment and management bungling. It backfired and humiliated the corporation. GM's chairman, Fred Donner, was out of the country at the time, but the president of GM, James Roche, was forced to acknowledge what GM had done and to apologize for it in Washington, D.C., in early 1966. The net result was a classic case of the worst kind of corporate public relations.

Forty years later, in a somewhat devastating déjà vu General Motors found itself the target of another potentially disastrous public relations situation when it was charged the company had put GM pickup truck owners at risk by placing gasoline tanks under side panels of those trucks. Critics of GM contended that more than 300 persons had become fatalities in side crashes that could have been avoided if the fuel tanks had been located behind the chassis frame, and not directly under the outside sheet metal of the vehicle, where it was said the tanks could explode on impact, causing serious fires.

GM challenged those assertions in court but was at a disadvantage in mounting a campaign to head off the growing volume of negative publicity. Then a remarkable thing happened that resulted in a major PR-plus for the company. NBC News, in an effort to dramatize an impact explosion, used an incendiary device to demonstrate ignition of the gasoline on impact, and GM was able to document what it charged was a rigged test. A mortified NBC management had to acknowledge tampering with the test demonstration and issued a prime time apology on its "Dateline NBC" show on which the initial faulty demonstration had been aired. GM then announced it had been vindicated. NBC was appropriately contrite, the NBC V.P. for news resigned, and the charges against GM lost much of their initial impact as doubts were created in the "court of public opinion," as to the right or wrong of the situation.

Only time will tell whether GM's position will be upheld long range from a legal as well as a public relations standpoint.

Several years ago, Lee Iacocca, chairman of the board of Chrysler Corporation, found himself and the company in a similarly awkward situation. It was revealed that some misguided employees had been turning back the odometers on company cars taken out of service and offered for sale as new products. Federal law prohibits such action, and it was an abject violation of the law — first denied by Chrysler and then admitted when it became painfully apparent that management had known what was going on. It was a major embarrassment, and a corporate public apology was made.

Ford Motor Company also had a serious problem when it was charged with engineering and design neglect following a series of fatal fires involving Pinto cars that were rear-ended in accidents. The accidents and some resulting deaths led to major litigation that gained worldwide attention. Those who sued said Ford, in a money-saving decision, had placed the gas tanks too far to the rear of the vehicle, and that they were easily punctured during a rear-end impact. Persons trapped in cars that caught fire often became fatalities or were seriously burned and disabled. Regardless of the corporate position that Ford had acted responsibly in its design production and marketing of the vehicle, a number of judgments were made in favor of victims or their families.

The human factor was overriding. Even though Ford's position was upheld in court, the company was judged guilty in the court of public opinion. Ford never apologized for what it considered a safe product placed at risk by human error and road hazards but settled each case on an individual basis. The image of the Pinto product suffered, however, and the overall result was a negative public relations experience no matter how well the company presented its story or how fairly that story was reported by the media.

More recently, the United Way of America received substantial negative attention when it became public knowledge that its president was not only receiving an inflated salary, flying in high-priced Concorde aircraft, and using an expensive New York apartment provided by United Way but also had allegedly arranged a high-paying position in a subsidiary of United Way for his son. Many UW contributors and UW affiliates all over the country found the actions unconscionable and self-serving. Within a short period of time following the revelations and the outpouring of criticism, the president, William Aramony, resigned and was replaced. His son also resigned his position, although he stated that he saw "no conflict of interest." Many UW affiliates, however, were threatening to withdraw their support and the drop in contributions to United Way throughout the country could have represented a major loss that would be felt for some time, though hopefully not permanently, in view of UW's unique public service role.

From the standpoint of personal public relations, Irish singer, Sinaed O'Connor, made few friends and caused an avalanche of negative reaction when she tore up a photograph of Pope John Paul during an appearance on the popular television show, "Saturday Night Live." She then left the country on an overseas trip, and when she returned weeks later to perform on a testimonial show for folk singer Bob Dylan, she was roundly booed and jeered by the audience and left the stage in tears. Tearing up the photograph of the Pope seemed intended to attract attention and cause controversy, but it resulted in an outpouring of criticism and rejection from people of all persuasions, religious and otherwise. It was a serious personal PR blunder that will be remembered for some time to come, and it should have been avoided. It could only reflect poorly on the young singer.

Somewhat similarly, Roseanne Barr, was pilloried in print and on prime time television for her unorthodox and raucous rendition of the United States national anthem during a West Coast baseball game. Roseanne compounded the negative reaction by intentionally scratching her crotch area as millions of viewers looked on. Her actions, coupled with a sharp negative comment from President George Bush that labeled her performance repulsive, landed her on front pages and TV news shows worldwide. Her personal PR took a nosedive and hit a low point. Following apologies, explanations, and changes in her subsequent public behavior and actions, there was some recovery of lost public support and approval. Whether or not she will fully recover remains to be seen. Fortunately, the public has a short memory.

And finally, the media circus that swirled around Mia Farrow and Woody Allen as they leveled charges of improprieties and questionable personal behavior at one another raised major questions of public disapproval. Because of the timing of their revelations, some observers contended it was all part of a contrived effort to launch a new Allen movie in which they both starred. One has to wonder if anyone in their right mind would subject themselves and their children to such unwarranted public exposure and scrutiny to achieve artistic or commercial success. Show business, however, is often a world unto itself.

Shifts in public opinion are sometimes difficult to anticipate and judge. Very often a negative event or experience is soon forgotten, but just as often it can linger on for years or forever, perpetuating a negative image or deep-rooted antipathy.

During the 1920s, following publication of anti-Semitic articles in the *Dearborn Independent*, a Michigan newspaper owned and controlled by the late Henry Ford, Ford Motor Company had a problem with many members of the Jewish community, and it persisted long after the newspaper ceased publication. To compound matters, in 1938 when Henry Ford received a medal from Adolph Hitler, delivered to him by Karl Kapp, Germany's Cleveland Consul, many people were further convinced that Ford was anti-Semitic. That was notwithstanding the fact that throughout his lifetime, he had received medals and other forms of personal recognition from numerous world leaders. Ford had major operations in Germany at the time as well as all over Europe and the rest of the world.

The Jewish problem persisted, however, and is the subject of comment elsewhere in this book. It presented a serious and continuing public relations negative for Ford Motor Company and Ford products for a number of years, regardless of its origin or justification.

During the past year, in other examples, Wal-Mart Stores suffered a major setback when it was widely reported it gave no more than lip service to a policy that proclaimed it favored American-made products in its stores, and the reputation of the Jack-in-the Box restaurant chain was seriously damaged by widespread news reports of sickness and deaths resulting from tainted hamburger meat served at some of its restaurants.

It is evident therefore, that public relations attitudes, for better or for worse, are always with us, particularly if an individual or an organization is in the public eye. And today we hear more often than ever that this or that statement or action is made or taken for PR reasons, which often suggests a shallow attitude toward what is said or done that is unfortunate. Equally unfortunate, is the fact that almost anyone can call himself or herself a public relations counselor. There is no legal way to prevent it, notwithstanding vigorous ongoing efforts by professional societies and associations in the United States and elsewhere to establish safeguards.

The professional PR associations and groups are to be applauded for their efforts to set and maintain high professional standards, but they are powerless to prevent misconduct and poor performance by anyone. Almost all have codes of ethics that are nothing more than guidelines to be hung on an office wall. I doubt many members have read them and can repeat them, and too few people who are engaged in public relations would allow the codes to influence judgments or actions that might conflict with their own interests or those of their clients.

Over the years, I've found the best codes of ethics are an individual's own personal values. What you believe and how you behave are what you are. Ethics and standards can be reduced to their simplest form by simply doing the right thing when decisions are made and actions taken. "Honesty is the best policy" is still a good rule to follow in all things. "Actions speak louder than words" is as valid today as when it was first written and the same applies to the Golden Rule of doing to others as one would have others do unto you.

No mystery, no mumbo jumbo, no unnecessary rhetoric, and yet I've seen entire conferences given over to wide-ranging discussions of the ethics of public relations. Long before I entered the field, the phrase "the customer is always right" had meaning for me. It still does, but it's rarely heard today. It deserves a rebirth.

People in our field also worry unnecessarily about their status as "professionals" and the subject is constantly addressed during meetings and seminars. "Is public relations a profession?" has been debated for decades. I don't think the label, as such, is important. I think what is important is that all the men and women in the field act and function in a professional way to reflect credit on themselves and what they represent. A book could be written on that subject alone but it would change nothing. Attitudes and performance are the bottom line where PR professionalism is concerned. The more PR people know their business and exercise good judgment in carrying out their assignments, the more they will be accepted, respected, and advanced.

To me, public relations practice is as much an inherent skill as anything; and it can be developed with education, training, and experience as surely as law, medicine and accounting. And where information and documentation on the practice of public relations barely existed when I entered the field fifty years ago, there are now libraries and research facilities with growing files of text books, case studies, and other written matter tracing the development, growth, and progress of the field from its earliest "roots" period.

The subject is now taught in colleges and universities throughout the world. But in the final analysis, acceptance and performance in the field will always be an individual matter. The universities and the organized societies and associations can help lead the way, but it is the individual who will raise the standards of public relations now and in the future.

If he were still with us today I'm sure "Tommy" Ross would agree. It is indeed "honest work," as Mrs. Ross put it, and her husband was one of those who reflected great credit on his chosen field.

Chapter II

A Railroad Flat in Brooklyn

Public relations was still in "swaddling clothes" when I was born on August 23, 1919. Depending on what you read or whom you talk to, the field is said to have had its beginning twenty years earlier, around the turn of the century. In 1897, for example, the Long Island Railroad hired a man named Hal B. Fullerton as a special agent to promote Long Island and the railroad by means of "photographs, speeches, books, pamphlets, and articles."

One of the more memorable attention-getting stunts of those early times was a race between a Long Island Railroad steam train and the noted bicycle racer, "mile-a-minute" Murphy. The event was held along a section of track on the railroad's Montauk run with Murphy peddling furiously behind the last car on plank decking placed between the rails. The railroad had conveniently built an overhang on the rear of the last car to provide a wind-free enclosure for him. This also offered a degree of draft, or suction, to help pull him along. The same technique is used by many race car drivers today when they tailgate the car ahead of them.

The uniqueness and novelty of the railroad's special event brought the sponsors substantial benefit in terms of publicity and public attention. It helped put Long Island and the Long Island Railroad on the map, and it has survived the test of time as one of the great publicity stunts of those early years of this century. During that same period, a number of racing contests and coast-to-coast automobile tours were staged to prove the reliability and durability of the motor car and convince the public that automobiles were safe. It remained for Henry

Ford, however, to prove that they could also be produced and sold at a price the public could afford.

The early press agents and publicists were also making their mark. In 1906 Ivy Lee, often looked upon as the "father of public relations" a title many are now attempting to attribute to Edward L. Bernays — became the spokesperson for the anthracite coal industry. He is best remembered, however, for his association with the venerable John D. Rockefeller. When Lee came into the picture, Rockefeller was widely regarded as an industrial "robber baron" and a grasping skinflint. Ivy Lee set out to change that image and to "humanize" his client, which he did rather effectively by having the old gentleman carry a pocketful of shiny new dimes to pass out to children during his constitutional walks. Thereafter, the Rockefeller image gradually changed to become one of "wholesome abundance" rather than greed, and it was increasingly marked by generosity and philanthropy. Much of that same improved image prevails today as the Rockefellers continue to endow numerous public and cultural activities, and members distinguish themselves in public life.

Hal Fullerton had been a pioneer photo publicity specialist, and his wife, Edith Loring Fullerton, was more the serious writer. Ivy Lee was a journalist turned press agent who recognized early on that there was more to what he was doing and intended to do than merely promote and publicize. He quickly saw the need for organizations and individuals to change policies that were objectionable to the public and to explain those policies to the press. The steps he took represented what are generally considered the earliest known forms of organized public relations effort, though there are those who hold that public relations can be traced far back in history. The founders of our republic certainly knew something about good deeds and favorable recognition of them. Think of George Washington and the famous cherry tree story, Franklin's inventiveness, or Lincoln's oft-quoted statement, "Public sentiment is everything. With public sentiment nothing can fail — without it, nothing can succeed."

Therefore, more than one case can be made for the first PR practitioner and for the time when public relations put down its earliest roots. The dawn of the twentieth century, however, probably saw the development of the specialists who would devote their time and talents to the practice of publicity, press agentry, and ultimately, the broader field of public relations.

Edward L. Bernays, who has survived all his contemporaries in the field, is still with us and reasonably active at the age of one-hundred-one. He is undoubtedly unique. On the occasion of his centenarian achievement in 1991, he was recognized by professional public relations groups throughout the United States and the world. Many now refer to him as the "father of public relations," a recognition some feel was self-designated. In truth, however, there is no one "father" of this field. Many individuals, some of them totally unrecognized have made their mark over time and added to an ever-expanding body of knowledge about the field.

Scott Cutlip, a highly respected academician and an indefatigable researcher and writer on the subject of public relations, says Ed Bernays was, in fact, the ninth person to open a publicity office in New York City. The Bernays office opened during the summer of 1919 in a remodeled house at 19 East 48th Street, close to what is now Rockefeller Center.

I made my own entrance into the world at that time in a railroad flat in the Williamsburg section of Brooklyn and would never hear the term "public relations" used until twenty years later.

A railroad flat consisted of rooms in a line that began with the kitchen in the rear of the building and ended with the parlor in the front. You had to walk through the bedrooms to get back and forth between the two. The bathroom was located outside in the public hallway.

I had a fortunate early childhood. Our family lived in a flat at 85 Stockton Street during my first four years, and I surprise myself that I still have a few almost subliminal memories of the period. Our neighborhood was homogeneous but largely a mixture of Irish, Scotch, and German people with a sprinkling of Italians and other ethnics thrown in.

My father, Benjamin Sattler, was a journeyman printer, and in those early years, he worked in the Park Row section of Manhattan, near the offices of the *New York World*, a newspaper of the time. The print shops at that time were located in vintage, rickety structures that were rather dismal, but the work provided a good living. Unfortunately, the ink, lead, and paper dust took their toll on his later life, and he contracted emphysema, aggravated also by an entrenched cigarette habit. My father was a good and honest man and a steady provider for the family.

My mother, Josephine Armstrong Sattler, was a handsome woman and a strong, steady influence on our family. She was of Scotch-Irish lineage, her parents William "Big Bill" Armstrong and Elizabeth Gallagher having immigrated to the United States just prior to her birth in Brooklyn in 1888.

My father's parents, George Sattler and Julia Matthews, were of Swiss-German and Irish descent. They were born in Brooklyn in the mid-1800s after their parents arrived as immigrants.

Coming from that Scotch, German, Irish background, I always attributed my penchant for work to the Germans, thrift to the Scotch, and for relaxation and blarney, to the Irish. Throughout my life too, I also always had some of the luck of the Irish, but still had to work to make things happen.

I had two brothers, Ben, Jr., and Joseph. Ben, born after Joe, died at the age of nine, shortly before we moved from Brooklyn. My mother told me his death was caused by sitting on a chunk of ice in the street, which "brought on pneumonia," but he also had a rheumatic heart. My brother Joe was nine years my senior. He died of heart failure at the age of sixty-nine in 1979 at our home on eastern Long Island. Our family members are all buried in St. John's cemetery, Middle Village,

Queens, within walking distance of the final resting places of some of New York's most notorious mobsters, including Lucky Luciano and the Profaci brothers. Some of them were early neighbors in Brooklyn. St. John's is an "equal opportunity" business!

Today Stockton Street has completely disappeared, and so has Floyd Street, which was around the corner. The old railroad flats were razed years ago for a low-cost housing complex. The only real remembrance I have of the area are two original street signs for Stockton and Floyd Streets, which I bought at a flea market some years ago. I also have a boxful of faded photos. My Aunt Louise and Uncle Tom Bourke lived on Floyd Street, and both our families moved to Floral Park Centre, Long Island, in 1924, where they built houses side by side.

But I still have those few subliminal flashes of a four-year-old playing with a toy hook-and-ladder fire engine on the kitchen floor, and the time I was dressed as Uncle Sam for a Maypole party in the Stockton Street backyard. Other than that those years are just a blur.

My brother Joe said he remembered horse-drawn fire engines coming out of the Ellery Street firehouse, but I don't.

Floral Park Centre was about as rural an area as one could find at the time and still live within commuting distance of Manhattan. Work and income, of course, were the bottom line then as now, and the normal work week was five and a half days.

My Uncle Tom and my father built their houses on weekends, even though my father was a printer and my uncle a "drayman" for the Borden Company. He drove a team of horses, and later a chain-driven Mack truck. He felt very important behind the wheel of the Mack. When he became a volunteer fireman, he insisted on driving the Mack hook and ladder in the annual firemen's day parade and wouldn't let anyone near it on those occasions.

Floral Park Centre was so "country," there were farms within five hundred feet of our houses, which stood virtually by themselves at the end of the slowly developing residential area. We were one mile from the Jericho Turnpike and its trolley line and another mile from the LIRR station, where my father and uncle caught a daily train to and from New York City and Brooklyn.

Water was from a well, and there was no electric power, so we used kerosene lamps. I still have the one from our living room. Coal and ice were delivered by horse and wagon, and a single "pipeless" furnace heated the entire house from top to bottom, on the principle that all heat rises.

That was only partly true, however. On winter days I would grab my clothes each morning and dress in the kitchen, next to the coal stove, standing on a chair to get off the ice-cold floor.

It's a shame every kid can't spend some time on a farm. It's an unforgettable experience. In those days it was back to basics in just about every sense — growing your own food, milking cows, hunting eggs in the barn, making butter, working in the fields and giving a team of horses its "head" as they ran for the barn at the end of the workday.

Dwyer's farm was just down the road from our house, and I was there every day after school and on most weekends. Two bachelor brothers, Morris and Bill, and three spinster sisters, Kate, Maggie, and Nelly, owned and operated the farm. Having a small redheaded kid around seemed to add something to their lives, although they might not have admitted it. But I had the run of the place, and it became an extension of home.

Down the road a few miles was the Filaski farm, a landmark operation. As growing communities pushed against it, the Filaskis sold out. The family kept moving farther east to the more remote sections of Long Island, where some members of the family are still farming today. But Filaski's Pond is still on the outskirts of New Hyde Park as part of the community recreation area. Gone are the barns, the workshops, the home, and the fields, and those who live there now could never imagine what it was like slightly more than half a century ago.

The same thing happened to the Dwyers, the Wicks, the Sabarras, and the Leahys. A busy intersection at the end of Willis and Hillside Avenues at the Queens-Nassau line marks the spot where the old Dwyer farmhouse stood, and buried under the roadbed and surrounding stores are the remnants of what once was a piece of rural America. I'm glad I experienced it, and to this day farm life and its trappings are still a small part of my lifestyle.

Little did I know then that one day I would move just as comfortably along the avenues of Manhattan as I did along the dirt roads and paths of the Dwyer Farm.

I would also move about in a world of intrigue and power far removed from the bucolic life of a "country kid." But it was a time in my life I always look back on with the fondest of memories.

If it's a struggle today, life was good and comfortable in those earlier days, or so it seemed. Crime was virtually unheard of, neighbors got along, and there was a can-do spirit that often seems to be lacking today. The volunteer fire department was the nerve center of our community, and Saturday night barn dances, minstrel shows, and socials were looked forward to with pleasure and anticipation. Dr. Looney, our local dentist, drove his sulky down the road every afternoon. He kept it in the barn behind his house, which also served as his office. Ice, coal, and milk were delivered by horse and wagon, and the deliverymen were an extension of the family.

Sundays, which always began with an early morning church service, were family days in the fullest sense, invariably ending with radio programs like Tom Noonan's Chinatown Mission, Father Coughlan's weekly sermons, the Eddie Cantor Show, or the Ford Sunday Evening Hour. "Death Valley" was my own personal favorite. Our Philco box radio was shared by the family, but I had my own earphones and small crystal set to listen to Friday night boxing, Saturday afternoon football games, and other programs. I thought at the time it would be great to be an announcer covering news and sports events, such as those broadcast by Clem McCarthy, Floyd Gibbons, and Lowell Thomas. I couldn't possibly imagine that I would one day meet some of those personalities and many others who wrote, reported, edited, and broadcast the news of the day.

Toward the end of what was so often characterized as the Roaring Twenties or the Jazz Age, I had a small taste of how life was lived in the "upper" world as well as in the "under" world. One Sunday, our two families had an unexpected visit from one of Jack "Legs" Diamond's bodyguards, and I later took part in the campaign to elect Al Smith president of the United States. I was to learn much later that the two worlds were not really that far apart and that they often came together in more ways than most people could possibly imagine, let alone observe or experience.

"Legs" Diamond was a notorious prohibition-era gangster. He and Owney "The Killer" Madden were among the last of the Irish "hoods." "Legs" was gunned down by rival mobsters in a Catskill-area boarding house while hiding out with a girlfriend. Before that happened, though, one of his lieutenants, "Lefty" Joe Burke, arrived at my uncle's house one Sunday afternoon with his girlfriend, Vera Farrell, and two of Vera's girlfriends, Sadie and Mazie. Vera was the daughter of old Brooklyn neighbors. She was a stunning brunette, and Sadie and Mazie, her friends, were synthetic blondes. All three would have qualified for the cast of *Guys and Dolls*.

Vera's brother Joe was an Irish cop, but it didn't make any difference in those days. Then as now cops and hoods sometimes joined in an unholy alliance for reasons best known to themselves. Burke was no relation to Bourke. It was simply a coincidence. Vera had planned a social call to show off her boyfriend and his fancy Packard sedan. But Burke never went into the house and never left his car during their visit. My uncle didn't know it at the time, but the Packard carried enough firepower to stock a small gun shop, and Burke's behavior reflected the hazards of his occupation. Several years later, he was put out of circulation by two hit men, who cornered him in a Brooklyn bar. The Packard was parked at the curb, out of reach.

My own brother Joe had a weekend job in those days parking cars and cleaning hangers at Curtiss/Roosevelt field, a long bicycle ride from our house. He was seventeen and I was almost eight when in May of 1927 Charles Lindbergh took off in his Ryan monoplane, the Spirit of St. Louis, for the thirty-three-hour flight to Paris. It was an electrifying event that changed the world and made us all feel a small part of history, because we lived so close to the airfield. Joe's big regret was that while he saw the plane, he never saw Lindbergh except in the newsreels. We often visited the field, which was primitive by today's standards. Later it became a huge shopping center and racetrack for trotting horses, but it kept the Roosevelt Field identification through the years.

Joe told us the Lindbergh plane was no bigger than most of the other planes at the field and that everybody called it a flying gas tank, because every spare inch of space was used for that purpose. It carried more than four hundred gallons on that historic flight.

Fifty years later, I welcomed a barnstorming pilot to the old Henry Ford Airport in Dearborn, Michigan, on the occasion of the Golden Jubilee of the New York-Paris flight. The pilot was flying a replica of the Spirit on a cross-country tour as part of the milestone observance. He visited Dearborn because of Henry Ford's personal friendship with Lindbergh and to help us observe Ford's seventy-fifth anniversary, then just getting underway. Both events were important pieces of American history and coming together, they provided a unique public relations opportunity.

When I saw the replica, I had to agree with my brother that such a flimsy plane seemed hardly capable of that remarkable flight. If anyone other than Lucky Lindy had been the pilot, he might not have made it. Lindbergh had overseen construction of the original plane during a sixty-day visit to the Ryan plant in San Diego, California, and he knew intimately every detail of its construction and operation.

The year 1927 featured a run for the presidency for the first time by a Roman Catholic, Democrat Alfred Emmanuel Smith. His republican opponent was Herbert Walker Hoover. As a strong church-going Roman Catholic family, we obviously favored Smith. My father plastered our old Nash sedan with "Smith for President" stickers, and we campaigned throughout the community. It was great fun for an eight-year-old. Al Smith had been governor of New York State and was a Tammany Hall clubhouse leader of the Democratic party. He was as Irish as a shillelagh and as streetwise as an alley cat. When asked by a reporter what schools he had attended, Smith quipped, "the Fulton Fish Market." He was earthy, ungrammatical, colorful, and he lost. Some people said it was because of his religion, but the Tammany label and Jimmy Walker's lifestyle as mayor of New York City didn't help.

I also had a good closeup look at prohibition in action and saw how the law was circumvented. My uncle, Lawrence Hoppenhauer, who lived on Autumn Avenue in Flatbush, Brooklyn, was a liquor salesman for the Austin Nichols Company, but prohibition limited his clients to doctors, hospitals, and similar controlled sources. He soon became a weekend bootlegger. I learned later that he had plenty of company and competition from the likes of Sherman Billingsley of the famed Stork Club and Charlie Berns and Jack Kriendler, who later parlayed their popular speakeasy into the renowned "21" Club in midtown Manhattan.

Uncle Lawrence also showed the family how to make "home brew," a concoction of malt, hops, brewer's yeast, and patience. It wasn't long before we had a series of ceramic crocks in the basement "percolating" away until the stuff was ready for bottling. I operated the bottle-capper but could never understand how anyone could enjoy the cloudy, amber-colored end product.

But they did, every Saturday night around the piano in the living room or at the firehouse community gatherings.

There wasn't much else to do in those days, or so it seemed, that far out in the country. Today, of course, the place is wall-to-wall suburbia.

Meanwhile, in Detroit and elsewhere in the nation Henry Ford was introducing his highly-touted Model A Ford after nineteen years of Model-T production. The new car received almost as much news coverage and public interest as the presidential campaign. Riding on the Fordson tractor at the Dwyer farm was great fun, but I couldn't possibly imagine that there was a Ford in my future or that one day I would work for Henry Ford's grandson, Henry Ford II.

outing for a Career

The stock market crash of 1929 barely touched us. My mother and father never played the market. Any spare money they had was used to build the house at 200 Willis Avenue with Pop doing most of the work himself. I hid out at the Dwyer farm whenever I could, and brother Joe was the principal "goffer." The end result wouldn't win any *House Beautiful* awards but both houses, side by side, were comfortable and quite livable. Fifty years later, I had to sell our house to support my mother in a nursing home. The new owner tore it down and replaced it with a modern two-family building. The Bourke house is still there, however, and today as I drive through the old neighborhood, the memories come flooding back. No one living there now could possibly realize what it was like in those earlier days and how it has all changed. Yet it seems like only yesterday.

We weathered the Great Depression quite well. In fact, we were considered well off by many in the community. The printing trades offered steady work, and Pop was a dedicated union man, a member of Typographical Union no. 6 — the Big Six, as it is still known. He was never without work until he retired in the mid-fifties. From then on, the emphysema regulated his daily routine until he died in 1963 at the age of seventy-five.

My brother Joe followed in his footsteps as a printer, but I had a lot of self-doubt, and my mother secretly hoped I would enter the priesthood. I knew, though, that wasn't "my call," so I studied printing while attending Sewanhaka High School. When I graduated in 1936, I was sixteen and felt I had no talent anyone would consider worth employing except in the most basic ways. I often sat in class and wondered how I could possibly apply the subjects I was studying to earning a living. I'm sure I must have had a lot of company. Jobs were not too plentiful, and even mature men were sweeping the streets as part of Works Progress Administration (WPA) "make work" jobs. Many young graduates had gone into the CCC, or Civilian Conservation Corps. They were at camps throughout the country, working on agricultural and reforestation projects. The pay was minimal but it was better than nothing at all. The outlook was not promising in 1936. Almost sixty years later, it appears just as bleak for many young graduates.

Since there were no family funds available for college, I had to find work no matter how menial. In that summer of 1936, I found a temporary job delivering meat for a local butcher and bought a bicycle for three dollars from a classmate, Charlie Brude. The delivery job paid two dollars a day for six full days. Of the twelve dollars, I kept two and gave my mother ten toward household expenses. That's the way we were brought up. Today our grandchildren don't understand that way of life. Two dollars wouldn't be enough for popcorn at the movies, but in those days we could go to the movies for a quarter or less, and an ice cream soda cost fifteen cents.

In the fall of 1936, I took a job as a "runner" for a brokerage firm on Wall Street in Manhattan. The pay was thirteen dollars for a five-and-a-half day week, and I sat on the messenger bench with graduates from Princeton, Columbia, Fordham and Yale. I got the job because I told the personnel manager I planned to enroll in evening classes at New York University to study finance. But I was laid off before I could enroll. Tuition money was in short supply. I was devastated and again filled with self-doubt. How would I ever break out of the rut I felt I was in and amount to anything? I felt like a marathon runner far back in the field who would never get close enough to the front to see who was leading the pack.

Then I saw a small classified ad in a New York newspaper for a messenger for a publishing company. The requirements and pay were the same as those for Vilas and Hickey, the brokerage firm that had laid me off. The advertiser was Printer's Ink Publishing Company. Since I knew something about printing, I applied for the job and was hired as a combination messenger and office boy. Things were looking up, but Manhattan on two dollars a day was a challenge when one had to eat and commute from Long Island.

But Printer's Ink turned out to be one of the major breaks of my life. Messengering was an education in learning the ins and outs of the Big City, and the office boy detail took me behind the scenes of a small, if aging, publishing business where everyone appeared to be hanging on for dear life. That was no surprise in those depression-era days, but lack of youthful, innovative thinking eventually led to "old age" and death of the company. That did not happen, however, until the period following World War II.

I enrolled in evening classes at New York University's School of Commerce, Business and Finance in a six-year program leading to a Bachelor of Science degree. I majored in advertising and minored in economics and found myself totally occupied seven days a week with work, school, and class assignments. Saturday night was my only leisure time for a number of years, but in retrospect, night college was one of the best investments of time I ever made. It taught me many things, such as personal planning, discipline, and sacrifice, and it was tough. But when it was over, I felt I had a better education than most who attended day classes and could enjoy campus life more fully than those of us who were night students.

The big value for me was that I could interact between school and work, and several of the executives at Printer's Ink took an interest in what I was doing — Henry Marks and Jacob Chasin in particular. Henry Marks, manager of the Readers' Service Department, encouraged me to try writing short articles for the "Schoolmaster" section of *Printer's Ink Weekly*. I did, and the articles were accepted for publication.

I was thrilled. They were my first published writing efforts, and I still have every one of them. At the time, it was pretty heady stuff for a nineteen-year-old. Jake Chasin helped me with letter writing. He was the circulation manager and wrote all the promotion letters for his department. Many years later, I would write letters for the signature of a world business leader, Henry Ford II, and be told by former President Harry S. Truman, "You write a very persuasive letter."

After two years at Printer's Ink, during which I received a two-dollar-a-week raise and had a number of Schoolmaster articles published, Henry Marks called me to his office one day and said he had a call about a job with a one-man advertising agency. Would I be interested? I interviewed the same day, and John Dugan hired me to work with him at Dugan Advertising Service, located on lower Fifth Avenue. Dugan specialized in advertising and promotion in the gift and art field. I became his "inside man," handling layout, copy, and production, while he serviced our clients. Most of them were located in the Gift and Art Building, a short walk from our office. The pay was nineteen dollars a week. There were no other employees, and we did everything but sweep the floor. But it was another modest step forward, a learning opportunity, and when I left Printer's Ink, Roy Dickinson, the president, told me something I never forgot. "John," he said, "always remember that while a rolling stone may gather no moss, it does gain an enviable polish."

Those early self-doubts were now a memory, but I knew that I had a long way to go to prove myself. I was still well behind the leaders in the marathon and on the bottommost rung of the career ladder. But I had had help and direction to "find myself," and I was greatly encouraged.

After a year with John Dugan, I realized the income was barely enough to sustain the two of us and that John Dugan had made a personal financial sacrifice to hire me. He simply couldn't do all the work himself, but paying the two of us was a strain. Additionally, he was supporting his brother, Neil. It was not "the best of times."

The depression appeared to be coming to a close but not all businesses were benefiting, especially those in the gift and art field, which depended on imports, particularly from Europe. Additionally, I had met my wife-to-be and we were talking marriage.

John Dugan was disappointed at my decision to leave, but understood when I explained my need for more income and broader experience. We parted good friends, and he brought his unemployed brother in to work with him on a temporary basis. In that sense it was a good move for all concerned, but John had to teach Neil the fundamentals of the business, and Neil was well into mid-life.

Within a week, an employment service specializing in advertising personnel sent me for an interview with Mark Vignate, advertising and promotion manager for the business division of the Boy Scouts of America. Vignate hired me to handle the department's production function, and on the strength of my writing samples, he said I would also start a public relations unit to serve the needs of trading posts and dealers in Boy Scout merchandise from coast to coast. I was to work with the trade press to publicize the business division's operations. The Boy Scouts already had a general public relations department headed by Leslie C. Stratton, who reported to Dr. James E. West, the chief scout executive.

My salary was thirty dollars a week to start, and I was very pleased. So was Elinore Richter, my intended, who was then employed by the Metropolitan Life Insurance Company, in its actuarial department. With our combined incomes, we were sure we could venture out on the "sea of holy matrimony."

More than fifty years later, our marriage vows are as solid as ever.

To celebrate my new job, I took Elinore, her cousin Irma Frebal, and Irma's date to the Capitol Theater, on upper Broadway one Saturday night to see a movie and a stage show featuring Sammy Kaye and his "Swing and Sway" band. Sammy's show featured a contest called "Do you want to lead a band?" He would invite five people from the audience to come on stage and direct the band in a number. Fun was the objective, but some volunteers took the whole thing too seriously. Elinore and I were in the balcony when Sammy spotted me waving a white scarf. He called me down, and in no time I was on the stage, baton in hand, being interviewed by the maestro.

"Why do you want to lead a band?" Sammy asked. "I wanted to see what you do to make all that money," I said. The band members guffawed, and so did the audience.

"That's good," Sammy said. "But what do *you* do to make all that money?"

"Well," I half laughed, "I do public relations for the Boy Scouts, but I'll soon be making fifty dollars a month working for Uncle Sam."

That was good for more laughs, and I had the audience with me. I was on a roll, and thank the Lord I didn't have to explain public relations to two thousand people.

I ended up winning the five-dollar prize and an autographed plastic baton, which I still have as a memento of the occasion. The prize money went for an after-show celebration for the four of us at Howard Johnson's restaurant on Queens Boulevard in Forest Hills. Today, it would barely buy one cheeseburger or a tub of popcorn.

As the Capitol Theater's stage descended into the basement, Sammy Kaye and I with it, Sammy thanked me, and Jimmy Ritz, a member of the then popular Ritz Brothers comedy team, jumped on from the front row seats. "That was pretty good, kid," he said. "You should go into the business."

I laughed but didn't realize until years later how prophetic his comment was. It appeared that much of what we did in public relations was, indeed, "show business."

Working in scouting was an unforgettable experience. In fact, I found it to be one of the most rewarding periods of my life, because the program we were promoting was so constructive and so beneficial to young people. During the two years I worked with the BSA, scouting enrolled its one-millionth boy. It was a major milestone in the history of scouting, which had come to America in 1915 from England, where it was started by Lord Baden Powell. The milestone observance was an opportunity to pull out all the stops in an advertising and public relations sense, and we made the most of it. In the business division, we planned major events for all of the official scout trading posts and gained full backup support from leading stores across the country that sold scout equipment and uniforms.

Les Stratton's department arranged radio salutes, interview programs, and special editions of newspapers and magazines, and the results were virtually unmeasurable in those earlier days. The occasion helped focus attention on all of the contributions of scouting at a time when there was growing concern about the role the United States might play in the defense of Europe. "Be prepared" was a scouting slogan that was taking on added meaning.

As a one-person PR unit, I was so fully occupied turning out radio scripts, news matter, and magazine articles for the trade press that another young man, Bill Most, was soon hired to replace me on production matters. Years later, his son Donnie Most would star in the TV series "Happy Days" with "Fonzie" and the gang.

Mark Vignate and the rest of the staff were turning out posters, commemorative advertisements, a new handbook, anniversary catalogs, and a range of other supportive promotional material. Meanwhile Ed Belason, head of our shows and exhibits staff, had his people on overtime creating displays and floats for major exhibits, public events, and parades.

It was a time of dedication, drive, and accomplishment for all of us and especially for scouting throughout the nation.

It saddens me now to see how some things have changed with the years and to hear and read of attacks on this great organization by some who would change its programs and policies. Scouting has always had strong moral and religious values that are not forced on those who identify with its programs and what they represent. It's a movement that reinforces patriotism and engenders respect for our country's heritage. It teaches young people how to better serve their country, their fellow man, and themselves. Unfortunately though, there are activist individuals and groups today that would destroy and eliminate those values from an organization that has successfully taught generations of young men how to live better, more fulfilling lives.

Currently, the Boy Scouts of America is engaged in a series of legal battles to defeat efforts to make changes in its membership rules, policies, basic programs, and even the Boy Scout Oath. Membership stands at more than five million, and one of scouting's greatest problems is finding qualified leadership during a period when young men are growing up without male role models in the home, let alone in a local scout troop. It's a sad commentary, and one can only hope that attempts to force unnecessary and unwise changes in the policies of scouting will be resoundingly defeated.

Recently, under pressure from activist interests, the United Way of San Francisco withdrew its support for Boy Scout Councils located in San Francisco Bay area. The reason given was that United Way could not support an organization that has "discriminatory policies." Bank of America and the Wells Fargo Bank also withdrew support for the same reason — "discriminatory policies." These actions have posed a major public relations and financial problem for scouting that could spread to other parts of the country. The national leadership of the Boy Scouts of America is adamant, however, that the policies of scouting will not be changed by this type of pressure, now or in the future.

Elinore Richter and I were married on George Washington's birthday, February 22, 1941. We took a few days of "honeymoon" time on the Jersey shore after a warm send-off by fellow workers and our families. Our small apartment in Hollis, Queens, was ideally located for commuting to and from our jobs in Manhattan. We worried for a time that parenthood or the loss of either of our jobs would result in economic chaos, but it never happened. What happened, instead, was World War II.

Chapter IV

Mooning over Miami

Everyone who is old enough knows exactly where he or she was when the news of the bombing of Pearl Harbor came over the airwaves. Elinore and I had just hiked from Hollis to Floral Park to visit my parents, and we were sitting in the living room listening to the radio when the news flash came. We were so stunned we all simply looked at each other. I finally broke the silence by saying, "Well, that's it. I guess I'm in." I wasn't sure what "in" meant, but I knew perfectly well that no able-bodied man would escape early draft consideration. I was eminently, if not imminently, eligible.

My mother began to cry, and my father was somber and totally out of character for a person generally in a good mood. Brother Joe seemed safe for the moment. He had a wife and two children and steady work in my father's print shop. I was married with no children and vulnerable, and we all knew it. Elinore was philosophical. Her concerns were masked, and she said, "I'll go too." As it turned out, she did — but not in uniform!

I had a delayed draft board status but immediately looked into what the services were offering. I knew I would have to suspend college and wondered if I would ever get back to it. But it was a postponable consideration. The Navy offered deck officer training for those qualified, and I picked up an application, but before I could complete it, I saw an item in the *New York World Telegram* about volunteer officer candidates for branches of the military. I decided to look into it that. It was then early 1942, and after a battery of tests and interviews, I soon found myself reporting for induction at my draft board with a rather tenuous indication that I would be considered for officer's candidate school somewhere, if "qualified."

On the morning of June 18, 1942, I arrived at the New Hyde Park City Hall for swearing in with one other VOC candidate, Frank Rutledge of Garden City. Our respective families were on hand to see us off, putting the best possible face on everything. We said our goodbyes, and I was sure we wouldn't be back. We had sent one of our BSA colleagues off with a rousing "draft party" some weeks before, and he was back the next day. He had failed the physical exam and was classified 4F. I was sure that wasn't going to happen to me, and it didn't. We were processed through Governor's Island in New York Harbor, were sworn in, took needles in both arms and the buttocks, and went to bed at Camp Upton, Yaphank, Long Island, for the night. The whole thing took fourteen hours. There were fifty men in our two-story Upton barracks — twenty-five on each side — assigned cots and footlockers, dormitory style.

Grown men could be heard crying. It was without question an unnerving experience. Many had never been separated from their families before, and particularly from their children. It seemed like a bad dream, until 5 A.M. the next morning, when all the lights went on and we were roused out of bed to reveille. We didn't need Irving Berlin to sing "Yip, Yip, Yaphank," or "Oh, How I Hate to Get Up in the Morning," as he had when he entertained at Camp Upton in World War I.

We settled into life at Upton quickly, however, and for those who made the fast adjustment, it was something of an adventure. I think I was one of them, but I readily understood that some men couldn't adjust. The "commanding officer" of our barracks was a regular army corporal named Montrey. He wore blue fatigues and an army campaign Stetson and carried a swagger stick. He had me digging a drainage ditch for three weeks, which was considered "good duty." I never forgot it. I had two hands full of callouses and a half dozen nasty boils from the abrupt change in lifestyle, food, and shots of medicine.

Frank Rutledge disappeared on a troop train about the second week of our stay, and I thought I'd never see or hear from him again. I had no idea where they had sent him. The following week I received a postcard from Miami Beach. Rutledge seemed to be on vacation. "John," he wrote, "This is the life. Swimming every afternoon. We live in beachfront hotels and sleep on mattresses. It's the Air Force Administration Program. Come on down!" I couldn't believe it.

At that point I was headed for the Signal Corps. As a kid in high school — which didn't seem that far back — I had raced homing pigeons, and I knew the Signal Corps used them for communication purposes. I mentioned the pigeons during processing and immediately got a Signal Corps assignment. All I was waiting for was the troop train.

When I got Frank's card on a Sunday morning, I lost no time in heading for the adjutant general's office to see if I could change my classification. It was closed, and I was about to leave when an AGO second lieutenant came up with keys in his hand. I saluted, and he asked if he could help me. I said I thought I'd been wrongly classified for the Signal Corps and wondered if there was a possibility I could switch to AAF administration. "Let's take a look," he said. He pulled my service card from a file tub and looked it over. "I don't see any problem here," he said and punched in a new classification code.

There, you're all set," he said. "Good luck." It was as easy as that! I thanked him, saluted, and left for the barracks. I couldn't believe how simple it had been and how lucky I was to have met that particular young officer at the right time. It not only changed my entire military experience but my entire life, as one thing led to another over the years.

Within a week, I was aboard an overnight troop train to Miami Beach. I felt so good, I volunteered for KP duty — kitchen police — in a baggage car that had been converted to a rolling kitchen.

The Virginia countryside was magnificent, and I had never been that far from home.

Before we left Camp Upton, however, I had an unforgettable experience. Young Joe Louis, the heavyweight boxing champion, and his sparring partner came to the camp one evening to entertain the troops with a three-round exhibition fight as part of a USO program introduced by Richard Conte, who was then in a play on Broadway. I think Louis was about nineteen years old, and I never saw a fighter in better condition. He was like a well-oiled machine. Arthur Donovan, a member of the New York Athletic Club, refereed the match, as he did so many famous fights in those days.

A number of years after the war, I met Cassius Clay (Muhammad Ali), and I thought back to Young Joe. How the two would have made history in a "dream match!" Could Ali have beaten Joe? We'll never know, but it would have been the match and the "gate" of the century.

The Upton USO show also featured a medley of Irving Berlin songs, some written at Upton during the first World War. I was to meet Irving Berlin three years later in 1945, at Freeman Field, Seymour, Indiana, when we were there with General Jimmy Doolittle, on a classified USAAF project. Doolittle, who now lives in a California nursing home, is ninety-five years old, and one of our most enduring war heroes.

Frank Rutledge was right about his life in Miami. When we reached Miami Beach, we were billeted in beachfront hotels on Ocean Drive. I spent two months in the Edison Hotel at Tenth Street and one month in the Breakwater Hotel next door. Our mess hall was in the Evans Hotel at the corner of Tenth Street and Collins Avenue. Today, the Edison, the Breakwater, and other nearby hotels are considered Art Deco landmarks, and they command a lot of attention and high room rates. They are much sought after by tourists who want to experience what remains of a bygone era.

A short walk down Ocean Drive from the Edison in those days were the old fishing pier and auditorium, where I unexpectedly met Al Jolson one evening on his way to entertain at the USO. Jolson extended his hand and asked, "Where are you from, soldier?" When I said New York, it got me a big smile and a front-row seat for the show. He said he had just come down from New York on the Seaboard Line to "take the sun and entertain the troops."

I had been "on the beach" for two weeks in a sea of green fatigues and khakis when one Sunday afternoon I had a few hours off and decided to walk up Collins Avenue. The timing was perfect! I spotted a familiar figure in a terrycloth robe crossing the street. Sure enough, It was Frank Rutledge. He was billeted in Haddon Hall, another beachfront Art Deco classic. We caught each other up on news and arranged to keep in touch.

In September 1942 we both entered AAF Officer Candidate School for the three-month program leading to "shavetail" status of second lieutenant. We were called ninety-day wonders, but getting the gold bars was an accomplishment. We sat up in blacked-out bathrooms part of every night, studying when we were supposed to be sleeping. It was simply impossible to get everything done — drills, formations, parades, classes, calisthenics, field exercises, homework, meals, guard duty. Sleep was for Sundays — maybe!

Frank and I graduated OCS on December 9, 1942, one year after Pearl Harbor. Frank was sent to England, where he served as a Special Services officer with the Eighth Air Force in the London area before being assigned to intelligence on the Continent. When he was separated in 1945, he returned to the *New York Daily News* and was there until he retired. Then he and his wife, Vera, moved to Vero Beach, Florida, where they still live. They are both in their 80's.

Meanwhile, prior to OCS and graduation, Elinore began the first of several moves when we found an affordable efficiency apartment at 1025 Meridian Avenue, on the beach. The rent was only seven dollars a week — half my military pay!

In time, Elinore found employment with a trucking company, and we were expecting our first-born. Regrettably, she had a miscarriage in the third month, the night of our graduation. I was shipped out the next morning to Oklahoma City, by way of Texas. After a week in St. Joseph's Hospital in Miami Beach, where I had to leave her, and a stay with landlord's, Aunt Rosie and Uncle Julius, she followed at the first opportunity. We rented a room in Oklahoma City, where I was assigned to the supply depot at Tinker Field.

Several months later, we moved again when I became the supply officer for the 405th Sub Depot in Fairmont, Nebraska. In view of my background, I was also a natural to serve as depot public relations officer. We all wore more than one hat in those days.

Elinore and I found accommodations in Geneva, Nebraska, a short ride from the air base, and I settled into my job of keeping B-24 and B-29 aircraft flying on training missions.

It was 1943, and at twenty-four years of age, I had the responsibilities and the accountability of a chief executive officer for a substantial business. It was hard to believe, but that was the way things were during wartime. At times I had to fight running battles with my superior officer, whose mistress was my chief clerk. He was a former stockbroker from New York City, who drove a Cadillac Fleetwood instead of a staff car and spent more on long-distance phone calls to his broker than he received in military pay.

They were trying times. Supply officers at some of the major depots in the Midwest often didn't want to part with critical and short-supply items needed to keep our training planes in the air, and that was a big problem for me. Our planes flew twenty-four hours a day, seven days a week, and those were also our own on-call duty hours. We weren't dropping the bombs, but we were in the front lines when it came to keeping our planes in the air.

When the bomb groups left our base after several months of training, they received new aircraft, which they then flew overseas to the combat zones. The 451st Bomb Group, our first under command of Col. Robert Eaton, went directly to Italy when it left Fairmont, and it distinguished itself in bombing forays over Austria, Germany, and Romania. Perhaps its most critical assignment was bombing the vital oil fields at Ploesti, Romania, one of the most hazardous missions of the entire war in Europe. The 451st gunners said you could almost "walk on the flak" from groundfire.

In fact, the 451st Bomb Group was one of the most decorated air units of the war. It was recognized with numerous citations for critical and hazardous missions, including three of the fiercest and most costly air raids of the war over Regensburg, Germany; Vienna; and Ploesti, from February through August 1944.

I developed a close rapport with members of the 451st at Fairmont, and while I didn't serve in Italy with them, they "adopted" me as an honorary member. I was an honored guest and spoke at their reunion at the Fairmont Air Base on September 7, 1990 — forty-seven years after we all served there. During the ceremony in front of the only remaining hangar, a lone B-24 came out of nowhere and flew low over the field in a dramatic "dèjá vu." Bob Karstenson of Scottsbrook, Illinois, the group's historian had arranged for that B-24. There wasn't a dry eye on the field.

Col. Bob Eaton, now a retired major general, came from Wilmington, Delaware, for the reunion, and delivered the principal address to the thinning ranks of veterans and their wives. It was a moment in history for all of us, and I was honored to have been asked to represent all who had served at the base almost half a century earlier.

It was at Fairmont while trying to keep 'em flying that I had one of my most unnerving experiences. We desperately needed generators and tires to keep the planes in the air twenty-four hours a day. There could be little down-time for maintenance, as we operated under combat conditions.

I located some of the equipment we needed at a major supply depot in Memphis, Tennessee, and additional items at Wright Field, Dayton, Ohio, and I decided to fly to both places to pick them up. I requisitioned a plane for that purpose through Ed James, a flight officer who spent all of his spare time in our depot maintenance hangar making mockups of B-24 fuel systems. James, a second lieutenant, reminded me of Lindbergh, with his mechanical and engineering background, and he knew a B-24 like no one else. He needed the flying time to keep up his flight pay.

We left on a Saturday morning and returned the following day.

What I didn't know at the time was that we would be flying in a B-24 bomber, since no other plane was available, that Lieutenant James would be flying it himself, and that I would be the only other person on board the aircraft. There wasn't going to be a co-pilot, and I couldn't fly a kite, let alone anything else that left the ground.

I didn't realize we were strictly a twosome until we cleared the runway at Fairmont, and I went forward to talk to James and the copilot. But I didn't see a copilot, and since those "flying boxcars" weren't equipped with lavatories, I knew instantly no one else was aboard.

"Where's the copilot?" I asked James.

"Aw, we don't need anyone else to fly this aircraft," he said. "Don't worry, I'll get you there and back. Sit down at those controls. You can be the copilot."

I stared at him in disbelief. Out of the corner of my eye, I could see Lincoln Air Base disappearing off to our left. We were on our way to Tennessee. I said a silent prayer that we would get there in one piece.

I was dumbfounded but too naive and busy to think about the situation again. We picked up what we needed at Memphis and then went on to Dayton, where we spent the night. The next day, with the final items on board, we left for home. And then the weather turned bad. We were cleared to Chicago, James said, and through a hole in the clouds I could see the city as we approached. But James made no move to land. He continued on to Omaha and then headed for Fairmont at altitudes that at times were barely more than five hundred feet. We were following Route #6, the main highway west, and I could read the names of the small Nebraska towns on the water towers — Friend, Exeter, and finally, Fairmont — but our field was socked in. Then, miraculously, James found a hole in the clouds and lined the B-24 up to land. Instead of landing, however, we went up again. There wasn't enough runway. By that time, I was fingering my rosary beads.

On the second attempt, we "burned rubber" and I felt like millions of passengers today who cheer and clap when their commercial airliner touches down in bad weather. What a relief!

I never said a word to anyone but my wife. It was nine o'clock that Sunday night and raining when I got home. "I was worried about you," she said. "So was I," I answered, in what had to be a world class understatement, and then I told her what had happened.

We both said our prayers with greater emphasis that night.

Two weeks later I learned that James would be court martialed. It seems the operations officer had gone to our base officer's club on the Saturday night we were away and ran into the officer James had falsely listed as copilot. When questioned about the Memphis/Dayton trip, the officer said he knew nothing about it. Ed James had listed him simply as an exercise in paperwork. The epitome of self-confidence, he had planned all along to fly the plane all by himself! He never doubted he could take it there and bring it back, and he did.

I thanked the Lord he didn't suffer from epilepsy — or worse — and realized how trusting and naive I was. I was never called to testify at the court martial, and James, for all intents and purposes, received no more than a slap on the wrist. He was grounded for six months, losing flight pay, and denied promotion for one year, but two weeks later his promotion to first lieutenant came through. It had been in the works and predated the court martial action. When I saw him again, we did not discuss what happened, and we remained friends. Frankly, I had a lot of admiration for anyone who could fly one of those megabombers all by himself.

Chapter V

Fighting the War at Harvard

Our time in Nebraska was memorable for a lot of reasons. Much of Nebraska is flat corn country with gently rolling hills. It is part of the great plains of the Midwest and beautiful in its way, but I believe most people would have to be born there to stay there. Our stay was about eighteen months, and we had no choice in the matter. When I was placed on overseas orders, the orders were canceled by our field command, because there was no replacement available and I had a critical military occupational specialty, or MOS. It was more important to keep those B-24 and B-29 planes flying than whatever else Colorado Springs headquarters might have had in mind for me. I never found out, but I was torn between the excitement and thoughts of far away places and my present job, which I knew was critical — not to mention being with Elinore. I've often thought about it, however, and I may have been damn lucky at that. I might not be here today.

Our firstborn, Sandra Lee, arrived on the scene at Fairmont in the base hospital, which was the largest hospital in the state and had just been cleared to handle military maternity cases. The nearest general hospital was in Lincoln, sixty miles away.

Fairmont, no more than a blip on the Burlington rail line, had a population of under a thousand people. Geneva, six miles away, had a population of slightly more than two thousand. Forty-seven years later, when I went back for the reunion of the 451st Bomb Group in 1990, Fairmont had grown by about fifty people, and Geneva had lost a few hundred. Life was again gentle and bucolic, and miles of corn and milo had replaced everything on the old base with the exception of a lone maintenance hangar and two old runways, which were still capable of handling a B-24 or a B-29.

When the 451st left for Italy, it was replaced by the 485th Bomb Group and then by the 504th VH (very heavy) group, which flew B-29s and was destined for the island of Tinian in the Pacific. It was from that island base that the Enola Gay took off in 1945 to drop the first atom bomb on Hiroshima, and some members of the 504th were included in that tragic mission.

I'll never forget the day the first of those 29s arrived at our field, and I went down to the flight line to sign papers and accept responsibility for it. None of us had ever seen a plane that big on the ground — or even in the air. I thought back to my growing-up years on Long Island. As I have already mentioned, we lived about ten miles from Curtiss/Roosevelt field. When Lindbergh took off from there one early morning in 1927 for Paris, he flew a Ryan monoplane. It would have fit on one of the wings of a B-29 with plenty of room to spare. The only airborne things I had ever seen that were larger than a B-29, were three dirigibles that flew over our house in Floral Park during the 1930s enroute to Lakehurst, New Jersey. They were the *Los Angeles*, the *Graf Zepplin*, and the *Hindenberg*. The last came by on the afternoon of its fateful trip from Germany shortly before it crashed and burned while landing. I remember standing in our backyard awestruck at the size of those huge craft as they floated along, looking for all the world like inflated cigars. For size, they were ahead of their time. For speed, they were dinosaurs, and like the dinosaur, they eventually became extinct.

When we had relaxation time at Fairmont, we played ball or went pheasant hunting if we could find shotgun shells. Every hedgerow had resident pheasants, and they grew fat on the corn for lack of hunters. Of course, there was always the base movie theater. That was about it for recreation and entertainment.

In the spring of 1944, I learned of a new program looking to the end of the war in Europe and acceleration of the war in the Pacific. Qualified officers were being sought to take training in handling war-contract termination and property disposal matters and the community and labor problems expected to arise as the war came to an end.

Actions taken to terminate or renegotiate contracts and resulting layoffs of workers were expected to create major public relations problems for the military and the federal government. I filed an application for the training and special assignment after clearing with our base commander and mission headquarters in Colorado Springs. Fortunately, my assistant at the time, 2nd Lieutenant Earl Thompson, was on hand to replace me. Within two weeks, I was accepted and told I would be sent to the Harvard Business School, Cambridge, Massachusetts, for "several months of indoctrination and training."

Elinore and I were ecstatic, because the move would bring us closer to our families in the New York area and enable occasional visits. In fact, however, since I had to be quartered at the school on a fulltime basis, Elinore went home with Sandra to stay with her parents, and I managed a couple of visits during the two-month program.

But leaving Fairmont had a sad side too. For several months, we had lived with a local family until we eventually found a small apartment over the offices of the *Geneva Signal*, the local newspaper. The Reichert family, with whom we stayed, were typical midwesterners — reserved, solid, and patriots to the core. We adopted one another and to this day, we still see and hear from them. Virgil, a building contractor, passed away some years ago, and Welcome is now approaching eighty. Their forebears settled the Nebraska territory, living in sod houses with the natives — mostly Oglala Sioux — as neighbors.

While Welcome Reichert has raised two children of her own during the time we've known her, a span of almost fifty years, she has also been "mother" to more than five hundred additional youngsters she helped bring into the world, and raise for others. We think of her as a kind of Mother Theresa of the Midwest, but in her humble and shy way, she shuns the recognition she deserves. She was horrified when I suggested telling the producers of the Charles Kuralt Sunday television show that she would be a perfect subject for its "Postcard from Nebraska" feature. "Too old and too late," she said, but I don't think so. The state of Nebraska, if not Washington, D. C. should recognize her with a medal for what she has accomplished.

(Sadly, Welcome passed away quietly, in late March, 1993, as this manuscript was being readied for the printer. We have lost a true and loving friend.)

Life at Dunster House on the Harvard campus provided the going-away-to-college experience I couldn't afford in the mid-thirties. It was spartan enough, but the opportunity to combine Harvard graduate-level education with military service was a real bonus.

The dean of the graduate school at the time was Donald K. David, and I was to meet him again when he joined the board of directors of Ford Motor Company some years later. It is indeed a small world.

When the Harvard program was completed, I was reassigned to the Air Technical Service Command at Wright Field, Dayton, Ohio. I had just turned twenty-five and had completed the Harvard program "with distinction," according to my diploma. I was a captain in the company of officers more senior in age, rank, and experience, and I wondered where I would end up in the new world of contract readjustment work to which we would all be assigned.

I soon found out. When I reported to the public relations staff of the ATSC, it was far from a warm welcome that I received from Major Julian Leggett, head of the unit to which I was assigned. Prewar, Leggett had been editor of a major magazine. A twenty-five-year-old captain, who had just finished what Major Leggett must have regarded as a cushy course at Harvard, ranked low in his priorities. I could see myself at the bottom of the barrel when it came to assignments.

"Before you say anything," he said, "Los Angeles and New York are out. Everybody wants to go there. [pause] I'll have to give this some thought." I nodded and thanked him, and said that under the circumstances, I understood and would go anywhere but had hoped for New York, since I had family there and might be able to take some evening courses at NYU, time permitting, to complete my degree work.

"That's probably out of the question," Major Leggett said, "but we'll take a look at it."

"Thank you, sir," I said, and left the room.

What I didn't realize was that within earshot sat the section chief, Colonel Gerry Johnson, working on papers and eavesdropping. The two of them discussed me after I left. It seemed they had a senior officer on their hands who had worked in advertising for the J. Walter Thompson Company. He was being assigned to New York, and they wanted to team him with a younger officer to avoid any conflict in age or rank.

It was another break for me, and I soon found myself headed for New York driving our Oldsmobile coupe which Elinore and I had loaded with personal items such as a crib and our pet dog, "Major," on the premise I would be assigned elsewhere in the country and not get back to New York to pick up those things. Elinore and Sandra were to join me by train in Dayton so we could all drive to any new location. It was a necessary bit of "forward planning" at the time.

With Major Jackson Matthews, the former Thompson executive, I reported to the AAF PR office in lower Manhattan at 67 Broad Street, corner of Wall. It was the International Telephone and Telegraph building and served as a military intelligence and communications command center of critical importance. Although Jack Matthews and I were on a special assignment, we reported nominally to Major Richard T. Nimmons, chief of the New York section, which included three additional officers and several civilians. It was a good and seasoned group, and I enjoyed working with them. Dick Nimmons had been a college fund raiser and had had several public relations jobs in Hawaii. Herbert M. Baus, then a second lieutenant, had served as publicity manager for the Los Angeles Chamber of Commerce and had written a primer on publicity work titled "Publicity, How to Plan, Produce and Place It." The other officers were former newsmen, and one had worked for the *New Yorker*. I felt I had moved into the ranks of experienced PR professionals, and I settled in with enthusiasm. It proved to be another of life's golden opportunities.

During the fourteen months I was in that office, I had the chance to handle a range of assignments that would have been impossible anywhere else. They included production incentive programs, community problems created by major contract cutbacks and terminations, layoffs, job walkouts, sabotage and espionage, air shows, captured enemy equipment displays, and one of the most frightening of all happenings, a military plane hitting the Empire State Building in mid-Manhattan.

Surprisingly, too, some of the news matter I wrote was appearing verbatim in the New York media. The editors might have found it too complicated to tamper with or felt they couldn't cut or rewrite it. There were times when I felt I was on a career racetrack and over my head — but that's the way it was in wartime. You were thrown into circumstances and could either sink or swim, and swimming was better, to paraphrase Sophie Tucker's favorite saying, "I've been rich and I've been poor, and rich is better!"

From time to time, I would join Henry "Hank" Greenberg, the former Detroit Tigers all-star slugger, on morale and production-incentive visits to area war plants. Hank was then a captain, had graduated with the OCS class ahead of mine, and he was on special assignment to our headquarters. He was courting Carol Gimbel, the department store heiress, at the time, and she occasionally joined us, along with any distinguished war heroes who might have just returned from the European or Pacific war theaters. The workers in the plants we visited never failed to bring down the house with cheers and applause as they caught sight of Hank and our entourage. In actual fact, though, we were there to cheer and applaud them for the job they were doing in the all-out drive for victory and an end to the years of death and destruction.

Meeting or traveling with celebrities was almost a common occurrence in those days, particularly where public relations activities were concerned. On the day I was enrolled in Class 42F at OCS, I received a personal hazing from actor and "upper classman" Clark Gable in the courtyard of the Boulevard Hotel. It was his duty assignment for the day, and he may have considered it ridiculous, but he went through the motions of being one of the boys while hazing the new recruits. When his familiar face, with GI haircut and minus mustache, was suddenly thrust in front of mine and I was ordered to "Brace, mister, suck in your gut and put your age in the number of wrinkles in your chin," I knew it wasn't the time to ask Rhett Butler for an autograph. Six weeks later, billeted as an upper classman at Sadigo Court, not far from the beach's famous Roney Plaza Hotel, I found myself doing the same thing with Gilbert Roland, a veteran though somewhat lesser known actor, who was a lower classman. Roland, also minus his familiar mustache, was often compared to Ronald Coleman, something his wife, Constance Bennett, told us he hated. The Rolands threw a big party when he graduated, but I missed it. I was already on the job in Oklahoma City.

I thought one of my best efforts during that New York assignment was staging an air show at Newark Airport as part of a campaign to recruit workers for changing skills requirements in New Jersey war plants. I thought an "air spectacular" might get the proper level of attention, and it did. I peddled the story and photos to the city desks of the *New York Times* and *Herald Tribune* and got a commendation from headquarters when they appeared on the front pages of both papers. That publicity in itself almost insured the success of the show. Several hundred thousand area residents turned out. They saw a Bleriot, which in 1909 was the first airplane to fly the English Channel and which we found in a crate in a Newark air base warehouse; and they saw "Thumper," a much decorated B-29 that had returned from the Pacific theater with its equally decorated crew, under command of Col. Charles "Pappy" Haynes. The crew's experiences while bombing the Japanese Islands were dramatized on "We The People," the highly popular Sunday evening radio show and were described in numerous stories regionally and nationally.

The *March of Time* followed later with a major takeout on our command, and I accompanied Jack Glenn, the producer and his cameramen to Wright Field on another harrowing flight in abominable weather. Those military pilots would fly anybody anywhere to log air time. On the trip from Newark to Dayton, Ohio, I felt we were flying through a sky full of flak as lightning flashed around us and the plane bounced every which way on the air currents. It was only a six-seat Cessna, a far cry from the huge bombers to which I had become accustomed.

On another occasion, I took a select group of national media people to Freeman Field, in Seymour, Indiana, to show classified enemy equipment — buzz bombs, V-2s, Messerschmits, Stukas, Zeros, and other items. Our party included Jimmy Doolittle, Irving Berlin and much-decorated war aces Colonel Francis "Gabby" Gabreski and Lt. Steve Pisano. The tour demonstrated, among other things, what our fighting men were up against in the European and Pacific theaters while carrying the war to the Germans and the Japanese. The captured German and Japanese aircraft had excellent performance characteristics, and the rockets were a taste of what might have been if Hitler's time schedule hadn't been interrupted by the relentless bombing of fortress Europe and the successful allied landings in Normandy.

Dick Nimmons and I were alone in the office one Saturday morning just before VE Day 1945 when I took a telephone call from one of the wire services. "We have a report that an aircraft has hit the Empire State Building. Can you confirm it?" the voice at the other end of the phone asked. It was the first of many calls I would receive during a long career when I didn't have a ready answer and would have to say, "I don't know, I'll try to find out and get back to you."

I took the name and phone number of the caller and almost didn't know where to begin. I told Dick Nimmons, who sat at a desk in the same room. (Our staff had now been cut to the point where there were only two of us and a secretary.)

It was news to Dick, so I called the police. "Yes, something has hit the Empire State Building. We think it might be a military plane but we're not sure," a precinct desk sergeant told me, "That's all I can tell you."

I told Dick they thought it was a military plane, so he decided to call our command at Wright Field with an alert. It was also news to them but he had barely hung up when they were back on the phone and so was Air Force Headquarters in Washington, D.C.

"Get up to the Empire State Building right away. Something's hit it, and we think it might be one of our planes," a voice from Washington said. "If it is, stay with it. Do what you can to get all the facts, but call back before you say anything to the press."

Nimmons went flying out the door as our phones began to ring off the hook. I was to be the communication center while Dick took charge at the scene of the disaster, which was already chaotic. So was my communication center for a good part of that day, Saturday, July 28, 1945. It was my first, but not my last, experience with a crisis public relations problem.

We soon learned that a B-25 light bomber from an air force base in New England was being flown to Newark Air Base by a lone pilot with two passengers. The pilot had become disoriented when he found he had faulty instrument readings.

He was supposed to be over New Jersey, but in fact he was flying down the center of Manhattan on a day when visibility was close to ground zero. The plane hit the world's tallest building on the northeast side of the seventy-eight floor. Part of the fuselage and the engines penetrated the building, and the rest, along with the tail section, fell to setbacks on the floors below. One of the two engines was torn loose from its mountings and sailed right through the offices of the Catholic Relief Services and into an elevator shaft, where it plunged to the bottom. Several fires that were started were quickly brought under control by the New York City Fire Department.

If there is ever anything fortunate about such an unexpected disaster, in this case it was the fact it happened on a Saturday morning when most offices in the building were closed or operating with reduced staffs. That was the case with Catholic Relief Services, but there still were injuries and ten fatalities in addition to three people killed on the twin-engine B-25.

We were in constant contact with all New York City departments involved, and Dick Nimmons and I spent the weekend and much of the following week servicing the press and our own command sources. It was laughable to think nothing should be said to the press without advance clearance from Washington. We knew better. That policy changed almost immediately, as just about everyone became an instant news source — the police, the firemen, office personnel, building officials, bystanders, and countless others. By quick action in organizing, getting facts together, and establishing a command-and-communication center, we soon became the official source for information from the scene of the crash. Our command center in the downtown office also became the source for new developments, and we put out regular bulletins whenever anything changed or when there was something new to report.

It was a big story but there was no unwarranted criticism of the Air Force for the way in which it had responded to its central role in an unprecedented and unexpected crisis. What little criticism there was, was leveled at the dead pilot for using faulty judgement. The LaGuardia Tower, which he had checked when approaching the metropolitan area, had advised a landing at that field, but Lt. Col. William F. Smith, Jr., the pilot, insisted on continuing his flight to Newark, to keep an appointment. He was advised to fly across Manhattan at no less than 2,000 feet. When he hit the Empire State Building, he was 913 feet above ground level, and the building's height exceeded 1,200 feet.

The media was fair and did not fault the USAF for pilot and mechanical error in the prevailing weather, but they did ask pointed questions about why the pilot was enroute from Bedford, Massachusetts to Newark, New Jersey, on that Saturday morning, and "why he was over mid-town Manhattan." The second question required a guess-work answer, and the response to the first was equally weak. "Col. Smith was on a authorized cross-country flight from his home base, in Sioux Falls, South Dakota, and had stopped off in New England, to see his parents." He was 27 years old and lived in Watertown, Massachusetts, prior to entering the service.

My guess, never actually confirmed, was that he was logging required flying time, like my old friend Lt. James, in Nebraska. Pilots had to log a certain number of hours in the air each month to sustain flying status and flight pay. But, it was a terrible tragedy and waste, all around.

And it was a PR "baptism of fire" for Dick Nimmons and me.

Twenty years later, I would invite members of the New York press and others to visit the public viewing promenade of the Empire State Building, one hundred and two stories high, to see a Ford car on display as part of a new-model-introduction program. The thousands of visitors who saw it thought we had put it up there by helicopter, but that would have been too dangerous. The car had been brought up in sections and assembled on the spot, overnight. As we showed the press around and enjoyed the view of Manhattan from that great height, I shuddered as I thought of that Saturday morning in 1945 and of how many more lives would have been lost if the accident had occurred during a work week. It was small comfort for a bad experience.

And, almost fifty years later a somewhat similar catastrophe would involve another major New York landmark, The World Trade Center, in lower Manhattan, when an incredible explosion occurred during the noon hour on Friday, February 26, 1993. Remarkably, while it was a regular work day, there were fewer fatalities than the Empire State crash caused, but vastly more casualties, due primarily to smoke inhalation.

The Trade Center's twin towers filled with smoke almost immediately following the explosion, and its power sources were immobilized, leaving the city's tallest buildings without lights and elevator service. As in the case of the Empire State crash, people visiting or working in the buildings had to leave by way of emergency stairwells, groping their way through smoke to street level from locations as high as one hundred and seven stories. It was incredible that more people weren't seriously hurt and that there were actually fewer fatalities than during the Empire State Building crash.

One major difference in the two disasters, however, was in the handling of the news immediately following both occurrences. While fire and police response was immediate in both cases, news coverage of the Trade Center explosion was almost on a "you are there" basis as the television cameras smothered the scene with action pictures. That was impossible during the 1945 disaster. Also, the Port Authority, responsible for managing the Trade Center, was delayed in setting up a news and information command center, as we had been able to do within an hour of the Empire State crash.

Meanwhile, local TV news anchors filled the void for several hours as occupants of the two towers began to call in with reports of panic and problems, and were given on-air advice and guidance by Jim Jensen, Chuck Scarborough, and Bill Beutel, local news anchors for CBS, NBC, and ABC. Nothing quite like that had ever happened before, and in some respects it reminded viewers of Desert Storm, the war in the Middle East, which was fought as they watched spell-bound in the comfort of their offices or living rooms.

Within a couple of months of the Empire State tradegy, Dick Nimmons left the service to join T. J. Ross and Associates and work on the Hawaii Employers' Association account. It was one of several major Hawaiian accounts the Ross firm had, including the Matson Line and the Pineapple Growers Association.

I then became the "chief" of EDPRO of the USAAF - the Eastern District Public Relations Office of the United States Air Force, which was more of a mouthful than an assignment. There was just the secretary and myself, and we were counting the days until it was all over. VJ Day signaled the end of just about everything, including my recommended promotion to major. The papers were in Washington but would not clear for months.

By October 1945, I was planning my own separation. Through a major who had been impressed with my handling of contract termination matters when I had to deal with the CEOs of companies like Piper Aircraft, Bell, Lycoming, and Curtiss-Wright, I had been offered a job with the Pulliam organization in Indiana. In fact, former Vice President Dan Quayle's grandfather, Eugene Pulliam, had signed a letter requesting my early release from service to join his organization. His company owned a number of radio stations and newspapers, including the *Indianapolis News*, its flagship paper. I was sorely tempted by the offer and grateful to Major Bill Worcester, the Pulliam executive who set out to recruit me.

But then, lightning struck. The phone rang, and it was Stephan Fitzgerald, former public relations vice president for Bell Aircraft. He had just joined Earl Newsom and Company, highly respected public relations consultants in New York, and Newsom was looking for new blood for one of its blue-chip clients, Ford Motor Company. Would I be interested? It didn't take me long to subway uptown to Madison Avenue and

Fifty-Seventh Street, where the Newsom office was located in the Fuller Building. I had to know more, and the sooner the better to make what would be a major career decision.

Chapter VI

The Ghosts of M1-5

When I called Bill Worcester to tell him I had decided not to accept the offer from the Pulliam organization, I knew he was disappointed. He had hoped we would be working together, and frankly so had I. The "chemistry" was right, but I couldn't reconcile life in Indiana vis-a-vis an assignment with Ford Motor Company that might take me anywhere in the world.

I had met Earl Newsom on the visit to his Fifty-Seventh Street, office and I was impressed. He reminded me of Abraham Lincoln as he sat behind his desk, and when I spotted the portrait of "Honest Abe" hanging in the office over Earl's head, I knew it was no accident. Lincoln was Earl's inspiration. They had the same gaunt, craggy features, and Newsom had read everything about Lincoln, quoted him frequently, and shared his ideals and values. I didn't know it at the time but Earl had only one good eye, which didn't deter him from being a voracious reader. When he looked at me during the interview in his office, with Steve Fitzgerald sitting at my side, I knew instantly the man personified honesty and integrity. I wanted to be a part of whatever it was he was doing. It was to be another example of public relations as "honest work," long before I ever met Tom Ross or heard him tell his story.

Earl Newsom gave his blessing for a trip to Dearborn, Michigan, where I would be interviewed by the Ford hierarchy. I made the trip in uniform within a week and was hired by John R. "Jack" Davis, a vice president for sales and advertising who had been exiled by Harry Bennett and brought back from the West Coast by Henry Ford II to become one of Ford's key executives. Jack Davis wrote a letter requesting my separation from service, and I was sent to Henry Ford II's office, where Ed Stephans, Mr. Ford's secretary, arranged a bedroom on the Detroiter for my return trip to New York. I had come to Dearborn sleeping upright in a coach, but I was going home in style with a job at double my military pay, a company car, and an expense account.

I called my wife from the Michigan Central Station as I waited for my train, told her the good news, and then treated myself to a Manhattan cocktail at the nearest bar. I might also have pinched myself. I'm not sure.

I was assigned to the New York office, but in fact, there was no New York office. Jack Davis just planned to have one, and I was to establish it — from scratch. And while I was to represent all of Ford Motor Company's public relations interests, I would be working directly for the northeastern regional sales manager, Charles J. Seyffer, an old-school veteran of Ford sales and marketing. But Charlie Seyffer wasn't so old he didn't recognize and couldn't adapt to changing times and circumstances, especially when the company president, Henry Ford II, was only twenty-nine years old and his newly assigned PR man was twenty-seven.

Charlie Seyffer had two sons close to my age at the time, but he always treated me like a respected and valued member of his staff, and that set the tone for all of my relationships with senior people. To all of them, including Mr. Seyffer, public relations was an unknown quantity, but it represented Ford Motor Company's new approach to doing business. Some of my new associates were visibly skeptical, however, if not downright negative. They preferred the status quo and didn't like the new look.

One Ford executive who got on the PR bandwagon right away was Nelson Bowe, an irrepressible New York district sales manager. Bowe had been an assistant to Jack Davis, in California, and had gone "hollywood"in dress, manner and flair for the dramatic. He took to New York like a Broadway headliner, but he provided a touch of humor to daily life.

One weekend I came up with an inflamed appendix and had to undergo surgery. Nels sent a flower-filled bedpan to my hospital room.

Another of his great put-ons was to approach a group of people, single out someone, finger that person's suit jacket lapels and say: "That has a nice feel to it, Kid, why don't you have it made into a suit?" Or, "I'll be damned, I didn't know burlap was coming back."

He craved personal publicity to a fault, and when his picture began appearing in automotive publications without our help, we found he'd appointed his chief clerk as personal publicist. That was a "No No."

He finally over-reached one day with the regional manager, Charlie Seyffer. He plastered the general and private office walls with large banners carrying the word GOYA. When the secretaries found out it meant "Get Off Your Ass," it back-fired and the banners came down faster than the Berlin Wall. Nels got "promoted"to Dearborn, shortly thereafter.

Under the old Ford policies, "The less said about anything, the better," was often the way things were handled. Many in the company in "old Henry's" heyday believed no news was good news. But that was about to change and quickly. Nevertheless, I was either given a wide berth or finessed by some senior Ford people in the earliest days, as word got around the plants and sales offices that I had "gone to school" with Henry Ford II. Nothing could have been further from the truth, of course. The only time I had seen Mr. Ford was when I went to his office in Dearborn the day I was interviewed, hired, and introduced to some of the management.

It had taken sixty days for me to have the paperwork processed and to report to Mitchel Field, Garden City, Long

Island, for separation after three and a half years of military service. That was on January 18, 1946. On the following day, I reported for work at my new office, 630 Fifth Avenue, wearing the only suit to my name. I had bought it the prior week off the rack at Finchley Men's Store on Fifth Avenue.

The New York Ford office was a small suite in the International building at Rockefeller Center. It had just been leased primarily as a New York office for Henry Ford II, and our public relations activity was an add-on. There were a few desks, some office furniture, a few working phones, and no staff.

We were starting from ground zero, for sure.

I soon learned that our office and some others in the building had been occupied by William Stephenson, and his staff of British Intelligence Operatives in the United States, throughout World War II. Known as MI-5, British Intelligence had started in a modest way when Stephenson was detailed by Winston Churchill to come to the United States and launch the activity with the full knowledge and cooperation of our government, including J. Edgar Hoover and his FBI and William S. "Wild Bill" Donovan and his newly-formed Office of Strategic Services (OSS).

The building at 630 Fifth Avenue had been a center of intrigue and mysterious comings and goings throughout the war. There were times thereafter, however, when I felt that some of the operatives had never left and could be seen on occasion riding the elevators with their briefcases, trench coats, and umbrellas or sipping a drink in the Mayan Restaurant on the ground floor. After all, it didn't hurt to have a lively imagination in the public relations field!

On a visit to the Ford New York PR office in February, 1993, again located in the International Building after four moves to other locations in Manhattan, I mentioned MI-5 and our early days to Chuck Oldbricht, the present PR manager.

"John, I think they are still here," he said. "I know the British news services are in this building, and I see Brits in trench coats in the lobby and riding the elevators all the time. I'm sure some of those old hands must be still around."

Chuck had a point. It always seemed to me that intelligence and journalism were never far apart where the British were concerned. I recalled that my old friend and former Ford colleague Sydney W. "Bill" Morrell had been a British journalist during World War II, but he was also blowing up bridges in Poland to slow the German advance through that country. Morrell told me he carried dynamite in his portable typewriter case, concealed in old, newspapers! At the time, Morrell was working with Maurice Buckmaster, based in London, who controlled agents all over Europe. After World War II, Buckmaster became public relations manager of Ford of England, and Morrell joined Earl Newsom and Company, prior to accepting a high level PR position with Ford, in Dearborn.

As I left Oldbricht that cold February day and passed the former Mayan restaurant, I thought for a fleeting moment I saw a familiar figure at a table in the shadows. Could it be? Stephenson? Intrepid, himself? But he was dead, wasn't he? Or was he?

Even before I could hire a secretary and requisition working files from Dearborn, in January, 1946, I had my first business call, and it was a doozey. It was from a reporter at the *New York Journal American*, who said he was checking a story possibility. "We understand Joe Adonis, the Brooklyn mobster, has the franchise to deliver all cars built at your Edgewater, New Jersey, plant to dealers in the New York area. Is that correct?" he asked.

I said I was new with Ford, that we had just opened the office, and that I couldn't confirm or deny what he said because I didn't know. I said I would look into it and get back to him, and I wrote down the particulars.

The response I was to provide later proved to be the first of several bum steers I would get from within our own organization, until I could develop my own dependable sources.

When I checked our Edgewater plant management, I was referred to New Car Carriers, the hauling company located near the plant. A call to New Car put me in touch with Paul Bonadio, one of the principals. I identified myself, repeated what I had been asked and identified the caller from the *Journal American*. Bonadio clammed up immediately. "Who did you say you were?" he asked. I told him again. "What's your number? I'll call you back," and he did in about twenty minutes, apologizing for the delay. The bottom line was that he denied everything, saying, "Mr. Adonis has no interest in this company." I relayed that information to the reporter, who was skeptical and said he would check other sources. The net result was that the *Journal American* carried a story the next day identifying Adonis as having a "sweetheart" contract to haul all local Ford car and truck production.

I had egg on my face, as they say, and felt bad about it. I felt better, though, a couple of weeks after my detailed report about the incident reached the right people in Dearborn. By appointment, Joe Adonis, looking for all the world like a well-groomed businessman, arrived at the Edgewater plant offices for a meeting called by John Bugas, former head of the Detroit office of the FBI, and then Ford vice president/industrial relations. Angus Harris, plant manager, and Charles Seyffer, branch manager, were also on hand. Polite, well-mannered, and almost polished, Joe Adonis acknowledged his "participation" in the haulaway franchise, and said that in order to avoid possible embarrassment to Mr. Ford, he would divest himself of his holdings. What we didn't know at the time was that Paul Bonadio and Charles Chiri, the other principals in the business, were related to Adonis. Therefore nothing really changed, but we could say Joe Adonis had divested himself of any ownership and participation in New Car Carriers operations.

Some years later when a major gathering of alleged mobsters took place at the home of Joseph Barbara in Appalachian,

New York, Charles Chiri was one of those apprehended by New York State troopers as he tried to flee into the woods. Joe Adonis had been deported to Italy by then, and Mr. Chiri was supposedly representing the interests of the Adonis family. Chiri was apparently in good company. They picked up Joseph Bonnano, Vito Genovese, Frank Costello, and a substantial number of other so-called syndicate types from all over the country, who said they'd "just dropped in for a social visit and a backyard barbecue" with their old friend, Joe Barbara.

The New York State Police and the Federal Bureau of Investigation didn't buy that.

Charles Chiri left the executive suite of New Car Carriers thereafter, but that was only the tip of the iceberg. As a result of Harry Bennett's influence on old Henry Ford, the company and its far-flung interests had been infiltrated by a veritable army of "hidden persuaders." I would uncover more of that in a short time.

Chapter VII

he Man in the Basement ffice

A man named Harry Bennett had a virtual hammerlock on the Ford Motor Company by the time Henry Ford II was mustered out of service to return to civilian life and help save the company his grandfather and father had built to international proportions.

Ford Motor Company was in dire straits as the United States went to war, and many say it was only the war that saved Ford. Henry Ford, Sr., had grown old and insulated and, for whatever the reasons, almost alienated from his only son, Edsel. Harry Bennett, a one-time navy gob and street fighter, had been hired by Henry Ford on the recommendation of Arthur Brisbane, the noted New York editor. He and Mr. Ford, had seen Bennett whip someone twice his size in a New York City street fight. "That's the kind of person you need at your company, Henry," Brisbane is reported to have said, and Ford hired Bennett on the spot to work in the Ford security department. It wasn't long, though, before Bennett saw better prospects for himself and made the most of his opportunities.

Henry Ford always seemed to take an interest in those who worked for him, and Harry Bennett was no exception. Soon Bennett was driving the Boss, as he called him, back and forth to work and elsewhere on the senior Ford's various daily rounds. He became the first Ford employee to see Mr. Ford in the morning and the last to see him when he took him home at night. He would call him later in the evening to see if there were any last minute instructions. He made himself indispensable, and he would stop at nothing to get things done and to please and impress the Boss.

One story often told is Bennett's quick action one day when Mr. Ford questioned the value of a company service station he spotted on Ford property while enroute to work in the morning. "Harry, why do we need that gas station out here?" Henry Ford is alleged to have asked, "I think it's an eyesore." The station had been used to gas and service company vehicles.

"I'll take care of it," Harry Bennett is reported to have said, and he did. By late afternoon when they were driving back to Ford's Fair Lane Estate, they went by the same location and the service station had disappeared. In the intervening time, Bennett had crews remove everything — structure, pumps, tanks, and anything else above ground level. Landscapers then moved in and put down sod, and planted trees and shrubs. It was virtually impossible to recognize the place.

"Good work, Harry," Henry Ford said. "You know how to get things done." He might have added, "Now, if I could only get Edsel to take action like that."

The senior Ford had a problem in understanding why his only son was "different." Edsel was a somewhat shy, retiring, and sensitive man who always deferred to his father. In part, he'd acquired that from being rebuffed so many times when he tried to take charge and advance his own ideas of how things should be done, how Ford products should be changed or company policies altered. Henry Ford usually would have none of it, showing great disappointment that Edsel wasn't more like him, as well as a distinct unwillingness to try anything new or change anything he, Henry, wasn't in complete agreement with.

It made for a miserable life for Edsel and for his wife, Eleanor, who came from two of Detroit's distinguished families, the Clays and the Hudsons. Henry Ford had blessed their marriage, but he rarely visited their home in Grosse Pointe, which is on Michigan's eastern shore. He couldn't understand why they didn't live in Dearborn or closer by, and he didn't trust Grosse Pointe "aristocracy" with its drinking parties and sporting habits. It all led to considerable strain in family relationships that didn't escape the interest and attention of the wily Bennett, who often played on it to his advantage, though he claimed otherwise.

In building up the security operations, Bennett had reached out for all manner and means of muscle — strong-arm men, football players and other athletes, ex-cons, and informers. He built them into a network of loyal and disciplined toughs whom he controlled from a basement office in the then Ford headquarters building at 3000 Schaefer Road. The headquarters was located across the street from the famed Rotunda, which had been the Ford exhibit showcase at the Chicago World's Fair in 1934. After the fair, Ford had had the structure moved intact to the Schaefer Road location where it was used as a multipurpose display and exhibit center. It was open to the public, and all tours of the famous River Rouge plant originated from there. Visited each year by almost a million people from all over the world, the Rotunda was an outstanding product showcase.

There was a tunnel that ran under Schaefer Road directly to the Rotunda from the basement of the company headquarters. It provided an excellent escape route for anyone at headquarters who didn't want to be seen leaving the building. Arrangements could simply be made to have a car waiting behind the Rotunda, and the return to headquarters could be made the same way.

Henry Ford had a formal Office of the President on the main floor of the headquarters, but he rarely used it, favoring instead a comfortable old office in the engineering building, where he was surrounded by the things he enjoyed and no one could bother him. He would visit Harry Bennett in the basement office at headquarters, however. There he could put his feet up on the desk and watch Harry shoot at targets on the wall of his spartan office. Bennett kept a gun in his desk drawer and liked to use it. He was also too smart to opt for a plush office in the executive suite that housed Edsel and the few vice presidents. There weren't many titles, though, as

Henry Ford didn't like titles. Harry Bennett knew Henry Ford liked unpretentiousness, and he played to it all the way.

As time marched on and the company founder began to slow with age, Bennett strengthened his hold on the old man almost to the point of total command. He kept people away from Henry and worked himself into the role of spokesperson. He acted and spoke for Mr. Ford, and few could challenge him, for they knew the role he played. He could say, "Mr. Ford wants, Mr. Ford says, Mr. Ford thinks, or Mr. Ford would prefer," and no one would know the difference. To compound matters, Edsel, the true heir apparent, died unexpectedly in 1943. Some said it was of a broken heart brought on by his father's callousness and Bennett's machinations. Henry Ford said it was from undulant fever, the result of drinking unpasteurized milk. Others attributed it to stomach cancer and alcohol, the result of personal depression and weekend efforts to get away from it all.

When I joined Ford Motor Company, there were still a number of senior Ford people around, like New York branch manager Charlie Seyffer, who had worked with Edsel over the years and had nothing but the best to say about him. They said his untimely death was a terrible loss for the Ford Motor Company, that Bennett would have been its ruination, and that Ford had come remarkably close to a Bennett takeover when the war was winding down in 1945.

John S. Bugas was chief of the Federal Bureau of Investigation in Detroit during the early war years at a time when the city was a hotbed of antiwar intrigue, Nazi sympathizers, and potential saboteurs. Detroit was the "industrial Ruhr" of the United States and vital to the war effort beyond measure. At its giant Willow Run plant, built from scratch during the first year of America's entry into the war, Ford was turning out B-24 bombers on an assembly line basis. By the end of the war close to nine thousand had been built. It was an unheard of production achievement, thanks to an all-out effort by Ford loyalists and full government cooperation.

Bennett knew and liked John Bugas and offered him a position on his staff at a salary Bugas could hardly refuse. J. Edgar Hoover gave his blessing as did Edsel's widow, Eleanor Ford, when Bugas went to see her in a private meeting. The government was in favor of the move owing to Ford's vital role as a war contractor. But it was a move Harry Bennett would one day regret, for instead of solidifying his role, it had just the opposite effect. Bugas brought seasoned FBI agents with him and placed them strategically throughout the company. He was biding his time while increasingly aware of the continuing deterioration of the Ford Motor Company through mismanagement, poor organization, intrigue, and political in-fighting.

It was probably his private reports to Eleanor Ford and her brother-in-law, Ernest Kanzler, that led to the release of Henry Ford II from the navy by Secretary Knox in July 1943. There was a greater wartime need for his services at one of the nation's leading industrial companies than at the Great Lakes Naval Air Station in Chicago.

Harry Bennett, of course, offered to do "anything possible" to assist "young Henry" in finding a "niche" for himself at the company, and Henry II graciously accepted his offer and that of anyone else. He was unpretentious, willing, and interested in doing whatever was necessary to hold the Ford Motor Company together for the major role it would have to play in the postwar world. After all, before the war it had employed several hundred thousand people in plants and offices in more than sixty countries. Since 1904 it had been a powerful factor on the world industrial scene when one year after its founding, it had established operations in Canada. Thereafter, it had expanded to England and the Continent and even China and Japan. It was an enormous and vital business, and it had to be saved.

Henry Ford, Sr., was becoming senile when Henry Ford II returned from the navy, but Harry Bennett's influence and control remained undiminished. Bennett still saw the old gentleman everyday or was in touch with him, whether or not

Henry, Sr., was well enough to leave his home. The same thing could not be said for Henry Ford II, or for anyone else. Bennett, the indispensable man, was still in control, still calling the shots, and it was then approaching the fall of 1945. Something was going to have to give, and at that point, it seemed unlikely it would be the man in the basement office.

Chapter VIII

Jncle Ernie and "Uncle Ernie"

While Harry Bennett felt himself comfortably entrenched, having eliminated just about all opposition in one way or another and considering Henry II too young to pose any serious threat, things were going on FBI-style behind the scenes with little fuss or fanfare.

Eleanor Clay Ford had been consulting with her trusted advisor, brother-in-law Ernest Kanzler, who had at one time been an executive of the Ford Motor Company and an ally of Edsel Ford. Henry Ford, Sr., didn't like Kanzler or the influence Kanzler had on his son, so he had found a way to get rid of him. That must have pleased Harry Bennett immensely. When he left the company, Kanzler became head of Universal Credit Corporation, which handled financing for Ford cars. He continued to maintain his close ties with the Edsel Fords and their children, however, to whom he was always "Uncle Ernie."

Also involved in the behind-the-scenes meetings, in addition to Henry Ford II, were trusted Ford executives John R. Davis — who had been returned from exile on the West Coast, over Harry Bennett's objections — Mead L. Bricker, a manufacturing executive, and John Bugas. The group decided it was time to make a move that would lead to Bennett's downfall and ultimate departure, Henry Ford II's election as president, and the necessary change in control of Ford Motor Company.

Ford was a privately owned company. All the stock was held by family members. It fell to Eleanor Clay Ford, as one of those owners, to take the lead in what they all knew had to be done. She went to see her mother-in-law, Clara Ford, Henry's loyal and dedicated wife and Henry Ford II's devoted grandmother. It was time for a change, she told Clara Ford. It was time to end all of the uncertainty and strife surrounding Ford Motor Company — strife that may have contributed to the untimely death of her husband and Clara's only son, Edsel, who had torn himself up emotionally and physically disagreeing with the things that went on at River Rouge and the Dearborn headquarters. Men had been beaten by Bennett's goons when they attempted to unionize the giant company's labor force. Theft and mismanagement were rampant. Private parties with women friends of some executives and company secretaries were being held in a fancy hideout on River Rouge plant property. Racketeers controlled food services, gambling, loan-sharking, and even some of the employment policies of the company. Something had to be done right away, Eleanor said, or everything they had been working for and that had been built up during the first half of the century would be lost. She, Eleanor Ford, was not about to allow that to happen to her children and Clara's grandchildren. She said Clara and Eleanor would have to speak to the aging and increasingly unpredictable founder and ask him to stand aside for younger members of the Ford family, or she would place her stock on the open market and take Ford Motor Company public.

The dramatic meeting was arranged, and Henry Ford, Sr., by then eighty-one years old, worn out and on the brink of total senility, capitulated. He would step down from the presidency and allow Henry Ford II to succeed him. It was a bitter experience for the old man, for in that moment, he too could see everything slipping out of his control. He agreed, however reluctantly, and a meeting of the board of directors was held on September 21, 1945, to finalize and legalize the action. When it was over, Bennett was advised by Henry Ford II that he was finished and would leave immediately with a company retirement pension.

Bennett was furious, accusing "young Henry," of contributing nothing to the growth and success of Ford Motor Company, while he, Bennett, had given his life to the company and its founder. What he didn't add, however, was that he had become a millionaire in the process and lived in a "castle" of his own in Ann Arbor, Michigan, equipped, interestingly enough, with its own secret staircases and tunnels that were part of escape routes in the event he and his family needed them. But it was all over — he knew it. And in a surprising gesture he offered to take Henry II and John Bugas on a tour of company property — an offer they accepted in the circumstances.

But the work of the Ford "rebirth" planning committee, as we shall call it, was not over. In fact, it was just beginning. Henry Ford II, at twenty-eight, needed a lot of help. He wisely recognized that, and he was willing to share responsibility and recognition with those who could contribute to the new era. It was a time of golden opportunity for anyone fortunate enough to join the team, even though the company was losing somewhere in the range of eight million dollars a month when I was hired in November 1945. When I went to work the following January, however, I simply didn't know that fact of corporate life. It was months later that the new executive vice president, Ernest R. Breech revealed the figures for the first time.

Ernest Kanzler, a seasoned corporate executive, and Eleanor Ford both had great respect for the talents and dedication of men like Bugas, Davis, and Bricker. They realized, however, that additional strong leadership and experience was needed immediately and could be found only outside Ford Motor Company. The man they chose to head the new management group, chiefly on Kanzler's recommendation, was Ernest R. Breech, a feisty General Motors executive, who had headed up GM's Bendix operations.

Ernie Breech was a financial powerhouse and a seasoned professional manager, but he probably would never have reached the top of the General Motors management heap, because too many senior people were ahead of him. On the other hand, he was well paid, successful, and happy, and he didn't exactly jump at the chance to join Ford when the No.2 job was offered to him by Henry Ford II, under whose titular leadership he would work. But "Uncle Ernie" Breech, as he was soon referred to by some, was a visionary. He saw all the possibilities and opportunities as well as the hazards, and it was a challenge he could not resist.

Ernest Breech came aboard as executive vice president on July 1, 1946, and brought additional key executive talent with him, including Harold Youngren, an engineer; Bill Gossett, a son-in-law of former Supreme Court Chief Justice Charles Evans Hughes; and Delmar Harder, a manufacturing executive. They went to work immediately to update and streamline the giant corporation, which had become moribund and muscle-bound, and it wasn't going to be easy. In fact, at the outset, Breech is said to have thought the problems almost beyond control.

I was already aboard when Ernie Breech and his team arrived on the scene. I had made a number of forays to Dearborn to explore the corporate and news operations files and by then could often provide immediate answers to information requests received by telephone in contrast to my experience with the Joe Adonis inquiry.

Ford had no public relations staff as such prior to 1946 when I started the New York office. There was only a Ford News Bureau, an excellent operation in Dearborn headed by C. E. "Charlie" Carll. Charlie's staff consisted of a half dozen former newspaper reporters, who covered the various activities of the company as they would cover beats for a newspaper — steel operations, engineering, manufacturing, sales and marketing, and so forth. Charlie also had on his staff an outstanding industrial photographer, Paul Dorsey, who supplied a steady stream of highly usable black-and-white photo and color material that was widely used in newspapers, magazines, and anywhere else applicable. One of Dorsey's most famous photographs would never be acceptable today. It showed the half-dozen landmark smokestacks of the famous Ford River

Rouge plant belching smoke into the sky as an indication of all-out production. Environmentalists from coast to coast, if not the world, would march on Michigan if that type of photo were distributed today. But it was a graphic and distinct message at the time and appeared all over the world to illustrate Ford production might.

Earl Newsom was our public relations mentor in those days. Working with Elmo Roper, the noted public opinion pollster and analyst, Newsom was diligently trying to change the image of the company from a labor-baiting, hard-as-nails employer to one of enlightened public- and self-interest. Henry Ford II, the new young president, would play the key role in changing the public image of the reborn Ford Motor Company under Newsom's carefully thought out plan and Earl would orchestrate it. The rest of us would also play on the team and occasionally turn in a star-quality performance. They were the Camelot days of postwar Ford public relations, and we were all Knights of the Round Table in King Henry's court. Above all, it was great fun. I don't think Henry Ford II would have had it any other way, and I know I wouldn't.

Harry Bennett had barely departed the scene, however, going on to California and Arizona to live, when some of the residue of his years of influence began to surface in awkward and embarrassing ways. I received a phone call one afternoon that would almost repeat the Adonis experience. Frederick Woltman, a noted writer on communism for the *New York World Telegram*, called to say that in response to one of his articles, he'd heard from a man who said he'd done a lot of "Communist investigation" for Ford Motor Company. The man also said he had handled other types of investigation for Ford, including a study of the sex lives of the DuPont family, whose company just happened to have a major stock interest in General Motors.

Did I know the man or anything about the investigations? Woltman wanted to know. I didn't and had to give him the routine reply of "newness" with a promise of a followup. Woltman told me the man said he worked out of the Ford Chester plant near Philadelphia. He never went to the plant, however, but met with a Ford representative in hotel rooms and was paid in cash. It sounded either kooky or criminal. I hoped it was the former.

A check with industrial relations at the Ford Chester plant brought almost the same response and routine I'd experienced with Paul Bonadio. "Who did you say you were? I'll call you right back . . . ."

A man by the name of Schmidt did call me back — said he knew the person involved but that the man actually worked for the military services and not for Ford. "Communist infiltration of war plants is a big military consideration," Schmidt said, "And this man works for the Army's Second Service Command."

Schmidt said he didn't know anything about the DuPont matter but that it might also be connected to military concerns.

I reported all that information back to Woltman but then received a call from the mystery man himself saying I had slandered him and that he proposed to sue me and Ford Motor Company. I advised Schmidt, who by then was very nervous and insisted on coming to New York to meet with me and the person involved to see if the problem could be resolved. Frederick Woltman was not to be included. That was fine with me.

When we met at my Rockefeller Center office on a Saturday morning, it was obvious to me that Schmidt had been lying. The mystery man was right. Someone connected with Ford had indeed arranged for him to get into a series of highly questionable investigations. Years later General Motors would undertake a similar highly questionable investigation against Ralph Nader.

At that point, Ford lawyers were brought in, and an out-of-court settlement was reached before the situation could become more inflamed.

Frederick Woltman never had occasion to follow up the matter after I apologized to him for providing the incorrect information I had obtained from my in-house source. It wasn't very good press relations, but I think Woltman understood what I was up against. Woltman said he didn't plan to write anything, which pleased me, but I always thought he missed a story detailing misguided corporate meddling in private and personal matters. From a public relations standpoint, however, it was the best thing that could have happened. Once again, honesty was the best policy when dealing with the press and others.

I never knowingly deviated from that policy during my entire career in public relations.

Chapter IX

Henry Ford is Dead in Dearborn

One of my principal press contacts in the early postwar days was an elderly reporter for the *New York Times*, Herbert A. "Bert" Pierce. In fact, the manuscript for this memoir is being typed on a gold-plated Remington typewriter I presented to Bert on behalf of Ford Motor Company at the Edsel introduction program in Dearborn, Michigan, in August 1957. The typewriter was given in recognition of Bert's fifty years of service as a reporter, many of them as an automobile writer. At that time, Bert was the automobile editor of the *Times*, and in the opinion of most of us, there was no other paper in the country with more clout and influence — something I personally believe hasn't changed over the years.

It wasn't any space-grabbing ploy on our part. We presented similar typewriters to two other reporters for the same reason, one to Leon Pinkson of the *San Francisco Chronicle*, and the third to David Wilkie of the Associated Press. All had been reporters for fifty years or more, and all had served as automobile editors and/or writers. It was a gesture we felt would be appreciated not only by the recipients and the press guests present for the Edsel introduction but also by those who would read or learn about the unique presentations through media news channels. We also thought the recognitions would add to the evening program, which featured Ray McKinley and the Glen Miller orchestra with its "big band" sound.

It turned out to be a super party, and Gayle Warnock, the Edsel PR manager, was ecstatic. Henry Ford II was more subdued but he had a great time whirling his wife, Anne, around the dance floor to the Miller band tempo. Bert Pierce and the other "Golden Oldies" beamed like presidential candidates as they came off the platform to waves of applause helped along by the bubbles in the magnums of Dom Perignon champagne. It was another of those memorable occasions.

It had been some years earlier that I'd received a phone call from Bert, who liked to sip rob roy cocktails at the bar of the Stork Club. He knew everyone in the club from Tony Butrico, the personable bartender, to the man himself, Sherman Billingsley. Billingsley would later have his own television show titled appropriately enough, "The Stork Club."

"Cheerio, Chin Chin," the voice on the phone said. "It's Bertie. I'm sipping a chilled rob roy at the Stork and wondered if you'd care to join me?" It was 4:30 P.M. I was beginning to wind down for the day and head for Garden City, where Elinore and I then lived. I hadn't planned on cocktails at the Stork. A call from Bert was almost a command performance, however, and the invitation sounded appealing even though I knew I would be picking up the check. I also thought it would be a good idea to establish my identity at the Stork, and I could have no better sponsor. After all, Walter Winchell, J. Edgar Hoover and his aide Clyde Tolson were regulars, and so were countless other movers and shakers of the world. It was one of the most exclusive "in" places at the time, and to gain entry, you had to get by "the rope" at the entrance, under the almost x-ray scrutiny of Ed Wynn (not the actor) and Chuck Harris, the "hosts."

Winchell and Hoover favored the Cub Room, from where they departed one evening to meet Louis "Lepke" Buchalter, the notorious garment district racketeer, who had been in hiding and had arranged with Winchell to turn himself in to the FBI. He thought it might lead to a reduced sentence. Something went wrong, however, and he subsequently died in the electric chair at Sing Sing Prison, fifty miles up the Hudson

River from Manhattan. Hoover had made no deal, reaped all of the press benefit, and then simply let the system deal with Buchalter.

I told Bert Pierce I was finishing some work and would join him shortly. I think I also called Elinore to say I might be home late, but there were times those good intentions were delayed or postponed until they were swallowed up in the gathering mists of the evening. Thank the Lord, Elinore almost always understood.

Bert was at the bar when I arrived shortly after five, waiting for any unsuspecting visiting automotive executive who might be good for a statement or a story. Automobiles were big news, and he knew K. T. Keller, the Chrysler chief, was a Stork Club regular when he was in town. Keller wasn't there that evening, however. And although I didn't know it, I was sitting on what would become the biggest news story of the day — totally unaware at that point of developing details. Henry Ford, Sr., the man who helped put the world on wheels and whose name was known in virtually every household, was in the final hours of his life in Michigan, at the age of eight-three.

Bert and I had several rounds of drinks at the Stork, and then went on to the Hotel Lexington, another one of his favorite haunts. We ended up getting something to eat, and I drove him home to Kew Gardens, where I dropped him near his home. In all the years I knew him, I never found out until the day he died exactly where he lived or that he had a wife. I always thought he was an aging bachelor who was wed to a solitary life of newspapering and socializing with friends like me. When I did meet his wife she presented me with the gold typewriter, which she couldn't use, as a remembrance of my warm friendship with her husband. She knew all about me, it turned out, even though I had never heard about her. I wondered if Bert had lived more than one life simultaneously. I insisted on paying Mrs. Pierce for the typewriter, however, and I have used it for special purposes ever since. In fact, in 1987 I took it to Indonesia on an assignment, and it created quite a stir. No one there had ever seen a gold typewriter, and come to think of it, very few have ever seen one here in the States.

When I arrived home from my evening entertaining Bert, close to midnight, Elinore had retired, and I slipped into bed just as the telephone rang. The caller was James W. Irwin, then head of our newly established public relations division. "Jack," he said, "sorry to call you at this hour but Mr. Ford just died, and Charlie Carll and I are on our way to the estate. How soon can you get to the office and open the TWX machine? This is a big story, and we have to stay on top of it. The phones will be ringing off the hook. Get in there and stand by until you hear from one of us when we reach the Ford home." I couldn't get a word in edgewise as Jim rattled on, never told him how long it would take to get to New York, or that I had just left the place about an hour ago.

When I put the phone down and started to dress, Elinore asked "What was that all about?" I told her and said I had to get right back to the office. "That's a crazy business you're in" she said. "What can you do about it? Mr. Ford is dead, isn't he?"

"Well, I'll have to help get the story out, I guess, and stand by for whatever develops."

It wasn't the last time that morning I would be asked, "What can you do about it?"

It was 1 A.M. when I got into my company car and headed for the city along the Grand Central Parkway. When I reached the old service station area in Queens, a police squad car caught up and pulled me over. The lone duty cop said, "You're in a big hurry. I clocked you at seventy-five. License and registration please." I knew I was in trouble, but tried to explain that Mr. Ford had died in Michigan and that I had been ordered to open my office immediately. "What can you do about it?" the officer asked. "He's dead, isn't he?"

I said I was in public relations, head of Ford's New York office and that there would be a lot of press interest, since Mr. Ford was a world personality. The officer looked at me for a moment, shook his head, and then said, "Well, I guess the police need public relations too. Take it easy. You'll get there, and we don't want two dead Ford people in one night."

That convinced me you can luck out with the police if they think you're on the up and up!

When I got to the office, the heat was off. It was March, and it was cold. I flipped on the TWX machine and alerted Dearborn to the fact I was there. An hour later, when I hadn't heard anything and hadn't received any press calls, I made a call to the Ford News Bureau and got the secretary, Charlene Heard. "What's going on, Char?" I asked. "It's terrible here. I'm dying for some coffee and there's no heat in the building."

What Charlene told me was almost comical. Jim Irwin and Charlie Carll had gone to the Ford estate, and when they got there, the gatekeeper wouldn't let them in. He said he didn't know them, and nobody was getting past him. They finally had to wait for Henry Ford II to arrive from his home in Grosse Pointe before they could gain admission. By then, it was all over. The story was on the news wires and probably in print in some places, if only with a big headline and a few paragraphs. The wires soon followed the news flash with reams of in-depth background. Feature stories about the legendary man ran in supplements and magazines for months thereafter.

I always thought one of the servants tipped Dave Wilkie, the veteran AP writer, within minutes of the old gentleman's passing, because they knew Dave and the senior Ford were good friends.

Henry Ford's life and death was a story with deep roots in America — the country boy who came into the world by candlelight and oil lamps and who had left much the same way. A severe storm on the day he died caused the Rouge River to overflow its banks behind his home, and the rising water flooded the powerhouse he maintained to provide electricity for the residence and estate. The flooding resulted in a total blackout as the man who had given mobility and comfort to millions breathed his last. Only oil lamps and candles were aglow in the house when Henry II arrived with Irwin and Carll in tow.

I spent the rest of the hours trying to catnap and do other things, including slipping out at one point to go to Times Square for the early morning editions of the New York papers.

The *Daily News* and the *Daily Mirror* carried front-page block headlines. "HENRY FORD DEAD AT 83" seemed to say it all.

It was a big story. Did we miss it? Could we have even handled it? The fact is, for a story like that, we weren't even needed. Veteran reporters like Dave Wilkie had been expecting it and were prepared. All we could have done was fill in a few details, but the wily Wilkie, with better news sources than we had, did that for us.

I never had a phone call until mid-morning the following day, and it was totally unrelated to what had happened the night before.

Chapter X

The Care and Feeding of the Press

Ivy Lee, Edward L. Bernays, and Benjamin Sonnenberg, those inspired pioneer press agents and publicists-cum-public relations specialists, knew from personal experience that communication was the life blood of what they were doing. It was all perfectly well to talk about changing policies and methods of doing business or even changing personal or corporate conduct, for that matter, but if no one knew anything about it, the job was only partly done. One of the simplified definitions of PR seemed to spell it out better than most, "Do the right thing and get credit for it." If no one heard about it, there was no credit.

You could build a better mousetrap, sewing machine, automobile, or dream house or develop a new toothpaste or whatever, but people had to be told about it to complete the circle. That was where the press agent and publicist — the public relations man — came in, along with the advertising, sales, and marketing specialists, and others. A good part of every PR job is to "get the message out," and that is why so many of the earliest people in this field were former newspaper reporters and writers. They knew what made news and what didn't and how to handle it from the idea stage right through to the printed and spoken word. Lee, Bernays, Sonnenberg, and other pioneers in the information field had cut their eyeteeth while generating and handling news, and they were increasingly in demand. It was much later that public relations began to broaden its base, became more sophisticated in its development; and got into such things as research, audits, and specialized functions — financial public relations, governmental affairs, lobbying.

Much of our PR work in the early days at Ford was the second half of the circle — communication. The first half was being handled increasingly well by Henry Ford II, who was our principal public relations figurehead and spokesperson, and by those who planned the corporation's policies and actions, the Ford Board of Directors and Ford Administration Committee. They were ably assisted by the outside counsel of Earl Newsom, Elmo Roper, and the veteran Washington, D. C., government affairs specialist, Arthur Newmeyer, Sr.

Newsom, Roper, and Newmeyer often had their heads together on changing Ford's public image and reputation and advised Henry Ford II and his board how to go about it.

One of the first major steps was a change in personnel and labor policies to offset the previous impersonal and antagonistic policies that had prevailed during the Bennett years. For a company that had pioneered the five-dollar day and shown early concerns for its employees and customers by paying high wages and offering low-priced products, Ford had slipped noticeably into third place behind its major competitors, General Motors and Chrysler. Many blamed it on Bennett and his undue influence on the senior Ford, but others felt Bennett merely carried out the bidding of a man who had grown old, embittered, and out of touch.

Ford did not like the unions and fought them tenaciously, while competitors took a more realistic approach in resolving any differences. It was Ford's obstinacy and intransigence that led to the bloody Battle of the Overpass at the Rouge plant when Walter Reuther, Richard Frankenstein, and other union organizers were beaten savagely by Bennett's "security" men. The stories and photographs of that incident on May 26, 1937, appeared on front pages all over the world, alienating the public and workers everywhere. The Ford women, Clara and

Eleanor, were badly shaken, and it was just such graphic demonstrations of brutality that convinced them things had to be changed.

When I visited the Ford Edgewater plant in early 1946 and met people in the local community, I heard a story about working conditions I never forgot. "That plant is run so cold-heartedly," a local tradesman said. "They stick a broom up your ass when you work the line so you can sweep the floor at the same time." Everybody laughed at that, but the message was clear. Ford supervisors were "whip snappers," and management approved.

I had a hard time convincing Hermione Davis, a reporter for the *Hudson Dispatch* in Jersey City, that things had changed. "I'll believe it when I see it," she told me. Her husband worked at the Edgewater plant and was a fledgling union organizer, so it wasn't going to be easy. But there came a day when Hermione did admit "the place has changed." It took about three years and a lot of what we called stroking and spoon feeding a recalcitrant press contact, but we did make a friend of Hermione, albeit a wary one. Where company and union interests were at an impasse, we couldn't count on Hermione to come down on our side, though she generally tried to be fair. She had heard and experienced too much to change her opinions too soon.

Our office treated the "outlying" press with the same degree of patience, interest, and attention we accorded the metropolitan press, or the big-city outlets. They may not have seemed equally important in some respects, but they were most assuredly important and especially those in company office and plant locations. Our employees read local and hometown newspapers, and they tended to believe "the locals" to a greater extent than they did the big-city papers.

Early on I hired Robert J. "Bob" Stone, wartime reporter for the army's Yank magazine and Stars and Stripes newspaper, and then a reporter in New Jersey, to become "our man on the scene" in working with suburban media. He did a superb job. In fact, all these years later, he is still one of the most effective PR media counselors I've ever worked with. Fair, objective, dedicated, and honest, Bob Stone may wear a public relations hat, but he becomes a part of the working press when there is a job to be done. I always rested easy when I knew Bob was on the job, whether it was a midnight fire at one of the plants or a wildcat walkout over some overblown or contrived issue.

My other early staff assistants in New York included Russell M. Hart, who had been handling automobile news for the *Herald Tribune*; William W. Hersey, who also came over from the *Trib*; and John D. Cameron, a well-grounded New Yorker who had come to us from the Fred Eldean Public Relations Organization and the American Petroleum Institute. Also aboard were D. C. "Chris" Whittle, who had handled PR for the military in Germany, and George Trainor, an ex-marine with a natural talent for making friends, and who eventually headed up our PR office in Washington, D. C., and Ford's international PR activities.

All were seasoned professionals when it came to handling news. All were personable, all could write, and all enjoyed the company of reporters and editors and had many friends in the press.

Together they were a class act that could be counted on for integrity, dependability, service, and performance. I was proud of everyone on our staff.

Stone eventually went on to a long and successful career in counseling, and is currently with the Dilenschneider Group in New York. Russ Hart headed up Ford field PR offices in Philadelphia, Chicago, Washington, and California, and retired to Florida. Bill Hersey also headed offices in Boston and Atlanta, and worked in governmental affairs in Dearborn before he retired to Florida. Regrettably, he died a few years ago after falling victim to Parkinson's disease. John Cameron eventually headed our New York office for a number of years before he retired to live in the Washington, D. C., area; Chris Whittle went on to teach at Cornell University and later entered the antique business in Ithaca, New York; and George Trainor bought a string of race horses and retired to Florida.

All of our staff, men and women, developed a host of working press friends during their years in Ford public relations. We never looked at the press as an adversary but as a potential partner in getting a job done. We worked assiduously to service and cultivate them. Some were crabby, crotchety, distant, aloof, and suspicious, and gaining their cooperation and respect wasn't done overnight but over years. Our New York office and the PR services of Ford Motor Company overall were held in high regard by those with whom we worked. No request was too trifling, and no service too demanding. It was an office and corporate policy that paid continuing dividends over the years.

It didn't take long to realize that the women in our office were invaluable when it came to dealing with the press, whether on the phone or in person. They would attend all press events and assist in hosting, entertaining, calming troubled waters, and handling all manner and means of detail. I was always very proud of Marge Hatzmann, Yvette Diaz Grossman, Ruth Koupal, Sally MacLaren, Cathleen Lyons McCarthy, Loretta Brown Luberoff, and Charlotte Bankwitz Urkiel. All these years later, we still keep in touch and visit with one another from time to time.

Our professional staff members would attend all manner and means of press-sponsored events whether they were outings, picnics, dinners, boat rides, or drinking parties, and the members of the fourth estate could consume more alcohol than just about any other group we ever came in contact with. Some of the parties following the annual New York Financial Writers' Follies went on interminably. The cast members, all financial writers, would work their hearts out to put on a good lampoon, but when it was over, all hell broke loose in the Astor Hotel, where the shows were held in the Grand Ballroom. I remember one year when Charley Sievert and I joined Franchot Tone, then in a play on Broadway, for Saturday morning eye-openers at the bar of the Piccadily Hotel across from the Astor. Sievert and I had been up all night, and it appeared Tone had too, but not with us. We ended up spending a couple of hours with him and wondered if he would make his next performance. We never found out.

Charley Sievert wrote a daily advertising news column for the *World Telegram* that was actually ahead of its time. Years later, the *Tribune* and the *Times* started similar columns that proved to be equally popular. Sievert was also the *Telly's* automobile editor and had a byline column, "Dining Out in New York at Night." He knew his way around and was a reporter in the old-school tradition — tough, skeptical, and fair. If Charley liked you, you could do no wrong. If not, all bets were off! Fortunately, Charley liked me, and our two families became quite close.

Our press contacts were not simply business contacts cultivated to see what they could or would do for us. We developed many lasting friendships, built on mutual respect, trust, and the pleasure of each other's company.

Nancy Sievert asked me to write Charley's obituary a few years ago when he passed away at the age of eighty, after a long illness in a New Jersey nursing home. I had visited him from time to time while enroute by car to and from Michigan and New York, and the two of us would reminisce until it became too much for both of us. Toward the end, sadly, I would sometimes have to tell Charley who I was. It was painful to see what the passing of time could do to a keen mind. In his prime, he rarely took a note, retaining everything in his head until he sat at his typewriter, sometimes hours later, to play it all back on paper for his column. I don't think we

will see many more of his type as the computer age takes
over.

Advertising and PR staff, Business Division, Boy Scouts of America, in 1940. LR: John Sattler, PR and production; Otto Steih, copywriter; Mark Vignate, manager; Al Peters, artist; Crawford Benedict, research.

To John —
with my best regards —
Capt. "Hank" Greenberg
February 15, 1945

Former Detroit Tigers baseball slugger, Capt. Henry "Hank" Greenberg, and Capt. Sattler, on 1945 "Morale Boost" visit to Republic Aviation, Farmingdale, Long Island, N.Y.

During a World War II air show at Newark airport, Capt. Sattler describes the operation of a remote-controlled gunnery system used on B-29 super bombers.

Captain Sattler, Irving Berlin and World War II flying aces, Col. Francis Gabreski and Lt. Steve Pisano, at Freeman Field, Seymour, Indiana, for 1945 press preview of captured German and Japanese equipment.

Ford Futuristic styling car on display at Chicago World's Fair, 1934. The almost identical design appeared later as Adolph Hitler's highly-vaunted "People's Car," — The Volkswagon.

Babe Ruth in Boston for "Jimmy Fund" dinner for under-privileged children. Seated behind Babe: Henry Strout, Ford District Manager, John Sattler, Jim Chapman, with security guard at wheel.

Eleanor Roosevelt, with late President's dog Falla, accepts delivery of Lincoln Sedan that saved her life. Charles Bonnell, right, owner of Park Motor Sales made the delivery at Mrs. Roosevelt's Greenwich Village Apartment.

The author at the wheel of 1947 Ford Sportman's convertible introduced publicly during the annual Easter Parade on New York's Fifth Avenue.

Elinore and John Sattler, with then Crown Prince Faisal, of Saudi Arabia, during a royal visit. Faisal, who succeeded his brother, as king, was assassinated by a deranged member of the Royal Family.

With New York Governor and later, Ambassador to USSR, Averell Harriman and his wife during annual Governor's Conference, Atlantic City, N.J., in the early ''Fifties''.

The professional staff of the Ford New York PR Office in 1955.
Clockwise, John Sattler, John Cameron, Bob Stone and Chris Whittle.

Henry Ford II, center, on a visit to Mahwah, New Jersey, to open new
assembly plant. Left, the author. Right, Charles Pfuhl, Honorary Mayor of
Mahwah.

Benson Ford behind the wheel of the Lincoln Futura "Dream Car", as it passed a horse-drawn hansom cab in New York's Central Park.

Christmas package with 1957 Ford Retractable Hardtop convertible and Mr. and Mrs. Santa Claus, at New York Coliseum for 1957 International Automobile Show "Grand Opening".

Henry Edmunds, Ford Historian, at wheel of 1909 Ford Model T race car which won turn-of-the-century "Ocean to Ocean" race from New York City to Seattle, Washington.

Ford PR staff members Marge Hatzman, Cathleen Lyons and Yvette Diaz, re-create the Floradora Girls of 1909, as part of "Ocean to Ocean Race" reenactment program in 1959.

Bert Pierce, *New York Times* automobile editor, leaving the Times building in a 1913 Ford Model T, enroute to his retirement party at the Overseas Press Club. Bob Price, *Herald Tribune* auto editor, is next to Bert. Anthony Despagni, Bert's assistant is next to George Munster, at the wheel.

Ford "Forty-niner" sedans pulled the floats in the widely publicized annual Macy Thanksgiving Day Parade, along New York's "Great White Way" — Broadway. Joining in the fun were the author and W.J. "Bill" Mitchel, Ford PR staffer.

Members of the Ford New York PR staff enjoying "Happy Hour" during an annual Christmas gathering at the Overseas Press Club, in the early sixties. Honor guest was retiring staffer Frank DeSimone, up front with guitar.

As 1962 President, New York Chapter, Public Relations Society of America, the author presented public relations pioneer Earl Newsom, with a distinguished service citation for professional leadership and "dedication to telling the American story abroad."

he Challenge of
Iuman Engineering

With Harry Bennett and his grandfather gone, Henry Ford II found himself in total command of his own destiny. With the help and counsel of Ernie Breech, he had taken the first steps toward realigning the top management of the Ford Motor Company, and the new look at Ford had created a great deal of excitement. He had first addressed himself to the festering problem of improved relations with employees and the unions. John Bugas, his trusted aide and confidante, had been placed in charge of all personnel matters, including the labor relations staff. The new approach was one of understanding and fair play.

With the continuing deficits the company faced from dated, if not antiquated, equipment and production facilities and the immediate need for fresh postwar products, Henry Ford II was not about to "give the store away" to establish better labor relations. But he gave every indication he would go more than halfway, and he did.

Roper's surveys, of course, had quickly spotted and pinpointed trouble areas, such as employee morale and the problems with the unions. There were other problems, however, and Earl Newsom was hard at work advising Ford management on what he thought had to be done. He was also developing a program of public relations strategy. Newsom was ready to move boldly to tell the world the story of the rebirth of Ford and the changes in its policies and leadership. Above all he wanted to establish Henry Ford II as a man for his time — the young determined leader of a reinvigorated industrial empire, which had just made such an important and essential contribution to the successful war effort. The Ford family, the company, and its workers could be justly proud of what had been accomplished.

In the few years since the late founder had reluctantly taken his somewhat aging production colossus into the all-out war effort, Ford had established an outstanding war record — thousands of B-24 bombers, so necessary to the success of the war in Europe, thousands of tanks, jeeps, trucks, and other military products. It was a record that could be looked on with pride, particularly since Charles Lindbergh had almost convinced his friend Henry Ford and others that Germany and its Luftwaffe were all but invincible. In the final analysis, Henry Ford, Sr., was a patriot and a believer, and he answered the call when it came.

Ford's war success story was not that well known, however, and it was overshadowed by the earlier negative image that came out of the Battle of the Overpass when Reuther and Frankenstein were so severely beaten during their attempt to bring better working conditions and a host of other benefits to Ford workers.

Earl Newsom wanted to emphasize the scope of Ford's wartime contributions, the need for its industrial vitality during the postwar period, and the "new look" of its management and products. It was a big challenge, and that very word — challenge — became almost a battle cry. Newson arranged for Henry Ford II to make his first major public appearance and initial public statement of corporate policy during a speech to the Society of Automotive Engineers in Detroit in early 1946, and our PR operation pulled out all the stops with the media.

The speech, titled "The Challenge of Human Engineering," was excellent. It had been written by the Newsom staff from Mr. Ford's ideas and his approach to his new task. Overnight that one speech put him in the forefront of enlightened business leadership. It appeared on the front page of the *New York Times* and just as prominently elsewhere and everywhere. People who hadn't been paying attention before suddenly took notice of the young man with the familiar name. What he said made eminent good sense — but did he mean it? And could he stay the course? The answer to both questions was to be yes.

All of us were enthusiastic about the "maiden voyage" speech — its meaning and content, the way it was received, covered, and commented on editorially in the press; and what it forecast for the company and its young leader. I felt confident as I made my press contacts and "talked it up." We were off to a good start in changing the public image of Ford Motor Company — "our" company.

I think Henry Ford II began to feel quite buoyant himself, for not long after, he almost got into a serious jam with the government and its Office of Price Administration over an announced price increase for Ford Motor Company products.

Ernie Breech and his sharp-penciled financial analysts quickly realized that Ford had to stem the flow of red ink or be faced with dire consequences. The immediate answer before enough cost-saving measures could be adopted was a price increase, and the action was taken as soon as possible and duly announced. The news was not well received in Washington, and it came at a time when Henry Ford II was going to Washington on other business. He was accompanied by Wilbur M. "Ping" Ferry of the Newsom staff who was then working on the Ford account. Ping Ferry was the son of Hugh Ferry, a former president of the Packard Motor Company, and came from a Grosse Pointe family. Earl Newsom felt Ping would be an excellent choice to work with the young industrialist. They had common background in a number of respects.

When Ford and Ferry landed in Washington a group of reporters was waiting. They had been trying to track Henry

Ford II all day and had learned of his travel plans. "Mr. Ford," one of them asked, "What do you think of the OPA's reaction to your increase in prices?"

Henry Ford said the increases were necessary, that his company could not lose money and expect to survive. "Are you prepared to tell that to a congressional committee?" he was asked.

"I'm prepared to tell it to anyone," Henry Ford replied with customary candor. The interview ended as Ping Ferry hustled the young president into a car waiting to take them to their hotel. But "the fat was in the fire," as the old saying goes. "Young Henry's" comments were not lost on Washington and particularly not on Chester Bowles and the staff of the OPA. They could see on the horizon a rash of increases throughout the economy if some action weren't taken. Henry Ford was immediately invited to make an appearance before a congressional subcommittee on pricing. That was the last thing Arthur Newmeyer and Earl Newsom wanted. It was a time for quick action.

I was summoned to Newsom's office in the Fuller Building, where Earl, Steve Fitzgerald, and Fred Palmer, who had drafted the "Challenge of Human Engineering" speech, were waiting. "We've got to get Henry out of that subcommittee hearing," Earl said. "I've talked to Arthur Newmeyer and with his help and his connections I think we can do it. I don't want Henry thrown to the political wolves in Washington at this juncture. He's a remarkable young man, but he's too inexperienced at this sort of thing for us to take the risk. We've got to respond, and we've got to get him excused at this time. I'm afraid he spoke out of turn, even if he was forthright and honest."

There followed several hours of anxious phone calls between Ford, Ferry, Newmeyer, and Newsom. The consensus: Henry Ford would respond to the subcommittee's hastily issued invitation with a considered and courteous reply that would lead to postponement of any appearance and eventual resolution of the problem. Ford sent a telegram to the subcommittee telling them he would be glad to appear at some future date if it would serve any useful purpose. He went on to explain the rationale and necessity for the price increases, pointing out that his company was faced with a number of serious problems as it entered the competitive postwar period.

Our small working group prepared the Ford telegram and a press statement, and when everything was ready, it fell to me, as the only company representative, to get it to the press. The carefully worded response was given major attention by the media, and with the passing of time, the matter of Henry Ford II's committee appearance died completely. All follow through contacts were limited to Ford Motor Company financial and pricing experts and the young president was not called again.

Henry Ford II had "shot from the lip" so to speak, in what would soon be recognized as his customary blunt, candid, and forthright manner. Over the years, his style would create more than a few problems for his public relations staff, and we would all be running around on occasion under "damage-control" circumstances, sometimes to his great amusement.

One damage-control assignment that came my way during that period was totally unexpected, at least by me.

The phone rang one day, and it was Henry "Hank" Lucking, then with Fawcett Publications. Hank was an ad representative, but he liked to associate with the editorial people and particularly with Charley Sievert and Joe Kaselow, the advertising news columnists. Kaselow wrote a regular and widely read column for the *New York Herald Tribune*. The three of them shared morsels of information and gossip that were useful to Sievert and Kaselow in writing their columns and to Lucking in keeping abreast of advertising developments and account changes. It was a beneficial relationship all around. Later, the group was expanded to include Carl Spielvogel, when Carl became the advertising columnist for the *New York Times*.

"John," Hank said, "I just ran across something that might interest you. Fawcett Books has a manuscript in the house from Harry Bennett. It purports to tell the inside story of what went on at Ford, and I understand it comes down pretty hard on Edsel Ford and your boss, Henry Ford II. I think Fawcett is planning to publish it."

What Hank didn't tell me was that he was planning to leave Fawcett for the *New Yorker* and he felt safe in tipping me off, as a personal favor.

Hank gave me all I needed to know. I thanked him for the tip, and immediately passed the information to Dearborn, and to Earl Newsom. Earl and I had almost a father-son relationship. His son Jack was about my age and was a sometime member of the Newsom staff, though I always felt his interests were somewhere other than in public relations. I soon became "Jack" to Earl, and it wasn't long before he had Henry Ford II calling me Jack, too. But Henry gave up when no one knew whom he was talking about. Earl never gave up, however, and I got used to it.

My report on the Bennett book started lights flashing and bells ringing in Dearborn. Bill Gossett, legal vice president, called Fawcett right away and demanded to review the manuscript or risk "any consequences" if it contained libelous statements or false accusations. That did it. Fawcett had no desire to alienate the Ford family or the Ford Motor Company or risk a suit for libel, misrepresentation, or character assassination. There was also the matter of possible loss of future advertising revenue to consider.

Lucking's tip proved fortunate, for the manuscript did contain some nasty and inaccurate references to young Henry and his father. It certainly shouldn't have surprised anyone that Harry

Bennett might take a parting shot at the reputations of the people he felt most responsible for his problems and for his dismissal from Ford Motor Company.

When the book came off the press, it was titled *We Never Called Him Henry*. The reference, of course, was to the senior Ford. It was published as a paperback, and I had occasion to pick up an old copy recently for fifty cents, so it's still around. The book never made the best seller list though Ford people devoured it to find out what had been going on behind the scenes. Bennett was incensed that his manuscript had been "compromised" on the basis of a leak, but he was powerless to do anything about it.

From a public relations standpoint, the book did no harm. If anything, it may have added to the mystique and excitement that surrounded Ford Motor Company and its new leadership as it entered a new era.

If Harry Bennett never called Henry Ford, Sr. "Henry," the same can be said about his grandson. He, too, was always "Mr. Ford." He expected it, preferred it that way and it would have been a serious error in judgement to address him otherwise. John Mayhew, who headed our international public relations operations at a point in time, said that "Late in the evening" on a trip to Australia, and after many rounds of good Australian brew, the Chairman said amiably, "John, you can call me Henny." John thought better of it and wisely so, for the next morning, as a new day got underway, and the Chairman came down for breakfast, Henry Ford II said, "forget anything I said last night" and the subject never came up again.

Chapter XII

A Ten-Million-Dollar Saving

Before World War II, the Ford Motor Company must have been run like a giant general store. It seemed to stock everything in its warehouses and on its "shelves," but no one was certain where everything was. Records were sparse, and theft and unauthorized "appropriation" was rampant. Houses were being built for executives with company labor and materials, equipment was used illegally, and millions of dollars in cash was stored willy-nilly in various places. Only a few insiders had access to those funds. There was said to be no accounting department as such, because the aging founder distrusted bookkeepers and accountants. Cost controls were virtually unheard of.

That was the situation that faced young Henry Ford II and Ernie Breech as they set about to right all of the company's wrongs in record time. It was a formidable task, but they had no alternative but to tackle it. The Ford Motor Company had to be put on a sound financial footing, or the bleeding would never stop. Ernie Breech was concerned that the whole situation was completely out of control.

A good part of the bleeding was due to the whimsical way the business had been run. Many business deals were made strictly on the basis of a handshake or an exchange of flimsy paperwork. The senior Ford's interests and actions transcended everything else. He had never forgotten the early years on the Ford farm in Springwells Township. (The township included Dearborn.) That period became almost a form of religion to him. He wanted to preserve it forever, and he came close to doing so. He moved the family homestead and untold numbers of antiques into the Edison Institute — now the Henry Ford Museum and Greenfield Village — and launched one of the earliest theme parks in America. Over the years it has been visited and enjoyed by millions of Americans who have come to see one of the greatest collections anywhere of early Americana. But it was costly, and while personally underwritten, it was also corporately underwritten, for Henry Ford was the corporation and vice versa. On his orders, company executives often went antiquing all over the country, looking for bargains. The acquisitions were things Henry Ford had seen or heard about but wouldn't buy personally because he thought he might be recognized, and the price inflated. Of course, many of those acquisitions are priceless today, but much of the original cost came out of Ford Motor Company, and it was never recovered, since the company was strictly a family enterprise.

Because of his interest in farming, Henry Ford had established a working relationship with Harry Ferguson, the Irish tractor manufacturer and inventor. Ferguson held patents on a tractor hitch and implement system that Ford adapted for sale in the United States. It was a relationship built on mutual trust and understanding, but it was a one way street — profitable only for Harry Ferguson, as Henry Ford II and Ernie Breech soon found out. Once previously nonexistent financial controls were put in place, it was obvious that Ford was losing money on every tractor it sold. Meanwhile Harry Ferguson was profiting handsomely from his patents and royalties.

It was also obvious that something had to be done about that arrangement. When the matter was discussed with Harry Ferguson, however, he bucked like a wounded steer. "No way," he said. "I have a legal understanding — a handshake agreement that predates your roles in the Ford Motor Company and it cannot be changed without my concurrence. I'll sue." And he did.

Of course Henry Ford II and Ernie Breech would not knuckle under to Ferguson's demand to continue the losing business arrangement. Nor would the company continue to absorb the substantial financial losses. At Ford and Breech's direction, the Ford board decided to form another organization that would develop and market tractors and farm implements. It was called Dearborn Motors. Ford management executives became its board members and principal stockholders. Harry Ferguson immediately launched his suit.

I became involved on two occasions. First, when it was apparent the hearings would be held in New York, where Ferguson filed his suit, and then when I came across some unexpected intelligence that helped save the company a substantial amount of money.

I'd been invited by a vintage-automobile collector and friend, Henry Austin Clarke, Jr., to be his guest for a social weekend and to attend the opening of his antique-car museum in Southampton, Long Island. Some New York editors and reporters had also been invited, and I drove several of them to Southampton in a newly introduced Ford convertible product. Austin Clarke put us up in beach houses for the weekend, and on Friday night, he hosted a dinner in Southampton's old Irving Hotel. That structure was razed some years later to make way for condominiums, a terrible loss of a charming landmark.

During dinner, I sat with Wallace Hughes of the *Journal American* and Bert Pierce. I noticed Henry and Anne Ford at a veranda table and slipped over to say hello and to brief Mr. Ford on what was happening. I also asked him if Bert could stop by to pay his respects. Bert, of course, was always looking for a story. Mr. Ford said that would be fine, and then he said, "Austin Clarke has invited me to that museum cocktail party tomorrow night. Do I have to go? It's a helluva bore, and besides I have a golf date in the afternoon." I replied

"Well, I'm sure Austin will be disappointed. It would be nice if you could drop by for a short visit."

I brought Bert over, and he received a friendly greeting, met Mrs. Ford, but got no news. When we returned to the table, I didn't have the heart to tell Austin Clarke he'd lost one of his key guests.

On one of the hottest, most mosquito-infested nights I have ever experienced in Southampton, most of us went to the beach to sleep. Saturday afternoon we assembled for the cocktail party opening the auto museum. Henry Ford II never showed.

Austin Clarke had quite a collection of cars, many of them beautiful old Fords. He was the scion of the family that founded Jack Frost Sugar Company, and I don't think he ever did much more than collect cars and go to automobile shows. He once told me his lifestyle highly displeased his father, who wanted him in the family business. Not that he was unique. Southampton had a substantial amount of inherited wealth, and those who had it knew how to enjoy it. Work frequently had a low priority with some Southamptonites.

The reception in Austin's quonset-hut museum was fun and well attended. Among the guests I met was a young man named Joe Ferguson, who said he sold classic cars for Fergus Motors, on New York's Park Avenue. I didn't make the connection at the time, but the next day Bill Hersey who was then the automobile writer for the *Herald Tribune*, told me Joe was a nephew of Harry Ferguson. Hersey said that Henry Ford II allegedly told Joe that he would gladly settle the Ford-Ferguson suit for twenty-million dollars, since Ford was "making so much money with its new Dearborn Motors subsidiary."

Hersey had heard that straight from Joe but didn't think he was going to write anything about it because it was speculative. I could hardly wait to get to the office on Monday morning. Whether or not Hersey considered it newsworthy, it was useful intelligence, and public relations is always a two-way street where corporate interests are concerned.

The intercom squawk boxes at Ford headquarters came alive when I telephoned my report on the Ferguson-Hersey conversation early Monday morning. Bill Gossett, vice president and legal counsel, went directly to Henry Ford II to find out what it was all about. Henry called Joe Ferguson immediately — probably on Gossett's recommendation — and told Joe he must have "misunderstood" and had "incorrectly quoted" him. He also said his company had no intention of settling a suit he thought was groundless and without merit. Ferguson told Ford it was no problem of his and he didn't want to get involved and lose Henry's friendship. After all, it had been only a "cocktail party conversation."

And that was that. At a minimum by quick action and good press relations, we avoided unnecessary press coverage, but I'm certain we also saved a lot of money.

Some months later Ford made an out-of-court settlement with Harry Ferguson for nine million dollars. I looked on that as a tidy saving, thanks in part to good old ear-to-the-ground PR work.

Ours was a happy life during that eventful period. I couldn't have been more satisfied with my work, and I loved my growing family. Elinore gave birth to two more children, Joan and Elinore, Jr., the latter always called "Lin," and we moved to our new home in Garden City, L.I.

It was an exciting time. In 1952 I took Elinore to Europe for six weeks, on our first real vacation ever. We toured ten countries and met most of the top Ford management group. When we returned, the new vice president for public relations, C. F. "Charly" Moore, called a meeting of all staff and field operations managers to brainstorm plans for observing the company's fiftieth anniversary the following year. It was going to be a challenging project. I couldn't imagine that twenty-five years later Henry Ford II would name me to head the company's seventy-fifth anniversary observance.

I had always been intrigued with what I observed and learned about the life of the first Henry Ford, his preservation of Americana, his relatively simple lifestyle even though he was, in his time, one of the richest men in the world. When I visited his Fair Lane home following his death, I had been taken through his bedroom, where his clothes still hung in the closets and his personal effects were still in the dresser drawers — drawers that still contained envelopes with crisp one hundred dollar bills and checks he had never cashed. The house also contained letters from all manner of people including royalty, customers and, remarkably, a testimonial letter from John Dillinger the gangster. Dillinger simply wanted to tell Mr. Ford how well his V-8 engine performed, enabling him to outdistance pursuers and make "quick getaways."

Ford's suits and jackets, with their narrow shoulders, looked like those of a fourteen-year-old, for he had been wiry and spare of frame. His favorite hat had once been a bowler but in later years it was a fedora.

I thought of those things as I sat in a room in Detroit's downtown Fort Shelby Hotel, where we began the exercise of planning for the Golden Jubilee. After all, the first fifty years of Ford Motor Company *were* Henry Ford. He started it all in 1903 with a handful of backers, all of whom were gone, and he almost made it to the fiftieth himself. He passed away on April 7, 1947. There was talk at that time of giving his home, his papers, and other personal memorabilia to the Edison Institute and Greenfield Village. The principal advocate of that idea was A. K. Mills, a former Earl Newsom staff member, who was put in charge of all Ford archival matters. "K" Mills wasn't at our meeting, and it's a good thing he wasn't. He would have given me stone-wall opposition when I said I thought the anniversary celebration should feature the opening of the Ford Archives, even though much of what they contained was of a highly personal nature and might not be under legal control of Ford Motor Company. Edsel and Henry Ford, who died in 1943 and 1947, respectively, had bequeathed a large part of their personal estates to the Ford Foundation. The archives would not be turned over to the family created Edison Institute until the 1960s. Whatever the complications, however, I was certain they could be worked out.

I knew Mills would strongly resist my idea, but Charly Moore saw the possibilities immediately and took the only course of action possible — he went directly to Henry Ford II and convinced him it was the right thing to do. That was that. Ford bought the idea, and Mills was told to work it out with Moore and the members of the fiftieth anniversary committee.

We were on the threshold of a media bonanza of megaton proportions, but it would take megabucks to do the job properly. Fortunately, Ford management stood ready to provide the funding. The bottom line influenced all major decisions and expenditures, and business was very good that year.

'he Golden World of Ford

I doubt that there has ever been a corporate anniversary observance to match the Ford fiftieth anniversary. It was in a class by itself and set a standard for all others to follow, including our seventy-fifth celebration, which was far more modest from a budget standpoint.

There was very little we didn't think of to put on paper even if much of the early brainstorming was simply "blue sky." When it was all thought through and refined, it was an impressive multimillion-dollar effort that few organizations could underwrite. And, it demonstrated that after some lean years, Ford Motor Company was again on a sound financial footing.

Keystone of the observance was the official opening of the Ford Archives even though, at first blush, the archives might have seemed like a somewhat stodgy story. It was, however, a story filled with all the ingredients of melodrama and one not generally known outside Ford Motor Company. It would have to be "talked up" to create the enthusiasm and interest we needed. Fortunately, the timing was good. Postwar growth was well underway, and the country was ready for nostalgia and romance. People were tired of war stories — at least for a time.

We also had a broad range of new products coming to market under the anniversary banner.

We had the full cooperation of the Ford family. Henry II, Benson, and William Clay Ford were busy at jobs in the company, and thanks to my location in New York, I had the opportunity to work with all of them from time to time. Each was different. Bill had recently graduated from Yale University, and I set up a modest press introduction for him when he attended a dealership opening in lower Manhattan. He was shy and unsure but took hold quickly. At the time of the anniversary, he headed the newly created Continental Division, the up-scale part of our business that had always held the interest of his father, Edsel.

Ben Ford headed Lincoln-Mercury and had been our host at a ground-breaking ceremony to announce plans for a new plant for his division in Edison Township, New Jersey, near New Brunswick. It was my first working assignment with Ben, and I was nervous as the day arrived with a forecast of rain. We were to have lunch at a nearby restaurant, where he would speak to press and VIP guests and make his announcement. Then we were to go to the plant site, which looked like a muddy playground. I ordered planks for a walkway, and they were installed while we were at lunch. An inscribed silver plated spade was waiting for Ben and the mayor to use in a symbolic ground breaking. It was not very imaginative, but that was before laser beams, satellites, and other electronic wizardry — and we didn't have a better idea at the time.

After lunch, we bussed everyone to the site. A light rain was falling. I sensed a complete pictorial disaster as the photographers went through the motions of taking stock photos of a spade being sunk into the mud. I was sure the negatives would end up in acid baths and stay there, but at least the press had the announcement release and the text of Benson's remarks. Then a miracle happened. Just as we were getting ready to get out of the rain and the mud, Charlie Seawood of Acme Newspictures spotted a surveyor's transit within arms length. Someone had forgotten to cover it. "Mr. Ford, would you mind looking through that telescope?" Seawood asked. "Sure," Ben replied, "Which end?" Everybody laughed. Ben squinted and the bulbs popped. The picture was good enough for the front pages of not only the New Jersey papers but New York's as well. The *Times* used it on its front page the next morning and captioned it "An Eye to the Future."

What no one knew at the time, including me, was that Benson Ford had one good eye and one bad eye. He was peering through the transit with his bad eye, and it was doubtful he could see anything!

But the young men at the helm of Ford — the three brothers — were catching the interest and attention of the press everywhere and the public as well. People wanted to know more about the Ford family, looking on them as a kind of American royalty, and we were prepared to encourage that, particularly during the golden anniversary year.

Life and *Look* sent top staffers like Phillipe Halsman to photograph members of the family in formal and casual activities and then ran extensive color layouts. We followed up with behind-the-scenes exclusives and select exposure of the personal papers and memorabilia that were part of the early history of the dynasty.

It was an exhilarating, dynamic time, and everyone in public relations got caught up in it. After all, we were in the front ranks of everything — planning, making it happen, and then proudly circulating the results. Heady times, indeed.

Events were planned for all over the country and the world, with Michigan and Dearborn as the focal point. There were plant open house programs, picnics for employees, community dinners, speeches and public appearances and, in fact, everything we could put in the grab bag of public relations attention getters. I even suggested putting giant electrified candles atop the rotunda to create a golden anniversary birthday cake and it was done.

The grand finale was a two-hour television spectacular produced by Leland Hayward and featuring a memorable song medley performed by Ethel Merman and Mary Martin. That alone became a collector's record. The TV show was a pioneering, award-winning event that by itself brought the company's anniversary story into the homes of millions. The follow-up coverage of the TV special — columns, features, and laudatory editorials — were a PR man's dream.

But before that, there was the public unveiling of Henry Ford's Fair Lane home, the display of archival historical memorabilia in Greenfield Village, the dedication of a new engineering center; the introduction of new product lines, including a series of dream cars; and the customary speeches, press briefings, tours, and receptions, concluding with a golden anniversary dinner for the three hundred members of the press covering the event.

I brought more than one hundred editors and writers from the New York area alone and also arranged a series of advance briefings for some of the New York-based media on a hold-for-publication basis, because they had to have lead time to plan and develop stories. One major opportunity fell into my lap by pure luck at the "21" Club one afternoon. I'd gone to "21" to meet Joe Willicombe, an old friend with the Hearst organization and found him at the bar with Larry Newman and Collie Small of Colliers; Burgess Meredith, the actor; and Eugene Black, an advertising vice president with *Life*. After introductions and some small talk I found myself standing next to Black and thought I would soft sell the anniversary story, even though I knew he was on the business side of the magazine. After all, Ford was a big advertiser, and say what you might about the separation of any magazine's business and editorial operations, they do talk to one another and work together when it suits their interests or purpose.

Gene Black was interested in what I had to tell him and seemed intrigued by the story of Henry Ford's private papers. He gave me his card and told me to make contact with Ed Thompson, *Life's* managing editor, and tell Thompson the same story. I did that the very next day, and a day or two later, a *Life* crew was on its way to Dearborn for a behind-the-scenes briefing and look. We did the same thing with the wires and some of the other select magazines and news services. It might have smacked of favoritism, but you simply couldn't wait until the last minute to pull up the curtain on a story with the depth and dimensions of fifty years of history. *Life* ultimately gave us fifteen pages of space, something quite rare back in that period.

To carry the press group to Dearborn for the three-day program, our transportation experts talked the New York Central Railroad into making a duplicate run of its crack train, the Detroiter. On its regular run that train left Grand Central Station at seven o'clock every evening and arrived at the Michigan Central Station every morning at seven. It was a favorite overnight trip for those who worked in and around the automobile business; air travel was far less available and dependable in those days.

We had a bar and lounge car, dining car, sleeper cars, and all the beverages and prime steaks we thought the group could consume. Wrong! We ran out of both in Buffalo and had to restock the train before it went into Canada, because the custom agents sealed everything not in the process of being consumed, at the U. S.-Canadian border, and the sealed cabinets could not be opened again for the rest of the run through Canada. Canadian customs didn't care about the food, but bottles of alcohol, unless about to be consumed, were impounded. Everybody had a few of those small bottles stashed somewhere. So there was very little sleep to be had that night, particularly by the PR hosts, who wanted to avoid untoward incidents or accidents.

During the three-day anniversary program, Western Union sent out the largest filing of news copy it had ever handled in Michigan. The pressroom had typewriters and teleprinters chattering day and night as our program moved from the nostalgia of Henry Ford and his era to the new look and leadership of his grandsons, and then on to the smart and sophisticated products that would soon be in dealers showrooms. It ended with a look at what the future might hold. There was something for everybody.

William Randolph Hearst, Jr., the editor-in-chief of the Hearst news-and-magazine empire, was among those at the final dinner along with one of his veteran reporters, James Kilgallen, (Dorothy Kilgallen's father). Jim was then in his seventies and had covered all of the big stories of his era, including interviews with the likes of Dillinger, Al Capone, Lindbergh, and on a number of occasions, Henry Ford, Sr. Julius Ochs Adler was there to represent the *New York Times* management.

I had become very friendly with Julie Adler and, in fact, with many of the people in the management hierarchy of the *Times*, leading to an invitation from the publisher, Arthur Hayes Sulzberger, to take lunch with him one day in his private dining room. The luncheon had actually been arranged by Orvil Dryfoos, his son-in-law and then heir apparent, who was married to Mr. Sulzberger's daughter, Marian. Nat Goldstein, the *Times*'s circulation director, and Orvil had come to my rescue one day when I got a last-minute request from Henry Ford II for world series tickets for his board members. Mr. Ford had planned a board meeting in New York for a Friday morning while the series was being played between the New York Yankees and the Brooklyn Dodgers. He wanted to take the board to the game at Yankee Stadium and then have them driven to his home in Southampton, L.I., for a relaxing social weekend.

In the group were Benson Ford, Ernie Breech, John Bugas, Jack Davis, Mead Bricker, and Harold Youngren, the latter two manufacturing and engineering vice presidents. Also included were Charlie Seyffer, my boss, and me.

But where do you get prime seats for a New York series two days before the game? Even bleacher seats weren't available.

A frantic appeal for help to Nat Goldstein brought nothing less than spectacular results. Enough box seats behind first base and home plate turned up to accommodate the entire Ford group, with Orvil, Nat, Turner Catledge, and other key *Times* executives sitting in the boxes with the Ford group. I never found out who had been displaced to accommodate our group, and I never asked. But I was able to return the favor on several occasions, and Orvil felt I should meet his father-in-law, the publisher.

The people at Earl Newsom's firm were impressed. John Sattler lunching with the publisher of the *New York Times*? A twenty-nine-year-old public relations manager? I had wanted my boss, Charlie Seyffer, to be included, and he had been invited but had to be out of town that day. I then asked if Bert Pierce could be included in Charlie Seyffer's place, and Orvil arranged it. Bert was overwhelmed at the invitation to lunch with *Times* brass. I felt more comfortable having him there, as we were joined by Edwin L. "Jimmy" James, the managing editor, and his assistant, Turner Catledge. Arthur Hayes Sulzberger asked me to sign the *Times'* VIP guestbook, and I did — under Edward, Duke of Windsor, who'd been the luncheon guest on the previous day!

Among the things we talked about at lunch, in addition to new management and policy changes at Ford Motor Company, Henry Ford II and Ernest Breech, new products and postwar car and truck sales, was the upcoming twentieth anniversary of Charles Lindbergh's trans-Atlantic flight. I brought the subject up, because I knew "Jimmy" James had been the *Times* correspondent on hand at Le Bourget Airport outside Paris the night the Spirit of St. Louis caught the glare of searchlights as it made its landing approach. For a few minutes, the drama and excitement of that historic night came to life again as one who was there relived the experience for us.

It was April 1947, and I invited the group to take lunch with our local Ford management at an early future date. "Let's do that at '21,'" "Jimmy" James said, but it never happened. All Ford operations other than public relations were soon moved out of New York City to an office in New Jersey, and the opportunity was lost.

That luncheon however was part of a long series of warm and friendly relationships with *New York Times* management that continued for many years, and I was not surprised when Marian Sulzberger Heiskell was named to the board of directors of Ford Motor Company some years later. Her former husband, Orvil, regrettably had died unexpectedly in 1963 after succeeding his father-in-law as publisher only two years earlier. Orvil was a warm and wonderful person, and I considered his death a personal loss. Marian Sulzberger Dryfoos eventually married Andrew Heiskell, a Time-Life chief executive.

After I moved to Michigan in 1967, I hosted a luncheon in one of our private dining rooms at Ford World Headquarters for Arthur Ochs Sulzberger, son of Arthur Hayes Sulzberger, who became publisher of the *Times* in 1963, when Orvil Dryfoos died. "Punch" Sulzberger, as he was known to close friends, was accompanied by a very young Arthur Ochs Sulzberger, Jr. who succeeded his father in 1992 as the publisher of that great newspaper. Following lunch, I took father and son on a personally conducted tour of the impressive, if aging, River Rouge operations, where they seemed especially impressed by the long river of molton glass being produced by the closely controlled pilkington process.

I was sorry we didn't have a VIP guest register for them to sign that day. The Duke of Windsor had made a similar tour when he was the Prince of Wales, many years earlier.

As had been the case with the *New York Times*, I felt I had developed an equally excellent relationship with the hierarchy of the Hearst organization, including Bill Hearst, Jr., and his key editors, including Les Gould, Paul Schoenstein, Sam Shulsky, and a young advertising news columnist and feature writer named Jack O'Dwyer, who went on to launch a newsletter in the public relations field that has grown into a small publishing empire.

Particular friends were Joe Willicombe, son of one of William Randolph Hearst's senior aides, and Bob Considine, a noted columnist and a member of the Hearst editorial task force, which also included Bill Hearst and Frank Conniff.

When Ford was experiencing a somewhat difficult period with dealers, press, and public during the mid-sixties, owing largely to Henry Ford II's frustrations with the Ford Foundation and his own personal life, we were casting about for ways to encourage upbeat activities and stories. Ted Mecke, our then vice president for public affairs, had called me to talk about it and ask, "What can we do?"

I knew that Bill Hearst was fond of HFII and considered his own role in life somewhat similar to Henry's, but I didn't want to go directly to Bill to ask favors. Instead, I went to Joe Willicombe, and outlined our problem. Joe then discussed it with Bill Hearst, who assigned Bob Considine to do an upbeat, updated "revisit" to Henry Ford II and his company. When Joe, Bob, and I played golf together at an artists' and writers' outing at the Westchester Country Club, we decided Bob would start by interviewing John Bugas. I introduced the two men, and it was fascinating to hear John Bugas, once again describe his basement confrontation with Harry Bennett the day Bennett was fired by Henry Ford II. We had been through it before, for André Fontaine, who did a major article for *Colliers*, in 1946, but I never tired of hearing the first-person details of how Bennett had moved Bugas's office furniture into a basement bathroom, of Bennett's loaded gun resting on his

119

desk as Bugas stood in front of him to carry out Henry Ford II's instructions, and the long, tense walk to the door Bugas made with his back to Bennett, who was then livid with rage. Bugas, of course, was carrying a snub nosed "38" under his coat. Fortunately, Bennett never made a move, and sanity prevailed.

Bob Considine put it all into a running series for the Hearst papers, and we reprinted the series in a booklet prepared for us by the Hearst promotion department. Copies were sent to Ford and Lincoln-Mercury dealers and others interested. It was a PR "ten-strike" at a time when we needed it.

Some months later, Bob served as "roastmaster" for a luncheon Hank Lucking and I organized to observe Charley Sievert's twenty-fifth anniversary as a business news writer and columnist for the *World Telegram and Sun*. The luncheon was held at the Overseas Press Club, and we had about two hundred of Charley's friends — press and PR types on hand. I made the introductions and read telegrams of good wishes from a range of people, including Jim Roche, the chairman of General Motors, and Henry Ford II.

On the way out of the house that morning, I had spotted a six-inch piece of grey slate in the driveway, got an idea, and brought it along to the luncheon. As I read congratulatory telegrams, I came to the slate and said, "And here's one from the twenty-five-hundred-year-old Brewmaster," a mythical figure used in a popular advertis- ing campaign for Ruppert's beer. That got a lot of laughs, but the crowd really roared when Considine came to the microphone, picked up the slate and said, "twenty-five-hundred-year-old Brewmaster? I thought it was Toots Shor's liver!"

Chapter XIV

No Business Like Show Business

Historically, the automobile business has been cyclical, and the car companies try to match production schedules with a multitude of considerations — new product reception, competition, production capacity, and above all, the economic health of the country and the rest of the world.

As for the economy, its like a seesaw — up and down and all around at various times.

That was the case in 1957. Ford had introduced some fine new products, but the economy was going sour. It was time to take a breather, but nobody in the business ever wanted to take a breather, because it meant downtime, layoffs, belt tightening and a lot of other things that were unpleasant.

If anything, the industry had a reputation for being upbeat even when the economic indicators said otherwise.

In that respect, it was not unlike President George Bush's pronouncements during the 1992 presidential campaign — "there's no recession " — "things are looking up," when everyone knew or thought otherwise.

You simply couldn't be downbeat and expect to generate business (or votes). Sales might be caving in, but you had to look for and play up the tiniest shred of good news. The public mood had to be buoyed by good news even if it had to be created, and it often was as we reached for anything and everything that might build confidence and motivate people to buy our products. It wasn't easy.

In 1958, when things were absolutely dismal, the industry launched a program to focus attention on the bargains that were available if only the public mood could be changed. The National Automobile Dealers Association came up with a series of promotion plans under the general theme "You Auto Buy — Now!" and all the manufacturers gave the program wholehearted support in every possible way.

The country was split into districts, and PR people from the major companies were assigned to work with action committees, organizing programs and events that would create excitement and direct attention to the retail end of the business. In short, to rejuvenate interest in car and truck sales and get people back into dealer showrooms.

General Motors had responsibility for working with the dealer associations in the greater New York area, and its New York PR staff was expected to come up with a plan. It did, but Joe Farlow, managing director of the New York Dealers Association, didn't like it. Basically, there was to be a pep rally in a Hempstead, Long Island, coliseum with speeches and whatever razzmatazz could be developed. Farlow thought it sounded deadly, that the dealers and their salesmen wouldn't bother to attend. He asked our office for help, but I didn't want to undercut Fred Collins and his GM group, with whom I had a good working relationship. Also, I didn't have an original idea at that moment.

When Joe asked me if I would attend the next planning meeting, I said I would. He asked me to think of alternatives to the Hempstead meeting idea, and again I said I would.

The next day, creative lightning struck as I was reading the *New York Herald Tribune*. I noticed an editorial-page item that included a picture of four elephants with their front legs up on each others' backs. The head on the story read "Unemployed Elephants," and the text indicated that things were tough all over. Even circus attendance was down.

If you couldn't sell circus tickets, how could you sell automobiles? But I got an idea. Why not work with Ringling Brothers and hold the meeting prior to the regular matinee circus performance in Madison Square Garden?

The prospect excited me and I called Joe Farlow right away. "Joe, I have an idea," and I outlined it for him. Joe was not a demonstrative person, but I could sense his enthusiasm over the phone. "Do you think you can pull it off?" he asked. I told him I knew Harry Dube, publisher of the official circus magazine, and that I'd arranged for a car for the circus to use in its famous clown act, where countless clowns come out of a compact car. Ford had loaned the circus the car in exchange for an advertisement in Dube's magazine — a quid pro quo.

Harry Dube like the idea and especially the fact that it wouldn't be gratis, that Joe Farlow's committee would offset any expenses the circus might incur, such as paying some of the acts for an extra performance and reimbursement for any other costs.

The deal was made, and the Ringling Circus provided the use of Madison Square Garden for a morning meeting featuring several acts, including the elephants that provided the initial inspiration. It was an SRO performance, as dealers and their sales representatives came from throughout the metropolitan area to see the mini show and hear inspirational messages from Bill Powers, GM's feisty, evangelistic sales manager, Joe Bayne, Lincoln-Mercury's sales chief; and a spokesman for the dealer organization. Powers ended the meeting by throwing new silver dollars into the audience to tell them it was just the beginning of a shower of sales if they'd simply get off their bottoms and get out and "look for the silver lining" — whatever that meant. If nothing else, it was good theater.

But the real capper came when we put Powers and two of the dealers on the back of an elephant, wearing safari pith helmets we'd brought along for the occasion. We'd found the helmets on Bannerman's Island in the Hudson River, where they'd been stored for years in mahogany cases. They were still in their original condition. Someone said they'd come from the Philippines, where they'd been used during the "Moro insurrection." True or not, that also made a good story.

The helmets were perfect for the occasion, and the cameras clicked and rolled as the three men raised their right hands in unison to the peaks of their helmets as though scanning the horizon. The picture went coast to coast with a caption that read "Searching for Sales," and the coverage exceeded anyone's willingness to pay for the clipping services.

We'd pulled a coup for a nominal investment. Everybody was happy, including the folks at Ringling Brothers.

From a public relations standpoint, it was almost a repeat of history. Many writers on the subject of public relations have said P. T. Barnum, the noted showman, was an early "PR type," but many serious-minded people in the PR business recoil at the idea of doing anything that smacks of circus press agentry. Personally, I've found an occasional stunt useful and newsworthy, and our "You Auto Buy" circus rally was one of the most successful stunts we ever carried out. It had an important objective, and it accomplished it in a novel, newsworthy way.

We reached into show business on more than a few occasions, like the time we were called on by our Lincoln-Mercury Division to create excitement and interest in a one-of-a-kind dream car they had built. Unlike most show cars at that time, it was actually driveable. Usually, the cars lacked drivetrains and were strictly for display at automobile shows and elsewhere. Some even had fake doors that couldn't be opened.

The LM car was called the Lincoln Futura and was well ahead of its time in styling and design features. It had a fighter-plane-type bubble canopy over the driver-passenger area, flare fins, and the streamlining of a spaceship on wheels. The division had invested a quarter of a million dollars in it to direct favorable attention to the styling capability of its design studios and its Star Trek quality was way ahead of its time.

The Lincoln-Mercury division management also wanted to highlight the improved contemporary styling of the then current lines of Lincoln products. They hoped there would be a lot of product identification rub-off.

The Lincoln Futura was a knockout, but introducing any product simply for press coverage was (and still is) risky. Sometimes nothing happened, and sometimes the results weren't quite what you expected. It was always a gamble.

I told John Millis, the PR manager for the LM Division, that I thought the Futura was a beauty, and I was sure we could do something special. I would have to give it some thought and get back to him with a memo.

John Cameron, Bob Stone, Chris Whittle, and I then went through the familiar brainstorming exercise. What could we do with that unique vehicle? We were working with black-and-white photos and did not actually see the car until it arrived in New York. But we could see from the pictures and statistics, that the flared styling made it low, long, and sleek. We were concerned about driving it in New York traffic, but it would be just another styling dream and display car if it weren't actually driven on the streets of New York City.

John Millis and Ben Ford bought what we proposed. We would start with an early-morning remote TV pickup from the Tavern-on-the-Green in Central Park, with Dave Garroway interviewing Ben Ford. Garroway would be in his studio on Forty-ninth Street and Benson in the park, behind the wheel of the Futura. We'd then have a press breakfast, primarily for photographers, where Ben Ford would describe the features of the Lincoln-Futura. A photo session would follow in the Tavern parking area, and then the drive from Tavern-on-the-Green to the Waldorf Astoria Hotel. It would be on display at the hotel during a major press luncheon, and Ben Ford and Bill Schmidt, the engineer/stylist who designed the car, would both speak. We would conclude our activities with a late afternoon reception for New York-area Lincoln-Mercury dealers and invited VIP guests.

It was quite a package, but Lincoln-Mercury liked it and found the money to fund it.

As is often the case, however, there were a few hitches. Ben Ford didn't want to drive the car in mid-Manhattan traffic, nor did we think it a good idea for him to do so. We settled on Bill Schmidt. "Big" Ed Sullivan, a press representative for Paramount Pictures, arranged for one of his Paramount starlets, Barbara Lawrence, to ride to the Waldorf with Schmidt and make an appearance at the press luncheon. Barbara was a blonde beauty, but that must have been the highlight of her career. Starlets were expendable, and she simply disappeared.

We also needed platform elevation for the photographers to track the car through New York streets, and nothing was readily available. Marv Runyon, a plant assistant manager, saved the day by building a wooden rack with three levels on the back of a flatbed truck. Marv left Ford many years later as a manufacturing vice president to head Nissan truck operations in the United States. He then became head of the Tennessee Valley Authority and currently serves as postmaster general of the United States. Quite a career path!

The worst planning problem we encountered was that the Futura was too big (too long, actually) for the freight elevator at the Waldorf Astoria Hotel and consequently couldn't be taken into the hotel for display in one of the private reception rooms. Then, Claudius C. Philippe, successor to the famous Oscar of the Waldorf, had a brainstorm of his own. Philippe, as he liked to be called, always resourceful where hotel revenue was concerned, suggested we rent the center court of the hotel's interior arrival and parking area, carpet it, landscape and decorate it, and display the Futura underneath the hotel, on the ground floor entrance level. Cost? Two thousand dollars, and Philippe would throw in the red carpet on which to drive the car in from the side street!

Claude Philippe was a polished banquet manager, with a bit of larceny in his heart, but we knew he could deliver, and the Waldorf was where we wanted to be. The Futura was an upscale product and had to be shown in a setting that was upscale in every way. So the deal was struck.

We knew Garroway would go for the Ben Ford interview and demonstration idea, and he did. Dave was a dedicated car buff and found the "big toys" irresistible. Everything else fell into place.

After the Garroway show, we left Ben Ford behind the wheel, and brought up the platform truck and a horse-drawn hansom cab from the Plaza Hotel for contrast pictures. Bob Stone assembled the photographers. As Bob went into the tavern to get them, the nervous horse reared on its hind legs, and all Ben Ford could see as he looked up were horse hooves. Startled as the horse came down on the pavement, and spotting me in front of the car he shouted, "For God's sake, Sattler, do you want to get me killed for this picture?"

I managed a grin and said, "Don't worry, Mr. Ford, he won't do it again." He didn't, fortunately. Public relations has never been a risk-free business!

The photographers then mounted the truck and "fired away" as Ben and the coach driver moved in tandem for about a hundred feet. We then switched to Schmidt and Barbara Lawrence for the drive down Broadway to Fifty-seventh Street, over to Fifth Avenue, Park Avenue, and the Waldorf. The resulting pictures were so good and showed such contrast they even appeared overseas. I saw one of them last year, forty years later, illustrating an article in the *Smithsonian* magazine.

One additional hitch developed at the press luncheon. Bill Schmidt apparently got carried away by the occasion and predicted solar-powered vehicles in the "not too distant future." When that statement reached Michigan on the newswires, top management had a fit. Ford was researching and experimenting with solar power along with a lot of other things, but it was years away and we had to put out an immediate clarifying statement.

All in all, however, the day was superb and a tremendous "image" launch for a car that would never go into production. The principal objective had been to focus favorably on the capabilities of the Lincoln design and engineering staffs, and we had done that.

Some years later, I was surprised to see the Lincoln Futura on television. It was being driven by Batman and Robin as the Batmobile. Chuck Barris, the Hollywood producer and entrepreneur, had bought it and found a use for it long after it had been moth-balled and sent to dead storage by the Lincoln-Mercury Division. The division probably recovered all of its costs by selling the dream car to Barris — even after all of the PR and promotional costs had long since been written off.

Good antiques have a way of increasing in value with the passing of time!

ord and "The Jewish roblem"

When I joined Ford Motor Company in early 1946, one of the first things I was told was that I had a major Ford public relations problem to deal with in New York.

"The Jewish people don't like Ford," I was told, "and will not buy Ford products." The reasons given almost always involved the company founder, Henry Ford, and the *Dearborn Independent*, a newspaperlike magazine that he once owned. In the early 1920s, it had published a number of anti-Semitic articles which members of the Jewish community found offensive, and rightly so.

Even if Henry Ford had nothing personally to do with the stories — as was claimed — the fact that they appeared in a publication he owned reflected the worst possible kind of judgment. That was the way most people felt, despite early protestations that it was all a misunderstanding and a mistake on the part of the editors.

It was said at the time that the vicious articles began following a period when Ford was strapped for cash. The bankers, some of whom were Jewish, wanted to exercise a degree of control over Ford Motor Company in return for putting up their money. Henry Ford would have none of that and was said to have developed strong negative feelings toward those who proposed it — feelings that encompassed more than just the Jewish bankers involved. They extended to Jews in general.

It was an unfortunate period, an aberration from Ford's long history of dealing fairly and favorably with people of all ethnic and religious persuasions. It had its beginning shortly after Ford bought the publication in 1919. During the early 1920s, the *Dearborn Independent* grew to a national circulation of 500,000 copies. It was available through Ford dealers and by direct subscription. One particularly unpleasant and damaging series of articles quoted The *Protocols of the Wise Men of Zion,* a publication that contended that Jews everywhere were bent on world domination through some form of international conspiracy. The document on which the protocols was based was later proved a forgery, but the damage had been done, and the very reproduction of it had far-reaching effects throughout the world Jewish community, and particularly in the United States.

Although Henry Ford later contended he was unaware of what was going on and that the editorial content of the *Independent* was the responsibility of others, he could not avoid the scathing criticism directed at him personally not only by the leaders of the Jewish community but by non-Jews of all religious persuasions as well, who were equally incensed by the vicious series.

The upshot was that Ford first replaced the management of the *Dearborn Independent,* and then ceased its publication entirely in December 1927, after eight years of ownership. Prior to that action, however, on July 7, 1927, with the help of his good friend New York editor, Arthur Brisbane, Ford made an abject public apology for any past attacks on Jews in the *Dearborn Independent* or "elsewhere." *The American Hebrew* reported at the time it was the first apology for anti-Semitism in history.

But that was not the end of it, for during the 1930s as Hitler's power was beginning to be felt throughout Europe and the world, reprints of some of the articles attributed to the *Dearborn Independent* began to appear, often under sponsorship of the Nazis and similar hate organizations. The continuing negative ruboff on Ford was impossible to avoid, and it was compounded toward the end of the decade when Henry Ford, on his seventy-fifth birthday, accepted Germany's Grand Cross of the Supreme Order of the German Eagle. It was presented to him at his home in Dearborn by the German Consul generals from Detroit and Cleveland, along with Adolph Hitler's personal congratulations and good wishes. It was said that Henry Ford had little advance notice of the dubious honor and that he accepted it rather than cause an international embarrassment at a time when his company was still hoping to control its operations in Germany.

It was quite obvious that neither Henry Ford nor those around him in a position to offer advice had thought through the matter of accepting any award from Adolph Hitler or Germany at that particular time, notwithstanding the importance to Ford of its German operations, which were substantial. It was another indication of the flawed thinking and misdirection of management policies that were prevalent at the time. Edsel Ford, who was company president, was deeply concerned but so insulated and so isolated from his father's daily decision making that he was incapable of stopping or changing any of his father's actions during that troublesome period. The short physique of Harry Bennett was casting a very long shadow at the time, and his influence exceeded Edsel's in many matters.

There is no doubt it was a period fraught with misjudgment in any number of ways, not the least of them participating in abhorrent behavior with respect to any religious or ethnic group. But Ford himself had become so successful and such a worldwide household name in the late teens and throughout much of the twenties, he may have considered himself above any level of criticism and reproach. That, of course, proved to be quite wrong. Sales of his seemingly invincible Model-T began to tumble, and he had to go back to the drawing board to produce an entirely new automobile — the Model-A, for the 1928 market — something considered unthinkable just a few years earlier.

Looking back, it is easy to see why a number of influential elements in the Jewish community were incensed at Ford during the twenties and why there was a carryover of the deep rooted feelings and animosity into the thirties. Following the end of World War II, however, and the beginning of a new era, it seemed to me as I took up my duties in New York that some people were never going to allow a bad piece of corporate history to be put to rest. After all, Henry Ford, Sr., was no longer a factor in the Ford Motor Company. He had been replaced by a grandson with a new approach to virtually everything.

Henry Ford, Sr., had been something of an enigma. A complicated man, with little education but inherent savvy, he seemed to trust few people, and he could be influenced by those he did trust. There is little doubt he harbored some degree of prejudice against those he felt were a source of problems for him and his company, and that happened to include Jewish bankers if not others of that faith. And yet he relied totally on Albert Kahn, a leading Jewish architect of the time, to plan and oversee development and construction of the huge River Rouge manufacturing complex, which was completed in 1924. Albert Kahn also handled numerous other major assignments for Ford, including design and construction of a series of car and truck assembly plants on waterways throughout the United States and elsewhere in the world. Henry Ford obviously had high regard for Albert Kahn's talent and capabilities and used his services throughout the period the *Dearborn Independent* was under Ford ownership. Similarly, when I joined Ford in early 1946, I found his regular New York driver was a man named Isadore Levine, who delighted in his job and had nothing but praise for his boss.

When I made a trip to Israel in November 1992 to revisit some of the areas I had seen following the Yom Kippur War, I met Eytan Lowenstein, son of the founder of the Palestine Automobile Company, founded in Nazareth in 1937 to distribute

Ford products in the Middle East. Eytan's father, Aryea, and Dr. S. Lipschitz were partners in that venture. They had contacted Henry Ford in the mid-thirties to represent Ford interests in Palestine and the surrounding area, had visited with him in Dearborn, and became his official representatives for Palestine, Jordan and Egypt. The business was sustained for forty years, until it was sold in 1977, to an investment company.

It was obvious, therefore, that all Jews were not bad Jews where Henry Ford was concerned. I felt the problem was being perpetuated to suit the interests of certain individuals and groups. Old Henry Ford had certainly made errors in judgment, for which he ultimately accepted responsibility, but he had also done many things that demonstrated his sense of fairness and liberalism towards all ethnic groups. The record shows that he often went out of his way to help and to employ minorities. Ford Motor Company always had African-Americans in its employ, and the senior Ford had a particularly warm relationship with George Washington Carver, the agriculturist, to the point that he had a replica of Carver's log cabin birthplace set up in Greenfield Village, near his own birthplace.

I wasn't familiar with all the background or the extent of the perceived ongoing problem with the Jewish community until shortly after I opened the New York office and was joined by Walter Rowcroft, a newly appointed New York Lincoln-Mercury district sales manager. His office was adjacent to mine. Rowcroft, who had been in the business in the New York area for many years, characterized the situation as bad and said as much one afternoon when Henry Ford II and Mr. Ford's personal assistant, Allan Merrell, dropped by our office for a visit.

We had a standby office for Mr. Ford's use, and Rowcroft and I were invited to join them there for a chat. The "Jewish problem" was one of the subjects. Mr. Ford was concerned about it, personally affronted because he had a number of Jewish friends, and he didn't want the company to face any continuing, inflamed situation. He said we had to make an all-out effort to identify the problem and resolve it, because the past was behind us and we didn't need that kind of encumbrance going into the future. "We have enough problems as it is," he said, and no one doubted that in early 1946.

Over the next ten years, while the problem didn't disappear, I did notice marked improvement in a number of respects. For one thing, we had an increasing number of Jewish dealers, though Ford had always had a fair number of them, going back many years — dealers like Sol Schildkraut in Jamaica, Long Island, who had me deliver a new Ford one day to Rabbi Jonah B. Wise, a prominent Jewish theologian.

I noticed, too, that some people appeared to be bent on keeping the subject alive to suit their own purposes. That included some of our local sales managers who would use the old crutch of the "Jewish problem" every time sales were down. New York was considered a strong Jewish market. I also noticed that the "interracial" and Jewish-oriented press would use it as a crutch to sell advertising. "Ford has a problem," their representatives would remind our advertising agencies and anyone else who would listen, and it was difficult to refute that pronouncement. We had even retained a consultant in Detroit, who was getting a handsome retainer to advise the company on steps to improve and correct the situation. He did not like the fact that I challenged him on some of the things he had us doing. I thought those actions might seem contrived — for instance, attendance at all Jewish affairs when no other companies were represented.

I finally wrote a public relations "white paper" one day in which I attempted to put the entire matter in focus. "We are continuing to live with ghosts of the past," I said, "because too many vested interests do not want to see this subject put to rest. One of our biggest problems is that Ford is not a public corporation. People who buy automobiles cannot buy Ford stock. The Jewish people are investment conscious to a greater extent than many other ethnic groups. If they own Chrysler or General Motors stock, it is unlikely they are going to buy Ford products. Additionally, lower-income members of the Jewish community are greatly influenced by what their leaders and affluent members do. Ford does not represent a good investment for them, and the situation is not helped by the fact that we have some quality and service problems that have been festering for some time."

In those early postwar years, we had not entirely lived down the Model-T or "tin lizzie" image, and Ford products had not kept up with the design and quality improvements offered by some of the competition.

The "white paper" didn't solve our problems, but I think it went a long way toward explaining where we had been and where we were, notwithstanding what some diehards wanted us to believe.

In reaching out to the Jewish community, Ford did a number of things that had a positive effect. With our Jewish dealers, we were always in attendance at major events sponsored by the United Jewish Appeal, the Federation of Jewish Philanthropies, and B'nai B'rith. We did no less for other ethnic organizations.

As a case in point, one day I accompanied Charlie Seyffer to the Waldorf Towers apartment of Julius Rosenwald, a prominent Jewish leader, to present a one-million-dollar check from Ford Motor Company toward renovation of a building in New York for the National Conference of Christians and Jews. Mr. Rosenwald was a charming, dignified man and gladly posed for pictures (which no one used). We had a delightful visit, and I always remembered the original Picasso small pen and ink sketch on the side table in his living room.

Ford also challenged prejudice and politics when it announced plans to start an assembly operation in Israel, an action that

135

brought a boycott of Ford products by Arab nations. That boycott went on for more than twenty years.

What the company and its management did was not contrived. Everyone, regardless of religious preference, political persuasion or skin color, was a prospect for our products, and we wanted to sell them anywhere and everywhere. The same attitude should have applied to employment practices but didn't, and these were changed, particularly with the implementation of affirmative action programs.

I've already mentioned Izzy Levine, who was the senior Ford's New York driver when I went to work in New York. He was a lively, informed company chauffeur, who seemed to know as much about the stock market as Sidney Weinberg and some of the other Ford board members he drove. Later, one of Henry Ford II's closest friends and confidantes, Max Fisher, joined him in a herculean effort to try to change the fast-deteriorating image of downtown Detroit. They worked together, traveled together, played together, and invested together. They were close friends, and there was certainly nothing contrived about that.

In early 1974 after I had moved to Michigan and after representing Ford in New York for twenty-one years, I was invited to accompany a group of predominantly Jewish journalists on a fact-finding trip to the Middle East following the Yom Kippur War. My wife accompanied me, and it proved to be one of our most unforgettable experiences. We visited Egypt, Lebanon, Syria, Jordan, and Israel (in that order because we could not go to Israel and then enter an Arab country). Our mission was to see for ourselves what was going on in that turbulent, festering part of the world, and we certainly did.

We were briefed by the Egyptian General Staff in the Sinai desert after examining the breached Israeli fortifications at Al-Kantara. The Egyptians were proud of what they felt they had accomplished. As we rode through the desert looking at the bleak, forbidding landscape, examining bombed and burned-out military equipment, it all appeared so futile. That feeling never left most of us as we bussed around those five countries looking for all the world like part of the cast from "The Ship of Fools." We felt relatively safe, with security provided by each nation we visited, but there were terrorists then as now, and the risks of a group such as ours traveling through hostile areas was something to think about. I was proud to be a part of that hardy, if somewhat adventuresome, band but relieved when we crossed the River Jordan, by way of the Allenby Bridge on our way to Jericho and Jerusalem. The security check by Israeli customs and armed forces was unparalled, I thought, even though we were a known VIP group. It wasn't our group they were concerned about but what we might be carrying that we didn't know about. Bombs, for example, as small as a personal letter.

During our fact-finding tour, we visited Palestinian refugee camps in most of the Arab countries and were besieged by those trapped in them, as well as by their leaders, to do something about their plight and the return to their homes in the Gaza strip and along the West Bank. It was a cry for help that was emotionally wrenching for all of us notwithstanding the monumental political considerations. An entire generation had grown up in those PLO camps, and the conditions were abominable. The habitats often consisted of scrap wood, cardboard, and tin huts that provided the most marginal of living conditions. The lack of proper sanitary facilities alone created major health problems, and water and food storage were below any accepted health standards.

I was personally incensed that in a supposedly civilized world, the countries we were visiting permitted such conditions to exist, making no effort to assimilate the refugees or at least to upgrade the living conditions. It was obvious that politics took precedence over everything else.

The Arab nations had no intention of assimilating refugees when those people could be held up to the world as a symbol or as an example of what Israel had done in creating a displaced-persons problem; no matter the Arabs had first attacked Israel. The history of that part of the world has kept repeating itself through the ages, and there simply is no easy resolution of the impasse.

I was afraid then that Israel had hunkered down with an intractable, inflexible attitude of no compromise, to prevent a recurrence of what took place in 1948, 1967, and 1973 when the Arabs made major assaults on that country.

I found that most in our party felt as Elinore and I did, that the shame and the blame had to be shared equally among all parties involved and that an early solution to the problem had to be found. Two decades later, as this is written, the situation is still unresolved, though moves are being made on both sides to seek that long-overdue resolution.

While in Israel on that 1974 press tour, I took the opportunity to look in on the Palestine Automobile Company-Ford operation. It assembled vehicles made in Great Britain that were shipped in containers as knockdown units so they could be assembled in Israel, — thus avoiding substantial taxes imposed on completed vehicles brought into the country. PAC had then been operating for thirty-seven years as the sole distributor of Ford products in that part of the world but was rapidly losing its market to competition. The Israelis were driving Fiats and other small, economical cars, and the Arabs throughout the region were driving Mercedes and larger cars because of their affluence and control of oil resources. There didn't seem to be many Fords in anybody's future at that time. Cars from Europe and Japan had begun to make serious gains in the marketplace.

The early advantage that PAC had when Henry Ford helped it get started in 1937 had all but evaporated. Nor did the fact that Henry Ford II helped it expand operations in 1967, even in the face of Arab pressure and a regional boycott, resolve the growing problems brought on by the added competition and Ford's limited supply of small cars. The Japanese imports delivered the final coup and PAC was sold in 1982.

Today, while you see a range of models and nameplates on the streets of Tel Aviv, Jerusalem, and elsewhere in Israel, the Japanese dominate the market, as they do in so many other countries around the world. And while Israelis may have had substantial Ford product loyalty in the late thirties and throughout much of the forties and fifties, it has almost vanished today, as price, choice, and availability have become the dominant buyer considerations.

During my recent visit to Israel in November 1992, I was surprised not only by the vast increase in traffic and the proliferation of vehicle types but also by the vast changes in the country itself. In the almost twenty-year period between my visits, Israel underwent a tremendous building expansion, particularly in the so-called occupied territories of the West Bank and Gaza. Now the hills around Jerusalem are studded with permanent settlements occupied for the most part by non-Arab,s and that development is bound to complicate any resolution of differences with surrounding Arab neighbors. The architecture is striking, the highway and road developments substantial, and the landscaping beautiful — and essential in the stark, barren hills of the area. Unfortunately, the Palestinians and nomads who previously occupied the area do not share the enthusiasm, as they consider themselves displaced losers, much in the way of Native Americans who found themselves confined to reservations as America moved westward during the nineteenth century.

There is still much to be shared in Israel, however, and with proper demonstration of goodwill and serious efforts to resolve the present impasse, there is no reason the Arabs and Israelis, working together, can't finish what has been so successfully undertaken to create a new environment and mutually beneficial life for all in that turbulent region. That shouldn't be beyond the realm of possibility in the land of milk and honey and in an area of the world where Mohammed and Abraham and Jesus spoke of peace and tranquility and the brotherhood of man.

Chapter XVI

A Distress Call from the Bluebird

I've always enjoyed being around water. I thank my father for taking me fishing when I was a kid. We'd go to Jamaica Bay for flounder or out of Freeport, Long Island, on open party boats for codfish in the winter. I tried to do the same with my own children as they were growing up.

When we settled into our routine in Garden City, the weekends provided the only time I could spend with the family that was meaningful. Owing to the nature of my work, hours and schedules were unpredictable. It was a three-to-four-hour daily commute even though we had company cars and parking space available in the Rockefeller Center garage.

Quitting time was irregular, and there were many combination business/social evenings that kept me away from the family dinner table. I give Elinore credit for her understanding and cooperation and for the way she raised the family, in many respects by herself. But I did everything I possibly could to make up for my irregular schedule by concentrating on family weekends.

To help do that I bought a used fishing boat that we could keep within reasonable distance of our home. We kept it in Freeport on the Woodclef Canal behind the home of Lebert Lombardo. The arrangement had been made by our yacht broker, Ben Minton, who was a good friend of the Lombardo family. Guy Lombardo's home, a rambling Mediterranean villa, and his vintage Chris Craft cruiser were two doors from Leeb's house, an old wood and shingle two-story. Both were on the canal.

Saturday mornings we would pile into the family station wagon and go to Freeport for a day on the water, returning home after the boat was washed down. We did the same thing on Sunday, and it got to be quite a drag with four kids. By then John Jr., had arrived and had to be strapped into one of the "fighting chairs" so he wouldn't fall overboard. In due time, the logistics led to a decision to sell the boat for a beach house somewhere but not until I had an experience that became another oft-repeated story.

I had gone fishing annually out of Brielle, New Jersey, with a group of press friends who enjoyed the same pastime: Charley Sievert, Hank Lucking, Joe Kaselow, Jim O'Gara of *Advertising Age*, and Joe Michalski of *United Press International*. We usually went for bluefish, which could be found all along the Jersey coast. I decided to reciprocate when we bought our Keasby fishing boat and invited a group for a Saturday fishing trip to the "acid slick," a deep water canyon in the Atlantic Ocean about an hour's run from Freeport. Only Sievert and Michalski could make it. Lucking, O'Gara, and Kaslow had to take a raincheck or cancel at the last minute.

I was a novice boat skipper, but I knew the basics and could handle compass direction and general safety regulations required by the Coast Guard. I also made sure I had a working ship-to-shore radio on board, which proved to be a godsend on that particular day.

We loaded up on gasoline, water, food, drinkables, bait and tubs of chum and headed out Jones Inlet in a generally southwesterly direction. We were going for "chopper blues," the big ones. It was a beautiful day with a slight breeze, clear sky, and a good forecast, and all we had to do, literally, was follow a procession of boats headed for the same fishing grounds. I never knew exactly what "acid slick" meant but assumed it was part of the dumping grounds for residue out of New York harbor. Whatever it was, it attracted fish and especially big blues.

Sievert and Michalski were enjoying themselves, and so was I as we cruised along at a good clip, the motor humming like a finely tuned machine. After two hours or so of cruising time, we arrived at the outermost edges of the fishing fleet, found an open spot, set our anchor, and began spooning chum to attract the fish. The slick moved out on the current, and it wasn't long before we had fish in the boat. It was going to be a great day.

The fishing slacked and then picked up again, and after a couple of hours, a stiff breeze developed and the ocean started to roll. We didn't pay much attention, as we wanted a few more of those big fish. After all, there were colleagues and neighbors to think about, and they all had freezers. I thought I detected a bit of drift and felt our anchor wasn't holding, so I asked Joe if he would go forward and check the line. Just as his head popped through the bow hatch, a huge wave hit us head on and lifted the boat almost out of the water. Joe hung on for dear life, Charley hit the deck, and I grabbed a last-minute hold on the cabin supports. We came down with a crash that scared the hell out of us. When we caught our collective breaths, Joe pulled in the line, and there was nothing on it. The line, which came with the boat and seemed to be in good condition, had simply parted, leaving the anchors (two of them) on the bottom. I figured they must have been set well enough or else they had caught on a wreck.

We had a smaller anchor and a short line, both of which were insufficient for any further fishing that day. So we pulled up all lines, secured everything and started the engine, which turned over immediately. I headed for home, and it was then that I noticed there were very few boats left in the area where we'd been fishing. I didn't realize it, but that was going to be another problem.

143

We hadn't gone very far when the engine conked out. That had never happened before, and I didn't like it but didn't anticipate what was about to happen. We started up again and the same thing happened, and then again and again. We had an engine problem or a gas problem, and while I wasn't sure which, either one spelled trouble and I wasn't about to try to work on gas lines or the carburetor in what was now a rolling sea. We were going to have to try hanging on, and without an anchor on the bottom, we started to drift in a running sea. I also realized we didn't have a sea anchor on board to keep us headed into the waves. We would be taking them broadside, and I was beginning to get a short course in off-shore emergency preparedness.

I immediately called the New York marine operator on the ship-to-shore, told her we were in trouble, and asked if she could help. "I'll sure try," she said, "but where are you?" I told her as best I could, and she said she'd alert the Coast Guard. That was all very reassuring. Another fishing boat came within hailing distance, and we told them we were in distress. They made no offer of a tow but said they would tell the Coast Guard at Freeport when they got in. We wished we were going in too, for by then there wasn't another boat in sight.

Joe Michalski was seasick by now and lying in the cabin. I was at the wheel and Charley in the cocaptain's chair on the opposite side. It was close to 3 P.M. and the waves, which seemed to be growing in size, were hitting us broadside and rolling the boat. I had a lot of faith in New Jersey-built fishing boats but prayed silently that the wood hull wouldn't spring a leak and add to our problems. I called the marine operator again, just as a huge Moran Brothers oceangoing tugboat hove into sight, pulling an enormous barge filled with what appeared to be garbage. The environment was going to take another beating, but I would have been glad to "hook a ride" with them if possible.

"We're having trouble positioning you," the operator said, and I told her about the tug and barge. "See if you can hail the captain of that Moran tug and ask him to call us and position you," she said. I grabbed the megaphone and yelled to the tug. A man came out of the pilot house, having spotted our distress flag (Charley Sievert's T-shirt) atop the radio antenna. "What's your problem?" he yelled, and I told him. He gave a somewhat reassuring wave and returned to the pilot house, and they moved farther out to sea. I was fascinated by the huge hawser line connecting the tug and the barge as it rose and fell with a regular motion into the air and deep into the water. Anything to get my mind off our predicament.

Hours went by. I managed a regular call to the marine operator, who I learned later had an exceptionally busy shift, with boats like ours in distress up and down the Jersey and Long Island coasts. But as far as we were concerned, nobody could be in as much trouble as we were.

By 8 P.M. the marine operator said they were sending a plane equipped with "Loran" out of Floyd Bennett Field, Brooklyn, to see if it could find and position us for the eighty-three foot Coast Guard cutter from Sandy Hook, New Jersey, that was searching for us. It was a needle in a haystack situation. "Please keep an eye out for the plane and the cutter," the operator said. She didn't have to say it twice.

"Do you have a light aboard?" she asked.

I said "yes."

"Good. Flash it when you see the plane overhead."

"Roger."

At about 9 P.M., after seeing several Europe-bound planes, we heard the navy PBY and began flashing the light even before we could see anything. Suddenly, there it was, and we hoped they could see us. About fifteen minutes later on the crest of a wave, we could see the cutter approaching. It was lit up like a floating playground, but there were no fun and games on board. We could see the orange-vested crew members scurrying around and getting ready to come as close as they dared without sending us to the bottom. It was like a scene out of a movie as the cutter rose on the waves and fell into the troughs. All we could see at times were the lights on its mast as our twenty-four-footer went deep into a hole of water. The cutter skipper, a long-service chief petty officer, told us later he had six men aboard who were seasick. Joe Michalski felt better when he heard that.

A crew member tossed me a "monkey fist," with a heavy towline attached, and I secured it to the bow for the trip home. Charley's legs had given out and he was hanging on from the chair. He didn't want to join Joe in the cabin. I steered as best I could as we moved behind the cutter. I would have to fight the wheel and the towline for the next six hours until we made port at the Coast Guard station in Sandy Hook. The cutter couldn't tow us through the Jones inlet to Freeport, because the inlet was far too rough that night. In addition, we'd drifted twenty miles from our first position. I realized how far out to sea we were when we passed both Scotland and Ambrose light ships on the tow to Sandy Hook. Those light ships guide the oceangoing liners into New York Harbor.

As the hours went by without sleep, Charley said to me, "John, I always knew I was going to go someday, but I never thought you would be taking me there. It's times like this when you wonder if all the insurance is paid up and what's going to happen to the wife and kids." We both laughed, and the world was a better place now that we were under tow.

Then a rain squall hit us, and we couldn't see the cutter anymore.

We arrived at the Sandy Hook dock at 4 A.M. Sunday. They gave us mugs of coffee and put us to bed in the barracks but not until the chief came aboard to make out his report. "Got anything to drink?" he asked and downed a good belt of Scotch before he went to work.

"You guys must be pretty important," he said. "This was an all-out effort from topside. We don't normally bring anyone into our own dock, but we're going to check everything out and get you on your way as soon as possible. Your wives know where you are."

"Well, thank the Lord for that," I said, but I called Elinore anyway and found out what was behind the chief's comment. As it got late, she'd heard from Ida Michalski and Nancy Sievert, and they kept in touch a good part of the night. Ida almost unraveled emotionally over Joe and called his bosses at UPI, who put out an emergency alert to the Coast Guard that a couple of important newsmen were in distress on a fishing boat called the Bluebird.

That got immediate attention, but the Atlantic Ocean is endless when you are out there in a relatively small boat and drop into the trough of a twenty-foot wave. All you can see is a mountain of water.

As we caught a bit of sleep in the barracks, the Coast Guard put a mechanic on board, cleaned the tank of some sediment that had clogged the fuel line, filled the gas tank, and sent us home to Freeport.

The following week Charley Sievert learned of an upcoming anniversary of the Coast Guard and used that to tell our story in a feature column in the *World Telegram and Sun.* "Semper Paratus," Sievert wrote of the Coast Guard motto, "is *always ready,* but unofficially it means: You have to go out, but you don't have to come back. Hats off to those grand guys in the Coast Guard on their one-hundred-sixty-fourth anniversary!"

After reading Sievert's column some of our needling colleagues said: "Hell, we know those guys, they went out and didn't know *how* to come back.

They were only half right!

Chapter XVII

Jew York, New York, 's a Wonderful Town

I've often thought I spent the "golden years" in New York — those of the city and of my own life. There wasn't a dull moment, as they say, during my twenty-one years there, handling Ford's public relations operations or anything else I was asked or expected to do.

I took to New York rather the way I took to Dwyer's farm — naturally. I couldn't get enough of it, and the Ford name was the "open sesame" to everything. Everywhere we went we had entrée, and we always went first class. That was the way Henry Ford II wanted it. When we were on the job, we were representing him, because he was the company. The two were inseparable.

I felt the magic of the name the first time Steve Fitzgerald called to ask if I had an interest in being interviewed for the job, and it never left me all the years I spent in Manhattan.

I suspect every passing generation feels the vitality of New York City and thinks of the good and not the bad. That's the way it was with me. It seemed I could go anywhere, anytime, and do just about anything I thought would be in the company's interests. And I tried to do just that. I made it my business to get around, become known, and reach as high as I could into the worlds of media, business, and politics. In public relations you simply can't be too well known or know too many people. Contacts were the life blood of PR then, as they are now, and that's one thing that hasn't changed a bit.

The world of New York has changed, however, under successive political administrations, financial pressures, and a plethora of problems stemming from economics, population growth, housing shortages, aging infrastructure, and countless other needs and problems that at times appear insurmountable. Yet "the city that never sleeps," seems to take it all in stride and always bounces back. "New York is where it happens" is not a hollow phrase, and during my years on the scene, I managed to get behind the scenes often enough to see how a lot of it came together.

I tried to dress like a diplomat in my early Ford days, with a dark topcoat, a matching homburg, a white scarf, and an attaché case. The police on duty at St. Patrick's Cathedral across from our office at 630 Fifth Avenue would often tip their hats when I passed, thinking I was a priest. That pleased my mother when I told her about it. But appearance was de riguer for entreé to the Stork Club, "21," El Morroco, or any other posh place in town. It was also good for visits to City Hall where what passed for an Irish face was always welcome in those earlier days.

I'd come to know quite a bit about how the "Hall" operated. When I was stationed in the downtown AAF PR unit at 67 Broad Street, we had a number of officers on the staff who had substantial political clout. That's probably why they were there.

When I first arrived, William O'Dwyer, a brigadier general, was the commanding officer. General O'Dwyer had just returned from Italy where he headed military government operations, and he was in a transitional mode. He didn't stay very long. He was about to run for mayor and he had plenty of support. "Billo," as his press secretary, Bill Donoghue, used to call him, had been the district attorney of Brooklyn during the heyday of Murder, Inc., the notorious band of thugs and racketeers who brought calamity to the city. The "Brownsville Boys," Murder, Inc.'s other moniker, had a penchant for taking contracts on people's lives. One of their leaders was the ruthless Albert Anastasia, friend of Louis Lepke Buchalter, who ended up in the electric chair after years of terrorizing the New York garment district.

Bill O'Dwyer had prosecuted the mob, as had Tom Dewey, and he sent a number of them to jail or worse. He developed a gang-buster reputation.

That propelled him to the forefront of candidates for mayor of the city of New York. But first there was the matter of World War II. He was commissioned and sent overseas, where he served in the military government.

While O'Dwyer was on duty in Italy, Vito Genovese, a deported mobster with a desire to return to the states, was said to have made a deal to get the New York crime families to give major support to an O'Dwyer ticket if he, Genovese, could return to live in the United states. He had been deported prior to the war, as an undesirable alien.

Vito Genovese was said to control black market operations in the Rome area and had ties to the military government in which Bill O'Dwyer had a prominent and influential role. Whether or not General O'Dwyer arranged an "accommodation," Genovese did return to the United States. He lost no time in picking up where he left off in a move to take over the New York rackets, then being managed by Albert Anastasia and others. He sent Frank Costello a message that Costello was no longer "prime minister of the underworld" and the mob's principal contact with Tammany Hall by putting out a contract on him. When a young thug creased Costello's skull with a bullet that missed its target, Frank got the message. He retired.

Anastasia ended up being assassinated in a barbershop chair at the Park Central Hotel.

There is no doubt Genovese played a leading role in the postwar Appalachian mob meeting at the home of Joseph Barbara in upstate New York. He was one of those rounded up by the New York State troopers as he fled through the woods with many of the sixty mob leaders who attended. A number were apprehended, but some got away. Genovese subsequently ended up in prison with fellow mobster Joseph Valachi, who feared for his life when Genovese arrived. Valachi's fear led him to speak publicly about la Cosa Nostra, and when he was released from prison, he asked to be put in the federal witness protection program. That pleased Attorney General Robert Kennedy immensely, since he had the entire mob in his sights.

Bill O'Dwyer was a mayor in the old Irish tradition, according to his press secretary, Donoghue. When City Hall became too hot for his comfort, Harry Truman named him United States ambassador to Mexico. It was reported at the time that President Truman had to get "Billo" out of town "for the good of the party," and that didn't mean some upcoming social event!

In many ways, it seemed like a reprise of Jimmy Walker's administration and the grand old days of Tammany, when the then mayor of New York was the toast of the town but ran a "Swiss cheese" administration. Walker and O'Dwyer were both well liked. I always remember my father telling me that the people of New York felt "when Jimmy was getting his, they (the people) were getting theirs," whatever that meant. I could only guess.

When John Cameron joined our staff, I was invited to numerous political and quasi-political activities that brought me to City Hall and a number of other gathering places around town. John was married into a family that was a political powerhouse on the New York Democratic scene. His father-in-law, Paul Rao, was a federal customs judge with a flair and a love for politics. He often invited Elinore and me to his townhouse on East 61st Street and his home in Mount Kisco for receptions, parties, and cookouts that featured a range of interesting guests, including Mayor Robert F. Wagner and his wife, Susan. Those occasions were always great fun and great "door openers."

I particularly remember a colorful political dinner in a lower Westside loft building, where the San Benito Wine Company had its offices and bottling facilities. The winery was called the Cellar in the Clouds, and Victor and John Dumbra (the owners) were our hosts. Tables groaning with fruit, cheese, and wine were set between the rows of wine casks. We were served a marvelous dinner and heard toasts, introductions, and remarks from various and sundry city bosses including Mayor Wagner, Fire Commissioner Edward Cavanaugh, Water and Electric Commissioner Armand DeAngelo, and Judge Rao.

But before we sat down for the meal and program, we all donned monks' robes, complete with hoods and heavy rope belts, and paraded around the wine barrels carrying lighted candles. It was about as close to monastery life as any of us ever got. But it was all great fun and there were always new movers and shakers or hangers-on to meet.

There were a number of similar fun occasions at Ruppert's Brewery, Térè a Segno (the Rifle Club), and elsewhere. It was an exciting period in city politics and in my own life as well.

When Ford reenacted a famous coast-to-coast automobile race in 1959, we had no problem getting the full cooperation and participation of everyone at City Hall, from the mayor on down. It was one of the most colorful and nostalgic programs our office had responsibility for planning and carrying out during my time in Manhattan.

In 1909, when the automobile was in its infancy and there were few roads across the nation, Robert F. Guggenheim, scion of a noted New York family, offered a trophy and a purse to the winner of an automobile race from New York to Seattle. It was a rugged undertaking, won by a Ford Model-T. The Ford managed to overcome raging rivers, muddy plains, almost impassable mountains, and other hazards, because it was light and durable, had high axles, and an under-carriage that was simple to repair.

The company's Ford Division wanted to reenact the historic event as part of its plans for introducing the 1959 new product lines. It seemed like another opportunity for a Golden Anniversary PR effort. Our job was to create and launch the re-enactment at the New York end, and we decided to try to recapture much of the color and excitement of the original event. The luncheon that preceded the race had been held in the Hotel Astor in Times Square in a room that hadn't changed since the turn of the century. It still featured a baroque ceiling that reminded one of the Sistine Chapel, and it still had the satin fabric wall coverings of the 1909 period, though not the originals.

Our luncheon featured clams on the half shell, beer by the pitcher, honky-tonk pianos, barbershop quartets, checked tablecloths, and a sepia-tone invitation in *Police Gazette* format. It was good enough for framing and actually became a collector's item.

The luncheon was SRO. The press loved it. Former Ambassador Richard Patterson, who headed Mayor Wagner's department of public events, served as master of ceremonies and was joined on the dais by an array of VIPs and city department heads.

Waiting outside the Astor Hotel to take us to City Hall was a cavalcade of vintage automobiles and apparatus from the city's Fire Department Museum that was rarely allowed out on the public streets. And dressed in the finery of the era were our staff secretaries, Marge Hatzman, Yvette Diaz, and Cathleen Lyons. They looked as though they were on their way to Delmonico's to meet Diamond Jim Brady.

At City Hall the vehicles were lined up behind a podium, where Mayor Wagner was to use a gold-plated revolver to start the race, as his predecessor had fifty years earlier. But first there were brief remarks and a telephone hookup that brought the voice of Robert Guggenheim, himself, to the occasion from his home in Washington, D.C. He was then in his eighties, not able to make the trip to New York, and he died shortly after the event.

When we found that the gold-plated revolver had been left at the Astor Hotel by accident, the mayor's police bodyguard emptied the chambers of his 38 revolver so the mayor could hold a gun aloft in a symbolic gesture to start the race. As he did, one of our staffers bent low behind the podium and roared, "They're off!"

Public relations is a field where the unexpected can happen at anytime, and often does. It pays to be resourceful and have a backup game plan! The "missing gun" became a story all by itself and moved nationwide on the Associated Press wire. The AP made it a funny and harmless story.

Those turn-of-the-century days in old New York were exciting and filled with wonderful happenings, and for a few brief hours, we were all back there reliving that colorful period.

There isn't any question in my mind when I say the years I spent in New York, half a century later, were just as exciting and eventful in their own way. Despite the fact that New York appears hopelessly burdened with a plethora of problems today, I'm sure that years from now, people will be rediscovering it and looking back with the same warm feelings about the city that I've always had.

Henry Ford's personal chauffeur in Chicago, and, later, Henry Ford II's, was a man named Joe Spedifor, who eventually was transferred to New York, as personal transportation supervisor, reporting to me. Joe carried a 38 police special handgun in a shaving kit, under his seat whenever he drove. It was a carry-over from his days in Chicago, during the 20's and 30's, when the company had him on special assignment demonstrating Lincoln sedans for the likes of Al Capone, Frank Nitti, Jake "Greasy Thumb" Guzik, Anthony "Big Tuna" Accardo, and Murray "The Camel" Humphreys, the aristocracy of the Chicago underworld. As a fellow Sicilian, Joe had special credentials, and when he made a "sale" the vehicle went right to the mob's armorers to be fitted with bullet proof glass, extra sheet metal and interiors capable of carrying a range of firepower in hidden compartments. Joe told me he found New York quite tame by comparison. Since he retired a number of years ago, he might not think so today as murder and mayhem are daily events on front pages and evening newscasts.

Experience and observation has told me there was, and probably still is, a kind of quid pro quo in the political system that reaches all the way from the underworld to the upper world in layers of contact and influence, encompassing everything in between. The underworld has always been well wired into the system and has provided a great deal of the funding for political action and favors. In fact, the underworld had its own political action committees long before that form of participation in government affairs was adopted by corporations and others with a need for entrée and support.

Claude Philippe and I were having lunch one day in the original Men's Bar of the Waldorf at a table next to one occupied by Frank Costello, Lewis Rosenstiel, the board chairman of Schenley's, and Bernard Gimbel, the department store tycoon. Philippe, who knew the three of them, told me they had just come over from the baths at the Hotel Biltmore, where business and politics were always principal topics for discussion. The Biltmore was headquarters for the Democratic Party of New York, the old "Tammany Hall."

People like Bernie Gimbel and Lew Rosenstiel apparently had no problem being seen with Costello, who was frequently referred to in the press as "the prime minister" of the underworld. Costello thought of himself as just another businessman, like Joe Kennedy, Gimbel and Rosenstiel. Frank favored the Waldorf, its Peacock Alley and barbershop, close by the Waldorf Towers, where his old associate Lucky Luciano once had an apartment. When Lucky was sent to prison by District Attorney Tom Dewey, he was later pardoned by Lt. Governor Charles Poletti, during a thirty-day period when Poletti was serving as interim governor. Lucky was exiled to Italy as part of the deal, but when he died in Italy, his family was allowed to return the body and inter him in a mausoleum in St. John's Cemetery, near his old colleague, Joe Profaci, and other departed friends. Even the dead have political clout, it seems.

One night, during a major city election campaign, a colleague and I were invited to attend a gathering at the Biltmore. We thought it would be interesting to see the elective process in action as the voting results came in. The place was packed with people, who seemed to come from all walks of city life. It was a real demonstration of democracy at work. I recognized Jimmy Breslin, a writer for the *New York Herald Tribune*, and a number of other reporters who specialized in writing about politics. After visiting with them, we sat with a group of people from the Greenwich Village voting precincts. Several were owners of bars and restaurants, and they invited us to join them later in the evening. We accepted, and it turned out to be quite a night on the town.

One of the places we visited was the Savannah Club on West Fourth Street, not far from New York University's School of Commerce, where I had attended evening classes. In those earlier days, I didn't have money to spare for a beer, let alone anything else.

Now we were given the royal treatment by our new-found friends and had a great time on the house.

The Savannah Club was a downtown version of the famed Cotton Club of jazz age fame, with a black chorus line and entertainment, and it was lively. I soon learned the place was owned by a notorious mobster with the alias "Three-Finger Brown," who lived along the Palisades in New Jersey. Al Anastasia was one of his neighbors. The manager of the club had a brother connected socially and otherwise to political power brokers who could reach right into City Hall. It was as simple as that — useful contacts at high levels. Today, we refer to that type of contact work in the PR field as "networking."

The Savannah Club was to gain substantial notoriety later, when Joe Valachi identified it in his "Valachi Papers" as one of his hangouts during the Genovese period, and when Vito got rid of Al Anastasia, he also got rid of Three-Finger Brown.

During that same era, I was invited to the grand opening of the Marciano Room, a restaurant and bar on Lexington Avenue in the mid-fifties. It was a Sunday-afternoon affair, and I was surprised to see Mayor Wagner turn up along with a number of other city officials including former Air Force General Roger Brown, who was a neighbor of ours in Garden City. The general had been named head of the city's purchasing department by his old friend and former military colleague, Wagner.

Also on hand were business leaders, socialites, judges, and Carmine DeSapio, the Tammany leader. It was DeSapio who got out of a taxi in which a brown paper bag was found that contained several thousand dollars of damp paper money. The

Tammany chief denied it was his or that he knew anything about it.

The Marciano Room was owned by the brother of the manager of the Savannah Club. Rocky Marciano, who was often around town in those days, didn't own any part of it. They merely used his name — part of the unholy alliance between boxing and "the boys."

Somewhat closer to home, one of our Ford secretaries married the son of one of two notorious Brooklyn crime kingpins, who had helped Al Anastasia control that borough's rackets. Guests at the wedding included prominent members of the judiciary and a number of city officials. Undercover law enforcement representatives stood in the shadow of the Brooklyn church to photograph the guests and did the same thing later at the Astor Hotel, where a reception and dinner took place in the Grand Ballroom.

It wasn't long after that, however, that the bodies of the bridegroom's father and uncle, Albert and Vincent Mangano, ended up in the wetlands of Jamaica Bay. They were victims of a contract hit just like their late associates, Anastasia and Three-Finger Brown. Vito was still "cleaning house." Crime is a one-way street filled with a lot of potholes, and those major rubouts had been high on the agenda of the Appalachian meeting.

You couldn't move about in the upper echelons of New York City politics and Manhattan night life without rubbing elbows with a wide range of personalities and learning a great deal about how life in the city came together. The "day people," (commuters and workers for the most part) only knew what they read in the papers or saw on television. The "night people," however, often had a box seat at what was going on and sometimes had a hand in making it happen.

Chapter XVIII

Winning One for "The Babe"

Public relations ideas are where you find them whether in the inner recesses of the imagination or out of something you read, hear, see on television, or simply stumble across.

So it was in 1947 when an idea that was sparked by a newspaper sports column led to the hiring of Babe Ruth as a youth consultant to Ford Motor Company.

The Babe had long since been out of baseball, having peaked in his playing career in the late twenties and early thirties. There was no one in the game quite like him. Sure, Lou Gehrig was a big favorite and there were many other outstanding players, but there was only one Babe. He'd had an amazing career for someone who had broken every rule of self-discipline and behavior, but now it was all over, or so it seemed.

Babe had wanted to manage, but it wasn't in the cards. He was star quality, a loner, and he couldn't manage himself, let alone others. Additionally, his health wasn't good. Still, he wanted to identify with baseball in a way that would keep him involved and useful. He was sixty years old.

It was at this point that Jim Chapman, one of my public relations colleagues at Ford, happened to notice a sports column that revisited Babe, his career, and his unwanted retirement. It said Babe was looking for something to do in baseball.

Ford at the time cosponsored American Legion Junior Baseball through its national dealer organization, in much the same way General Motors and Chevrolet sponsored their remarkably successful Soap Box Derby program. Legion baseball was a purposeful thing to do, and it brought people into dealers' showrooms to arrange participation. That gave dealers an opportunity to meet "mother and dad," to get to know them, and perhaps do business with them.

When Jim Chapman saw the column about the Babe, he got one of those ideas that public relations people get paid to generate — could Babe fit into the American Legion Junior Baseball program? The more we all thought about the idea and its various ramifications the better it sounded. I saw only one possible hitch, and that was Babe's health. He was not in the best of health, and that was generally known in sports circles and by the sportswriting fraternity. We could not afford to be put in the position of appearing to exploit a sports hero or risk his health no matter what the cause or how mutually beneficial the arrangement.

Babe was being counseled by two old and close friends, Paul Carey who owned a New York limousine service and a string of barbershop franchises, and Charles Schweifel, manager of the Gramercy Park Hotel in lower Manhattan. Babe was a frequent guest at the Gramercy Park, but at the moment he lived on Riverside Drive with his wife, Claire. Two other close friends were consulted, Mae and Peter DeRose. Peter was a composer, best remembered for "Deep Purple," one of Babe's favorite songs. Mae's family owned the Skirvin Towers Hotel in Oklahoma City. Babe's doctors were also consulted.

All agreed involvement in the program, within reasonable physical limitations, would be beneficial and therapeutic for Babe, who was personally very enthusiastic. So was everyone else, including American Legion management at legion headquarters in Indianapolis.

Jack Davis, who hired me and was still much involved in giving direction to Ford advertising and public relations interests, found the money for us to sign the Babe. It was almost as much as Col. Jacob Ruppert paid him in his early days with the Yankees. As part of the arrangement, Babe also received a burgundy Lincoln Continental with his monogram on the front doors, and I delivered it to him at his home on Riverside Drive. The car was a beauty, and I wish I had it now — both for nostalgia and as a collectible, for its value today would far exceed everything Babe was paid during the period he was under contract to Ford.

But first there was the matter of an announcement and a press conference for the official contract signing.

I picked the Waldorf for a number of reasons, not the least the convenience for the Babe, who could come in under the building and take a private elevator to the press conference location. The conference was held in the Waldorf's Perroquet Suite, large and comfortable. We could have gone to Ruppert's Brewery, but that would have pointed the story in the wrong direction. We were selling kids and cars, not beer.

I sent letters of invitation to the press and frankly was surprised to see my letter used as the basis for speculative news stories and sports columns. There was that much interest. I had been as forthcoming as possible without tipping our hand, but I obviously had to mention Babe and a press conference. On hand for the signing were Jack Davis, Benson Ford, and the national commander of the American Legion, with Babe in the "cleanup" position. Fourth at bat, he was to hit another homer.

Remarks were kept to a minimum, and after Benson Ford spoke Babe spoke briefly. It was touching to see him sitting at the table in front of a bank of microphones, somewhat hunched over, his jacket indicating the loss of weight from his huge frame. His voice was hoarse, since he was under treatment for throat cancer, and you could see the effects of the radiation treatment in his color and the partial loss of his hair.

But it was Babe Ruth back in the limelight, and if any of the hard-bitten reporters had to steel their emotions or wipe a tear, it had to be momentary as he wisecracked his way through brief remarks. He brought down the house when he said, "Well, I started out in sand-lot baseball, and here I am right back where I started, but it's going to be a lot of fun." He didn't have to say another word but he went on to thank all concerned and say how happy he was to be returning to baseball.

The story was big news, and the public relations value to Ford and the American Legion was substantial. It was like wrapping oneself in the American flag at a time when doing that was still considered patriotic.

I saw quite a lot of Babe during that period, visiting with him at his apartment and traveling with him to baseball dinners and events, where we would meet sports figures like Connie Mack, and Ted Williams. As Ford's goodwill ambassador to baseball, Babe would sit on the dais, wave, and say a few words, never failing to get a standing ovation that seemed endless.

Driving to Philadelphia one afternoon, Babe was thirsty, so we pulled in at a roadside tavern for a cold beer. He loved beer, and liquids gave him some strength, since he was having trouble handling solid food. The bartender's eyes went wide as saucers as he took our drink order. He never said a word, but four men at the other end of the bar spotted the familiar figure in tan polo coat and matching "Pee" cap. "Hey, it's Babe Ruth," one said, and they came bounding over to meet an idol and asked for his autograph. Babe gave it willingly, of course, and it was a moment none of them would ever forget. If that bar is still there, there's probably a plaque on it commemorating that surprise visit!

In Boston for the annual traditional Jimmy Fund dinner to honor a deceased young player, we took a suite at the Statler Hotel and filled an old-fashioned galvanized washtub with cracked ice and beer, which by then appeared to be Babe's sole sustenance. He would toy with food but never really do more than pick at it. I learned later that the "nurse" traveling with us was really an old girlfriend, but she was charming and attentive and did a fine job of looking after Babe. In his younger days, he'd had big appetites, and it was obvious he hadn't lost all of them.

The night Babe passed away at Memorial Hospital in New York City, I was one of the last people to see him. We were standing by at the Stork Club waiting for a call from Paul Carey and didn't want it to come.

"You better come up right away," Paul said. "Claire and Charlie, Mae, Peter, and I are here. The doctors say he won't last the night. You can only have a few minutes, like the rest of us."

Jim Chapman and I jumped into a cab, and the ride was depressing. So was the sight of Babe in an oxygen tent in intensive care. No one said much. We paid our respects, said a personal prayer, and left. He was on oxygen and sedatives and didn't know we were there. Within a few days we sat in the center aisle of St. Patrick's and said goodbye. He had lain in state at Yankee Stadium as thousands of fans from all walks of life passed his coffin.

An era in baseball history had ended forever. Every kid's hero was gone. I had never expected to meet him, let alone become a friend, and it had been all too short. My notes from Babe, autographs, and photographs are all personal treasures.

Ford was to continue its interest in youth programs for a number of years. It was manifested in many ways, through support of programs like Junior Achievement, the Ford Industrial

Arts Awards program, and a unique program to encourage young people to consider journalism as a career.

For several years, we offered college scholarship support to young people who were sponsored by a newspaper or a magazine and who would be brought to Dearborn at our expense during model-introduction time to report on the new products. It was a self-serving program in many respects because those participating would be writing about Ford cars and trucks, but the participants and their media sponsors liked it and gave it enthusiastic support.

One of our most noted finds, as it turned out, was Michael Crichton, who was sponsored by *Advertising Age* and went on to become a best-selling author after he completed medical school. His book *The Andromeda Strain*, was a runaway best seller and he has been at the top of the list with all his books ever since. His latest is *Jurassic Park*. Lawrence "Larry" Sanders, another best-selling author, was also a regular attendee at Ford press events. In those days he was an editor of *Science and Mechanics*.

The Industrial Arts Awards program was always one of my favorites. It was sponsored by Ford's Educational Affairs Office to encourage youngsters with mechanical aptitude and related creative talent. Some of the young people who participated in the program were at or close to the genius level (I thought), and I never ceased to be impressed with the projects they entered in that fine program.

Each year I would go to Dearborn for a couple of days and look over the best of the program entries. I picked those I thought should be brought to New York, along with their creators, for display and demonstration at a press conference. The nature of the items usually dictated where we would hold the event, and sometimes it was in Central Park or in the ballroom of a hotel. The demonstration shows we put on with those young people and their winning entries never failed to get substantial media attention. For several years we regularly made the "split page" of the *Times* and the *Herald Tribune*. There were remote-controlled lawnmowers, one-of-a-kind sports cars, space rockets, and talking robots along with a range of other unbelievables all created and put together by teen-age boys and girls.

One year we had a robot that was rigged to talk, so we cut a record, made the robot the master of ceremonies at our press luncheon, and programmed it to welcome press guests by name. The next day the *New York Herald Tribune* ran an editorial taking note that a robot had "conducted a press conference." With a touch of wry humor, the *Trib* observed: "Take it from us, that wasn't the first time a 'robot' ever conducted a press conference. Our reporters go to them all the time!"

It was an observation that shouldn't have been lost on anyone working in the public relations field. All too often management people were stiff and uncomfortable when they met the press. Today there are special PR-sponsored programs to teach executives how to relax when they meet the media and how to handle themselves under pressure during interviews and press conferences.

Panel of judges at famous Stork Club selects the Ford "Quality Queen". LR: Band leader Kay Kyser; Radio hostess Jinx Falkenberg McCrary; Model mogul John Robert Powers; Actress Georgia Carroll Kyser; and TV showman, Ed Sullivan. Others are Ford and agency executives.

Charley Sievert, left, Joe Michalski, center, and the author, pledge to uphold U. S. Coast Guard's rules of good seamanship following near disaster aboard the Bluebird.

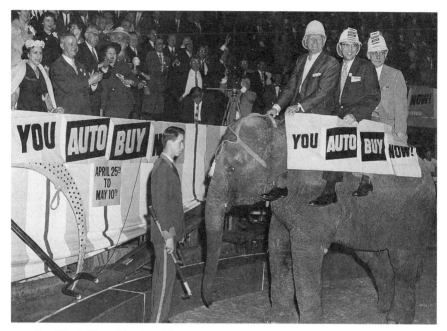

On "Safari" at Ringling Circus to end 1958 auto sales recession, were L.R. GM executive Bill Power, and dealers Ken Wellner and George Ashdown. Picture appeared all over the world.

Veteran showman Walt Disney describes operation of the Ford Pavilion's "Magic Skyway" to John Sattler, Jr., as the skyway is constructed around the outside of the Ford Rotunda entrance.

The author discussing Ford plans for the 1965 season with Robert Moses, Chairman and President New York World's Fair Corporation.

Mayor Robert F. Wagner presents Proclamation to launch N.Y. World's Fair 1965 season to Jim Judge and John Sattler, Co-chairmen, Fair Exhibitors Committee, and International Pavilion hostesses.

Walter Reuther, UAW President examines Ford show vehicle during Ford Pavilion visit. It was one of the last photographs of the Reuthers, who were killed later, in a plane crash, in Michigan.

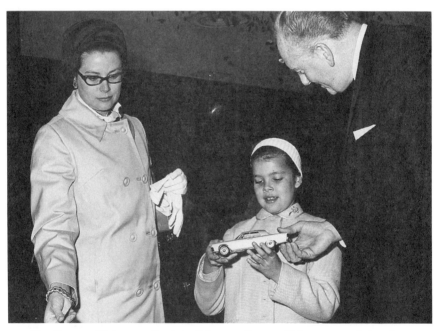

Her Serene Highness, the late Princess Grace of Monaco, and daughter Princess Caroline, visit Ford and receive a model car radio as a memento.

The author, with Sammy Davis, Jr., and Sandy Bain, PR Vice President, Restaurant Associates, planning gala to launch New York World's Fair 1965 season.

The author cutting cake in the design of the Ford Pavilion, during 46th birthday party at the World's Fair. Family members shown, LR: Lin, John Jr., Joan, Elinore, Sandra Lee, John Sr., and Kevin.

The author describes satellite built by Ford's Aeronutronic Division, to Muhammad Ali, boxing champion, as Ford's Larry Washington, looks on.

On Hollywood set for production of Ford's 75th Anniversary Show with Ford spokesman Bill Cosby and Shirley Eder, movie columnist, Detroit News.

Chapter XIX

The Russians Are Coming

As a leading worldwide corporation, Ford was frequently called upon to be supportive of the various interests and needs of our government and its agencies. The same thing applied to individuals.

Over the years, I had the opportunity to assist and work with the Secret Service, the Federal Bureau of Investigation, the Agency for International Development, and others, including the Central Intelligence Agency. It always gave me a sense of pride and usefulness — something I feel is often missing in too many of our citizens today who don't realize they live in a paradise compared with many other places in the world.

The United States State Department would occasionally contact us when it needed help with some program or to get a message across that might get more attention through identification with the Ford name, which was so familiar and represented so much in so many corners of the world.

That was the case one day when I received a call from Washington, D.C., asking if it would be possible to arrange a visit to our Edgewater plant for two defectors from the Soviet Union, Petr Pirigov and Anatoly Barsov. Pirigov and Barsov were Russian pilots who had defected to the West by flying their military aircraft over the border in Berlin. They were debriefed and subsequently brought to the United States under the auspices of our intelligence services and the State Department. The trip to New York was to be a combination holiday for them and a "PR propaganda opportunity" for Washington. Ford was well known in Eastern Europe for its overseas activities and specifically in the USSR, where an attempt had once been made to help the Russians establish car and truck assembly and production facilities.

The Edgewater plant was convenient for such a visit. It was located in New Jersey on the Hudson River south of the George Washington Bridge, within easy reach of Manhattan. I made all the necessary arrangements, including a morning plant tour and news conference followed by lunch at the New York Athletic Club, where I was a member.

At the Edgewater plant, we easily found a Russian-speaking supervisor, since a number of Eastern European languages and dialects were understood and spoken by our workers. The State Department encouraged us to invite the press, and we did, from New York City as well as New Jersey.

It turned out to be a fascinating day. The two men seemed like peasant types to me, and I marveled at the fact that they were pilots who opted for the West. I wondered if they were "plants" and the whole exercise a ploy to have them reject the west and return to the East. One of them did eventually go back but not for a couple of years. Anatoly Barsov became despondent after a year or so when all of the hoopla and VIP treatment ended and the two were left on their own. Adjusting and finding employment was difficult-to-impossible, and our government services eventually lost interest in them.

On the day of our tour, however, they were a great curiosity and enjoyed the attention. They smiled and waved, but they were also reserved. The story was a natural — Russians and Americans in a friendship mode, workers on the line waving and extending greetings, the two pilots behind the wheel of a newly assembled car coming off the line, and a salute from them to American workers everywhere. It was all upbeat.

By the time Anatoly Barsov opted to return to Russia it certainly had nothing to do with us. His return was attributed to homesickness and a desire to see family members he had left behind.

The Russian Embassy in Washington received him with open arms, and I don't know what happened to him after that or to Peter Pirigov, for that matter. Barsov may have ended up in a gulag in Siberia or some Soviet "mental hospital."

I never had a chance to ask Nikita Khrushchev about them because I didn't get that close to him the day he addressed an assortment of New York politicians, press, and VIPs at the Commodore Hotel. The speech followed his appearance at the United Nations, where he took off one of his shoes and pounded the speaker's lectern to make his point.

A chance to see the head of the USSR close up, particularly in view of the news he was making on that particular visit to New York, was highly prized. Ambassador Dick Patterson had arranged VIP tickets to the luncheon for John Cameron and me, since the luncheon was arranged by his office and the city was the host. Ambassador Henry Cabot Lodge, who introduced Chairman Khrushchev, represented our government, as the United States ambassador to the United Nations.

John Cameron and I decided to go to the hotel early to get good seats. We knew our way around many of the hotels, and we headed for the ballroom by way of the Commodore's kitchen and backstairs. Looking like a couple of plainclothes detectives, we ran into a bona fide detective from the police commissioner's staff, who recognized me. He'd been one of my students at City College of New York, where I taught evening classes in basic public relations. He was also editor of the official police magazine, *Spring 3100*, which happened to be the telephone number of police headquarters. On this day he'd been pressed into service as part of the security force.

The young detective was surprised to see me and asked where we were headed. When I told him, he took us into the ballroom and seated us at a table within fifteen feet of where Nikita Khrushchev and Henry Cabot Lodge would sit on the dais. We were joined later by an assortment of people I was certain included KGB agents and some of our own operatives. Henry Modell, the well-known owner of a sporting-goods chain and major contributor to the Democratic party, also ended up at our table.

When the dais filed in, the national anthems of both countries were played, and a remarkable thing happened. Everybody seemed edgy and tense. After all, Chairman Khrushchev the abrasive leader of the Eastern bloc, was on a self-imposed war path. He had taken to the balconies of the USSR consulate on upper Park Avenue to demonstrate his own brand of diplomacy, in addition to the shoe pounding harangue at the United Nations. His public posturing and remarks bordered on arrogance, and everyone wondered what might happen next. They weren't quite sure they wanted to experience, it but they were fascinated to be there in the circumstances. So were John Cameron and I.

Short, stocky, petulant, Khrushchev had the demeanor of a Benito Mussolini, but he had a great deal more to back it up — or so everybody thought. People were nervous, if not timid, and as the strains of the "Star Spangled Banner" began to fill the room, there was dead silence. Suddenly, as if in a rising tide of patriotism, many in the room began to sing the words to our national anthem. What started out as an uncoordinated, uncertain murmur of voices, gained strength and volume as virtually everyone joined in. Everyone but Nikita Khrushchev and the KGB agents, that is. They stood stone-faced. When the anthem ended, there was a crescendo of enthusiastic applause, and it was a moment to savor.

I felt much the same way two years ago during the reunion of the 451st Bomb Group in Fairmont, Nebraska, when a B-24

Liberator bomber roared out of nowhere to thunder over the heads of the guests and dwindling ranks of veterans on hand for the occasion. It was a vivid reminder of our proud heritage and stirred emotions and feelings of patriotism to the point of tears.

Henry Cabot Lodge, in full command of the occasion and with all the dignity and assurance of his position, introduced Chairman Khrushchev and responded to the chairman's remarks with direct and firm language. It seemed to many of us that the Russian leader suffered from a major case of a nationalistic inferiority complex. He wanted respect and recognition for himself and his country and felt that playing the role of tough guy, was the way to get it. In doing so, however, he created a mood of unease and uncertainty that was to prevail, not only in that room for one afternoon but in the world for some years. In the end, however, he proved less dangerous and more of a leader than those who followed him as chairman of the USSR — or so it seemed to me.

My wife and I made a trip to Russia after that visit, and I could hardly believe what I saw. While we were carefully observed all the time we were there, I had an opportunity to move about and make a number of personal assessments of what I experienced and saw. And frankly, I simply could not believe I was visiting a "superpower" when I saw people lining up at kiosks for a portion of undersized Mediterranean fruit, drinking at public water fountains from a common community glass, and buying lumps of frozen, unappetizing fish, unrefrigerated meat, and the limited produce displayed in the local markets. Bamboo and other rickety scaffolding on buildings that had obviously been under repair for years was as primitive as anything I had seen in southeast Asia or in many Third World countries. I fully recognized the imbalance caused by the diversion of so much of the USSR's gross national product to the military but still shook my head in wonder at what appeared to be behind it all. It was a grey, glum society, and years later I was not surprised at the ultimate collapse of communism — only the speed with which it eventually happened.

Working with our government services gave me a sense of pride for what they did in our interest as citizens. The people I met and worked with over the years were honest, hard-working, and dedicated. It has saddened me to read from time to time the criticism directed at some of them — criticism, unfortunately, too often justified by ineptness or bad judgment on the part of a few who brought into question the reputations of many.

In my early years in New York, I worked closely with Secret Service chief Al Whittaker on a number of occasions involving presidential visits and the use of our products. Sometimes the service would bring special units up from Washington, and sometimes we would provide backup equipment in New York.

I also worked with Jim Rowley, who went on to head the service in Washington, D.C., and who completely reorganized it. He died last year at the age of eighty-four, after a long and distinguished career.

One day Jim Rowley stepped in to put Grover Whelan in his place with utmost diplomacy when we were meeting in New York in connection with a visit by President Harry S. Truman. Whelan had a super ego and was a bombastic and vindictive man. He told me during the meeting with Rowley and others that "the president will not ride in a Lincoln automobile, because we have a perfectly good Chrysler parade car he can use."

Whelan was upset with me and Ford Motor Company, because Ford had not taken a $25,000 advertisement in the official program for a city-sponsored event he was chairing, and he said so in no uncertain terms. He was so petty and needlessly embarrassing that Jim Rowley spoke up and said ever so politely, "Mr. Whelan, arrangements for vehicles for the president are a Secret Service responsibility, and I will have to handle them." Whelan scowled and went on to other matters relating to the president's visit. I said no more, and Jim Rowley quietly arranged to have the president's armor-plated Lincoln brought to New York for the occasion. The Chrysler parade car ended up being used by Grover Whelan and an aide.

Cartha "Deke" DeLoach, a former *New York Times* reporter, was the public relations coordinator for J. Edgar Hoover. I had occasional contact with him, but my close friends Ray Bell of Columbia Pictures and Charlie Russhon, who worked for Cubby Broccoli in producing the James Bond film series, were always in touch with him. Russhon and I were in the air force reserves together along with Mayor Bob Wagner, Maxwell "Mac" Kriendler of the "21" clan, and a number of other New York area people in the advertising, PR and communications fields. Charlie Russhon worked closely with all the military and government services, and it was no accident when Bond used an exotic form of military or naval equipment or armament to thwart Goldfinger, Dr. No and others bent on 007's destruction. The services were usually glad to participate on a quid pro quo basis, and Charlie always saw to it that they were recognized in appropriate ways, including credit lines in the films.

Charlie Russhon never seemed to have an office of his own. He operated out of telephone booths, the "21" Club, his hat, or more often than not, our Ford office. Our administrative manager, Ruth Koupal, always accommodated him and often took his phone messages. I think she liked to listen to Russhon stories, which were liberally sprinkled with his own Bond-like experiences. Or, perhaps it was his alias that intrigued her, "Charlie Vanilla."

As I've said so often, in public relations, you can't know too many people. You never know when you might need them.

Chapter XX

The Edsel Affair, and Others

In our Ford public relations operations we never, but never, lost sight of the fact that it was the products we sold that put the money in our paychecks. We might get involved in a lot of things, some appearing rather remote from what went on day to day in the retail end of our business, but moving the merchandise was the bottom line of everything, and we never forgot it. After all, we were not in the public relations business, we were in the transportation business, with a multitude of side and peripheral interests. Sales and service of cars, trucks, and tractors was the bread and butter of everything we did.

And working with automotive products was exciting. They were big-ticket items that touched everyone at some point in his or her life, and they represented personal items everyone wanted. The same can't be said of all products offered to the consumer. I often wondered if it would have been as much fun working in the food services, financial, or pharmaceutical fields, and I came to the conclusion it would not. Of course, I know there are many satisfied and well-rewarded people handling PR matters for all of them. I always felt lucky to have been where I was, and that was one of the big reasons I stayed. I had been offered opportunities and bigger titles elsewhere, but it simply wouldn't have been the same, particularly while I was in New York. By the time I went to World Headquarters in Michigan, I was too committed to seriously consider anything else, and I never did.

Working with automotive products offered a lot of latitude when it came to providing promotional and marketing support to the various areas of our business, and we didn't spend much time thinking about public relations "purism." There were many times when the lines between press agentry, publicity, sales promotion, and marketing became blurred to the point of indistinctiveness. We never worried about it. Many colleagues in the PR field take themselves rather seriously. They are forever writing "think tank" articles for the professional publications about how public relations is principally a policymaking function that belongs at the highest levels of management, or about the need for PR people to sit at the elbow of the president or CEO and advise on what to say or do to enhance the organization's public acceptance and reputation.

What we were primarily interested in, in those days, was how PR activities could be reflected in the bottom line of the balance sheet. That is what we wanted credit for, public relations' contribution to the company's overall success and financial health.

The philosophy that public relations is largely counseling and policymaking generally doesn't work out in practice. Of course, the public relations activity should be a part of, or have access to, the top levels of management and offer counsel on actions or developments that influence public attitudes. That's basic, but the real test of public relations occurs when management does not need to be told what to do or say but simply does it instinctively, knowingly, and correctly. When that point is reached, public relations has really done its job.

But there will always be the need for the day-to-day basic operating functions of PR no matter what goes on in the executive suite. Press contacts should be made and maintained, news and information matter must be developed and distributed, inquiries have to be answered, and countless other work details handled that have little to do with policymaking "think tank" activities.

Shortly after the war and during the company's "rebirth" period, Ford's product showcase opportunities were almost incalculable. Immediately after World War II, products were at peak demand. Henry Ford II delivered the first car off the postwar assembly line in 1945 to President Harry S. Truman in an out-and-out publicity coup. It was October 26, 1945, and a photograph told it all. The war was over, and Ford was back to peacetime production. Everyone, it seemed, needed a car, and because of that a real PR boner occurred in New York City just before I came aboard — a few months after the Truman delivery at the White House.

Someone from Ford news operations thought the Truman press bonanza could be repeated on a grand scale by arranging a "mass delivery" of new Fords on Sheeps Meadow in New York's Central Park. One of our Broadway dealers, with a penchant for self-promotion, produced a number of celebrities for the occasion. They all wanted new cars, but there wasn't a war veteran in the crowd.

Actor Walter Huston; Sherman Billingsley; Walter Winchell; Hildegarde, the chanteuse; and similar familiar names made up the list of those who were to receive "expedited" delivery.

When it was learned, after the fact, that there wasn't a war veteran on the list, all hell broke loose. Letters poured into Ford offices, veterans' groups were up in arms, and the substantial initial coverage of the "mass delivery" was followed by scathing criticism in editorials, columns, and other comment. What was conceived as an attention-getting action ended up as a major PR black eye.

Ford couldn't reverse the action or wipe the slate clean, but when I became aware of the situation, after I joined the company, I asked our sales department to give priority where possible to the needs of returning veterans. Then I learned through our service manager, Jim Campbell, that a company in the New York area had developed a mechanical device that would enable disabled people to drive cars as long as they could use their hands and pass all other licensing requirements. Availability of the special hand controls was little known then but was to become a major boon to people with leg problems and particularly returning war veterans who were paralyzed from the waist down (paraplegics). They were among the most disadvantaged, it seemed to me, and I wanted to give them the highest priority for new-car deliveries.

I did some research and found a number of paraplegic veterans in rehabilitation at Kingsbridge Hospital in the Bronx and at Halloran General Hospital on Staten Island. I arranged group deliveries of products equipped with the hand controls to veterans who were waiting for cars or who would place an order if they could get delivery. It proved a "ten-strike," and helped substantially to overcome the earlier setback from the deliveries to Billingsley, Winchell, and other celebrities.

That didn't mean, of course, that we completely stopped delivering or expediting cars for VIPs and well-known personalities. What we did was try to exercise better judgment. I took part in a number of deliveries to people like Margaret Truman, Edward R. Murrow, Jack Dempsey, and Eleanor Roosevelt.

Meeting and spending time with Mrs. Roosevelt was a particularly delightful experience. Charlie Bonnell, our Manhattan Lincoln-Mercury dealer, and I called on her at her Washington Square apartment on a Saturday morning. We had tea with her and played with the late president's Scottie, Fala. The Lincoln four-door sedan we delivered actually saved her life at a later date when she was involved in a head-on collision on a Westchester parkway while enroute to the family home in Hyde Park, N.Y. Her Lincoln sedan was totaled, as were Mrs. Roosevelt's much photographed teeth, but her life was saved by the durability of the vehicle, and she recovered to carry on her many public service activities for some years. Everyone agreed at the time that had she been driving a less substantial product, her injuries would have been far more serious, if not fatal.

When the Ford sportsman convertible, with all-wood sides, was announced, I had Mr. John, the noted hat designer, create two hats with small cars running around the brims. I hired models and "green-talked" the police into letting us drive the car in the Easter parade on Fifth Avenue. It was the first and only time (to my knowledge) a car was unveiled during the parade; though a lot of other zany things have since made the Easter parade a target for publicists, press agents, and exhibitionists.

When the retractable hardtop Ford convertible came to market in 1957 and was shown for the first time at the International Automobile Show in the New York Coliseum, I made a proposal to the producers of the Garroway show to display that vehicle in a unique way in front of Garroway's Forty-ninth Street studio. It was during the Christmas season and we found an old gentlemen by the name of Lucky Squires, who looked more like Santa than old St. Nick himself. We also hired a pert brunette, dressed the two of them in Mr. and Mrs. Santa outfits, and had them "Christmas wrapped" with the car, in a huge transparent box. We then carted everything to Garroway's studio on a flatbed trailer. As Dave Garroway was talking about the novel Christmas package outside his studio window, Lucky Squires touched a switch on the dashboard of the car and the roof went up, bursting the cellophane top. The roof then slid into the trunk of the car, and Mr. and Mrs. Santa stood up and waved to the television viewers while the crowd on Forty-ninth Street watched the action.

When I was asked what would have happened if the top refused to work, I said it was a calculated risk worth taking and just one of the hazards you face when making risk-taking PR decisions. I had heard Henry Ford II say one day when he was being interviewed on television, "Well, some you win, some you lose, and some get rained out." I doubt he would have made that same philosophical comment, however, if he'd been watching Garroway and the retractable hardtop got stuck in mid air!

We repeated the same demonstration a couple of hours later in front of the Coliseum to help open the International Auto Show. All we had to do was repackage the car and its contents. As we rode up Fifth Avenue to Fifty-ninth Street, Ernie Breech, the Ford board chairman, came out of the Sherry-Netherland Hotel and looked on in amazement as our little procession went by. He didn't expect it and didn't see us following in a car, but we saw him, and while it was a luck-of-the-draw bit of timing, it helped make a big score that day for our office. Breech told Henry Ford II and PR vice president Charly Moore all about it.

On most new-car launches, you work for months brainstorming ideas, repeating some of the good ones on occasion but always trying to come up with something fresh and new. That was the case in planning the introduction of the Edsel line, a project that has been thoroughly chronicled by my former colleague Gayle Warnock in his book *The Edsel Affair*. Gayle was PR manager for the Edsel Division, and all of us worked with him and the division in getting that new line of cars launched. I even ended up in a feature by Lillian Ross that ran in the *New Yorker*. I spent months tapping every possible media source in the New York area, and there was no end to the things we did to create interest in that new line.

What went wrong with the Edsel? Well, that gets a lot of attention in Warnock's book. In my own judgment, it was primarily a case of bad timing. The economy was going into a downturn when the four different Edsel models were introduced in showrooms of the newly franchised Edsel dealers. It was virtually impossible to overcome the bad economics no matter how fine the product or how brilliant its introduction. I thought the Edsel was a fine product, even though it was plagued by early quality problems. The name didn't help, but I doubt that it hurt. Calling it the Edsel was Ernie Breech's way of recognizing Edsel Ford's self-sacrificing contributions to the Ford Motor Company, and Henry Ford II and Edsel's widow, Eleanor, went along with the idea.

St. Patrick's Day was always big in our New York PR Office. On one St. Patrick's Day, Nina Rao Cameron gave birth to a fine bouncing baby boy which the Cameron's immediately named Scott, and not Patrick. That didn't stop us from going over to Tim Costello's saloon, on Third Avenue, and holding an "Irish Wake" for the Scotch, with green beer. Judge Rao, a bed-rock Sicilian, was unfazed. Always the politician, he said, "Well, at least this gives us a balanced ticket!"

On another occasion, we sent a green Lincoln out to Kennedy Airport, to pick up Robert Briscoe, the Jewish Lord Mayor of Dublin, who was to be an honored guest in the parade down Fifth Avenue. Bob Stone was our ambassador. He took the Mayor to lunch and Briscoe opted for cream cheese, lox, and bagels instead of boiled potatoes, corned beef and cabbage. He probably had his fill of potatoes and the rest of it, in Ireland!

When we were getting ready to launch the Edsel series, we hired several "wee people" dressed them as Leprechauns, and sent them around to the city newsrooms with a release about the Edsel "E" insignia, which was highly stylized and had an emerald green background. The little guys were practically escorted into the newsrooms, where they were photographed and caused a lot of commotion. The releases they carried, however, must have ended up in the "round file." The story drew a complete blank.

For a lot of reasons I wish the Edsel had succeeded. But frankly, it cannot be judged a total failure even though it is often held up as an example of a product disaster. Edsel cars are much sought after today as car-collectors' items, along with numerous other vintage makes and models, and they still have a classic look despite the "horse collar" grille that provided so much grist for the humor mills of Johnny Carson, Bob Hope, Milton Berle, and others.

As collectibles, the Edsel car line is still with us and will still be here, ever increasing in value, long after the jokesters and what they said about it have passed into history. Unfortunately, however, the name has taken on the negative connotation of "disaster," and I doubt that any amount of public relations effort can change that. On the other hand, as the Edsel experience becomes more and more a part of history, fewer and fewer people will remember it.

Credit for the successful launch of any new product is collective, for many heads and hands are involved and no one can actually take personal credit (though some do).

All Ford PR offices were involved in the successful launch of the Mustang, in early 1964, for example, when Henry Ford II approved giving the bulk of the credit for that new line to Lee Iacocca, then head of Ford Division. That alone opened a pandora's box of PR credit-seeking.

Lee deserved much credit for the introduction of that new line, although there was no way he was "the father of the Mustang," anymore than Ed Bernays is "the father of public relations."

Lee was then emerging as a corporate management star and a charismatic media personality, and both Time and Newsweek decided the Mustang introduction warranted serious cover consideration. When both magazines actually did cover stories the same week, however, everybody wanted credit for that coup. (The two magazines cried "foul" and hinted at double-dealing, but that was a false charge.)

Many of us had had a hand in laying the ground-work, but Bob Hefty and his Ford Division PR staff deserved much of the credit for persistence, and follow-through.

Almost thirty years later, I am amused when I read or hear that this PR person of that one "pulled off the great Time/Newsweek cover coup." It simply wasn't so. The story was there for the reporting and that is why both magazines put it on the cover.

Later, when it was all over, I felt certain Henry Ford II had second thoughts about his decision to let his young vice president stand alone for that media blitz. It all added up to the beginning of a never-ending drive for power that would reach a climax a decade later.

The passage of time has a way of changing a lot of things, and sometimes helps to modify or improve a once disastrous public relations image and reputation. President Nixon is finding that out as he diligently works at improving his role in history despite the Watergate disaster, and many observers feel he has made noteworthy progress. President Bush was similarly engaged with a range of PR-type actions during his last months in office, trying to leave the White House on an up-beat note, despite his defeat at the polls.

Only time will tell how history will treat both former presidents over the long term.

Chapter XXI

"What Do I Do Now?"

Henry Ford II liked New York. He liked the city and its ambiance although he may have preferred London, where he felt he was just another face in the crowd. In fact, he arranged for private offices in the city of London so he wouldn't have to go to the company offices in Warley, outside London. He also eventually bought an English country home with a lot of charm and history from Prince Stanislaw Radziwill, the former brother-in-law of Jaqueline Kennedy Onassis. Radziwill had been married to Jackie's sister, Lee. The place was called Turville Grange, and it was a hideaway for peace and relaxation.

Mr. Ford had a private office and a country home in New York as well. His New York City office was located for a number of years at 477 Madison Avenue, and our public relations operation was an extension of it. It was also an office for liaison with the Ford Foundation, located at that time in the same building. Henry Ford II had taken the space on the twenty-first floor to make a statement to those who ran the Ford Foundation and to have his presence felt. It was convenient for him to take the elevator between floors when he chose to, and although his office was considered spartan by comparison with some CEO offices, it served his purpose well. It was paneled in ebony wood, and trimmed with teak, and it overlooked Cardinal Spellman's quarters in the chancery of St. Patrick's Cathedral, at the corner of Fifty-first Street and Madison Avenue. In fact, we could see the Cardinal's colorful vestments being aired from time to time atop the flat roof area of the chancery.

Chairman Ford fought many battles with Ford Foundation management over policies and programs even though he had some hand-picked supporters in the management of that organization. The foundation was actually independent of Ford Motor Company. It had been funded by the sale of Ford stock and in later years did everything possible to distance itself from the company and its president, and later Chairman, Henry Ford II.

Among those who headed the Foundation in the early years were Paul Hoffman, Henry Heald, and McGeorge Bundy. Bundy presented the biggest problem of all for Henry Ford II. The chemistry was bad between them, and Bundy had no intention of allowing the grandson and son of the two men who made the foundation possible in the first place — Henry Ford and Edsel Ford — to exercise any influence over Ford Foundation grants and policy decisions. It lead to a total break in any personal or working relationship between Bundy and Henry Ford II. In the end, Henry Ford II resigned any connection with the foundation and walked away from it in a personal pique. The foundation had divested itself of all Ford Motor Company stock and built a new building in the United Nations area on the East Side of the city. As far as Henry Ford II was concerned, the situation was a major disaster for him, his family, the Ford Motor Company and its dealers, who were on the receiving end of endless complaints about the foundation and criticism of it from Ford owners and community leaders. The feeling was that it had superliberal leanings. Henry Ford II, in fact, had hoped at one point, that there might be some way of depriving it of the use of his name, but that was not possible.

In the end, after Henry Ford II publicly renounced any role in the foundation, and McGeorge Bundy was eased out of his position as president, things took on a less controversial and confrontational dimension and eventually achieved a degree of normalcy. Today, the Ford Foundation is one of the world's wealthiest and most respected philanthropic funds.

Because he liked New York, the Ford chairman would often accept a speech invitation that brought him to town and enabled him to spend time in his New York apartment or go on for a weekend in Southampton, Long Island.

On one such occasion, he was to address financial supporters of the George Junior Republic, a youth home in upstate New York, which functioned somewhat on the order of Boys' Town in Nebraska. Also on the program was Thomas E. Dewey, the former New York governor, who had been a candidate for president of the United States. Mr. Ford's speech had been written at company headquarters in Michigan and not by the staff of our outside PR counsel, because an effort was being made at that time to handle more speech writing and related PR matters in-house. My office had handled distribution of the text of the speech, and I accompanied Mr. Ford to the Waldorf Astoria Hotel, where he was to speak following dinner in the hotel's Empire Room.

I sat at the press table and excused myself occasionally to find out what was going on and to check in with Mr. Ford on the dais. Ruth Lloyd, who handled PR and press matters for GJR, told me at one point she'd learned Tom Dewey was going to speak off the cuff. She said she had no idea what he would say, and I immediately advised Mr. Ford. "What do I do now?" was his immediate reaction, and I was put squarely on the spot. I assumed he obviously did not want any negative comparison with the experienced former district attorney, who would speak extemporaneously while he, Henry Ford II, followed a prepared text.

Charly Moore, our PR vice president, wanted Henry to use the speech his staff had prepared. He was anxious to demonstrate that speech writing for the chairman and other top people could be handled in-house, rather than by reliance on the Newsom organization, and I knew Earl and his staff would also be watching the outcome. In fact, Charly Moore had called me just before I left the office to meet Mr. Ford and asked me to call him at home when the program ended to let him know how things went.

I was in a difficult situation, and I new it. There was no time for all those things to go through my mind, however, and I responded the only way I could in the circumstances. I said: "Well, you're the boss. I think you should do whatever makes you feel comfortable. You have an excellent speech, there's news in it, and I'm sure it will be well received by the audience, but if you decide otherwise, please try to cover the main points in the text." I had no idea what he would do, but I guessed right, as it turned out.

I went back to the press table where I was sitting with Russell Porter, a top reporter for the *New York Times*.

When dinner was over and various housekeeping details out of the way, Mr. Ford was called on first. He rose to his feet and forgot all about the text. He rambled a bit, caught the measure of the moment, and then went on to deliver a fine talk about his experiences at the United Nations where he'd been serving as a delegate with the United States mission. He covered, in his own way, what he felt was significant in the prepared remarks.

He didn't get a standing ovation, but there was strong applause, and it was obvious the audience liked what he had said.

Russ Porter looked at me somewhat bewildered and said, "What do I do now? His text is in the paper." I said, "Russ, Mr. Ford stands behind every word of the text, and essentially that was what he was saying in his own words." Porter rolled his eyes but made no move to go to a phone. When Tom

Dewey got to his feet, he began his remarks by complimenting Mr. Ford on what he had said and the way he said it.

"Ladies and gentlemen" Dewey said, "I happen to know Mr. Ford had a prepared text and set it aside to speak his own mind. It's a pleasure to be in the company of a young businessman who knows what he wants to say and how to say it." There was an immediate round of applause, and Mr. Ford waved to acknowledge it. He had lucked out albeit at some risk.

I headed for Times Square to pick up the first edition of the *Times*, and there was the speech on the first page with Russ Porter's byline. I called Charly Moore right away to fill him in. His reaction was almost unprintable. "That son of a bitch," he said. I think Charly considered it a rejection of his staff's work, but it wasn't. It was Henry Ford II deciding he wanted to be his own man in what he regarded as an awkward situation for him personally. After all, he was just starting out, and Tom Dewey was a seasoned campaigner. He had made the right decision in my judgment, and forget the bruised feelings of Moore and the speech-writing staff. But I obviously didn't put it that way when I made my report to Charly on the phone.

The next morning I received a phone call from Earl Newsom asking how things went. I told him, and I gathered he lost no time in calling Dearborn to needle Moore. I then received a call from Bill Morrell, Charly's assistant. Bill had served with the OSS in World War II and later with UNRRA, the United Nations Relief and Rehabilitation Administration before joining Earl Newsom and then Ford Motor Company.

"John, Charly's nose is out of joint. Why did you call Earl Newsom and tell him about Henry's speech decision last night?" I realized then that I simply couldn't win no matter what I said. I had left to Mr. Ford the decision on how to handle the speech, as I knew I should have. I told Bill Morrell I had duly reported to my boss, as requested, and I hadn't called our PR counsel with any report, because it had been the other way around.

"I told Charly that," Bill said. "I was sure Earl called you but there are a lot of sensitivities at the moment." I told Morrell I understood but ended up having an uncomfortable day. The discomfort eventually passed, however, as it almost always did. But I occupied an unenviable position between my immediate boss, our outside PR counsel, and the boss of all bosses, Henry Ford II.

No one could really tell Henry Ford II what to do or say. No one. He was simply that type of individual. He would listen to you, he would accept advice, and he always respected opinion or comment, or seemed to. He hated phonies — "boot lickers" — and those who curried his favor. He had a good mind of his own, and he operated on a combination of common sense, intuition, and instinct. I found him to be fair, blunt, candid, and even sorry if he felt he had unnecessarily bruised someone's feelings. He was a big man both physically and in his approach to life. I never found him petty, but he could be vindictive, and he could concern himself about detail to an extent that was incomprehensible.

Shortly before I retired, I had responsibility for Ford's participation in a major program in Detroit. It was a World Energy Conference that brought leaders in that field to Michigan from all over the globe. The Arabs, who were very much in evidence, of course, had brought a huge delegation and all of their own food. The Saudi Arabian delegation was headed by Sheik Ahmed Zaki Yemani, advisor to Saudi King Fahd. Yemani, one of the principals of OPEC, had attended my school, New York University. It gave us something to talk about and helped me out of a tight spot the night of the conference banquet, which was held in our guest center pavilion.

Mr. Ford wanted to know everything that was going on concerning the banquet down to the last detail, and it was a situation fraught with problems of attendance, seating, food service, transportation, logistics, and protocol, among other things.

On the day of the dinner, the chairman had me in his office going over everything. He was particularly interested in who would be seated with him and was irritated when I couldn't give him every name at that particular moment. Other activities were scheduled for the same evening elsewhere, and we lacked a final acceptance from a key member of the British delegation.

"I have a problem," I said. Before I could finish he looked at me over his half glasses and said, "I know you have a problem, but who is going to sit there?" I gave him the name of the British delegate. "Fine," he said, but I was winging it. I never did hear from that person, and she did not put in an appearance at the dinner.

At the dinner reception, in a special tent we'd constructed leading into the guest center, I spotted Sheik Yemani with a gorgeous female companion. Yemani was to sit with Henry's wife, Cristina, but I had no seat arranged for the beauty with him. She was an added starter. I went over to Yemani, was introduced to his guest, and immediately said, "Oh, yes, of course, you'll be sitting at Mr. Ford's table. Yemani looked at me as though I had just hit him below the belt. "And you, Sheik Yemani, will be sitting with Mrs. Ford, of course." He nodded and I took them to their tables for introductions.

It was a fine evening under the most difficult of conditions, since we had to cater everything from a specially organized field kitchen. But the chairman didn't like it. He gave all of us a good blast after the guests had departed and he was winding down with a dubonnet-on-the-rocks in the guest center lounge.

"It wasn't very good," he said. The "steak was cold," the "ceiling was too high," causing a sound problem not apparent to the rest of us, and the tables of ten "didn't allow for intimate conversation." He never mentioned a word about the pretty Saudi dinner companion.

At the root of it all were marital and other personal problems he was having at the time that put him in a foul mood. I should have recognized the situation earlier in the day. His marriage was almost on the rocks, and he was involved in a serious relationship with Kathy DuRoss (who would eventually become wife number three). It would not be long before he moved out of his house, first to a suite above his office in the World Headquarters building and then to the Edgar Allan Poe cottage behind the Dearborn Inn, near Greenfield Village.

The Poe cottage was where we had arranged for Arthur Hailey to stay when Hailey was finalizing research for *Wheels*, his book about the automobile industry, which later became a movie. I also worked with Harold Robbins when he researched *The Betsy*, another book about the motor industry, and both Hailey and Robbins were joint luncheon speakers at the Public Relations Society of America National Conference in Detroit in 1972. They filled the ballroom of the old Book-Cadillac Hotel in one of the best luncheon programs PRSA has ever sponsored.

Chapter XXII

A *Fair in the Meadows of Flushing*

Robert Moses made a herculean effort to establish a major city park in Flushing Meadows after the 1939-40 New York World's Fair, but for lack of funds the park was never finished — at least not the way Robert Moses envisioned it.

The fair itself, coming at the tail end of the Great depression, with war clouds gathering in Europe and then, in its second season, on the threshold of America's entry into the war, was considered a success as an attraction but a failure as a money maker. Most world's fairs are, in fact, financial losers. The fair had given a lift to the American spirit after a grueling economic depression period and made people feel good for a change, but the treasury was empty when all bills were paid and the demolition and cleanup completed.

All that remained at the Flushing Meadows fair site in 1941 were a few buildings that were taken over by New York City, and some promenades and walkways, and that, of course, was a big disappointment to Robert Moses, the internationally acclaimed public servant, bridge builder, and parks planner. He had overseen the development of the metropolitan area's updated highway system, construction of the Grand Central Parkway, Jones Beach, the Triboro Bridge Authority, and numerous other projects. But the showcase he'd dreamed of for Flushing Meadows fell short of objective, and it wounded his pride. He would not forget it.

The 1939-40 fair had been well attended and well supported, but the cost of doing things kept going up and up. The man "out front" on that fair had been the pompous and ebullient glad-hander, Grover Whelan. In his own way, Grover Whelan was a prominent figure on the world stage, and with an ever-present carnation in his lapel, he gloried in his assignment as New York's official greeter.

In contrast to Grover Whelan, Bob Moses was more the behind-the-scenes operator, the thoughtful, calculating planner who knew how to ram a project through from blueprint stage to opening day. In my opinion, neither New York City fair could have happened without him.

For the second fair, the 1964-65 extravaganza, Robert Moses was everything, not just the man who could and did get things done. In addition to mover-shaker, he was also the new fair's "man out front." And that caused some problems.

Working with Robert Moses in a somewhat secondary role was Thomas Deegan, a former *New York Times* reporter who had entered the public relations field and established a name for himself as PR counsel to Robert R. Young, the railroad tycoon. Together, Moses and Deegan seemed like a perfect combination. Bob Moses could be demanding and abrasive, while Tom Deegan could be charming and considerate. It was a reversal of the earlier roles played by Whelan and Moses, and everybody thought it would work. For a few short months, it did.

Ford Motor Company was one of the many major corporations, countries, and other entities invited to participate in the first major post-World War II fair. Ford had also participated in the prewar fair. True, it had been only two decades since the 1939-40 fair was held on the identical spot, but a whole new generation had been born and the time seemed right to have another party. Bob Moses, of course, was far less interested in the party than he was in finally completing his plan for the park. He saw success within reach and convinced the city fathers to undertake sponsorship through a New York World's Fair Corporation with a board made up of distinguished leaders from all sectors of city life. Robert Moses and Tom Deegan were at the top. Mayor Robert F. Wagner held an honorary role, as befitted his position.

The postwar years had been good to most business interests and certainly to those in the transportation field. There had been some down years like 1958, but systems were pretty much on a go basis when Ford, General Motors, Chrysler, General Electric, AT&T, Pepsi Cola, IBM and others signed on for the fair in 1962. Charly Moore, who was still our public relations chief, had convinced Henry Ford II and the Ford board that Ford had to participate. He had to overcome the objections of the financial people — what Lee Iacocca always called the bean counters. As it turned out, Ford played a major role in the fair, and the fair was a super showcase for Ford, its people, and its products.

But beyond the decision to participate, all that existed at that point was a contract with the Fair Corporation. There were no specific plans.

Charly very wisely came to the conclusion that Walt Disney and his staff were the people to plan and produce the Ford Pavilion and its ingredients, and a good choice it proved to be. Disney had already been in contact with Ford and with Charly in an effort to interest Ford in a display at Disneyland in California, and everybody thought the two organizations were made for each other. Both were respected American success stories as family-oriented as apple pie and ice cream. They seemed to go together.

Walt Disney liked the idea, Henry Ford II liked the idea, and a deal was made. It was to be a multimillion dollar undertaking, the Disney organization to receive close to one million dollars as its fee for developing the plans for the pavilion and show. Then Walt Disney came up with a novel idea — Ford could forget the Disney fee and apply it to participation in Disneyland after the fair closed. Although appealing, that feature of the arrangement was put on hold. The contract was signed, and all systems had a green light.

I had the distinct privilege of being among those from the company who were assigned to work with Walt and his team in the early planning stages, even though I was in New York and would continue to manage the New York office. It was an added assignment that I could attribute only to the fact that I had demonstrated some flair for show biz. After all, hadn't I led Sammy Kaye's band on the stage of the Capitol Theater and won first prize?

I began making regular trips to Pasadena and Burbank, California, along with Ford colleagues who had other assignments like design, engineering, and architectural liaison. My role was to help in the overall planning of the show with particular attention to where Ford fit in. We didn't want to end up with a major Disney production that didn't do justice to Ford, which was the sponsor and bill payer. The Ford story had to be an integral part of a memorable entertainment feature, and that's the way it was.

Of course, it wasn't as simple as that. There were periods of stress and strain as all of the elements went through a gestation period, and brilliant ideas on paper had to be turned into a reality. That wasn't easy. Some things had to be scrapped, some added, and many changed before opening day.

The general theme of the show was a ride through history in Ford convertible automobiles from the beginning of time to the present and into the future. Disney "imagineers" and master mechanics had created audio-animatronic figures that moved and emitted sound, and you saw them as the action was being described on the car radio. The final sequence, "The World of Tomorrow" turned out to be a grossly oversimplified sequence of scrim, sounds and flaky props. Here we ran into budget problems and had to cut and improvise. But the key elements all hung together in what proved overall to be a highly entertaining experience with a solid Ford PR and commercial message.

I enjoyed working with Walt Disney. Dressed in a sweater, slacks, and loafers, he was the epitome of relaxation, friendliness and warmth. He was so interested in the end result of everything his staff did that he had to be pried loose by his brother, Roy, whenever we got around to the nitty gritty discussions of "how to" and "how much." To Walt the show was everything regardless of cost, and he had actually gone broke several times in his early career by over-spending in his quest for perfection. His brother Roy, who was the financial chief of the organization, was not about to let that happen again — ever. Roy or one of his people would always be on hand when money was discussed, and Walt would excuse himself to go to the restroom or elsewhere and never return. We finally caught on to the routine after a while.

One very major cost problem involved the roof and the exterior design of the rotunda-type pavilion entrance. Initially it was to have been an actual operating waterfall cascading down from the roof with multicolored lights playing on the water at night. When Welton Beckett, Disney's architect, brought in the first concepts, however, the cost projections were out of sight. The weight of the water on the roof structure was also a major factor, and that idea had to be scrapped.

We were sitting around a conference table in Burbank, California, one morning trying to figure out what to do, noodling and doodling when I roughed out a "Jello mold" concept that caught the eye of Disney creative guru, John Hench. John had started out as an animator with Walt and was one of Walt's most valued executives. The *New York Times* referred to him in a feature story in 1991 as the "éminence grise" of the

Disney organization. He is emeritus today, but he was in his creative prime during the World's Fair period.

In fact, Hench and others were dividing their creative time between our project and the planning for Disneyworld in Orlando, Florida. The land in Florida was being bought through third-party channels, and the major elements of the principal exhibits and show features were already on paper. Naturally Walt and his management team hoped we would participate in Disneyworld as well as Disneyland after the New York Fair, but neither ever happened. That was one time the "bean counters" had their way and convinced company management we were in the transportation business, not show business!

"John, let me take a look at what you have there," Hench said that morning. "I think that may have possibilities." What I had done was a rough design, a rather crude "crown roast," with the ribs rounded inward at the top to simulate a reverse waterfall. Behind the arched exterior columns, the outside wall of the rotunda would be surfaced with seagreen glass. And that was it. John Hench quickly produced a finished rendering that everyone liked. The concept was subsequently approved by Ford management, came in within budget, and soon went into production on the site.

When finished, the building was unique and outstanding, and so was the show it contained. It took about eighteen months from concept to completion. In the spring of 1964 we were ready to go.

When I finished my assignment in California, for which I'd been commuting back and forth from New York and Dearborn, I immediately went to work on plans for the press and public launch of the show. Ford had a great household name in the transportation field, but the Disney name was entertainment magic, and we played that up heavily. Editors and writers who either never or rarely covered show business or automotive news were on hand with their wives and children for a Sunday afternoon private preview planned as an all-family event. An earlier VIP reception and preview had brought out the likes of Jim Farley, Sophie Tucker, Buddy Hackett, Red Buttons, and Julie Andrews and a pavilion full of politicians, publishers, financial and business types, and other so-called VIPs. We were off to a running start.

On press preview day for the pavilion and magic skyway show we covered all of the Mustang convertible models on the Skyway ride with special car covers for teaser effect. They were not to be removed until Monday (the following day) when automobile editors and writers from all over the country would see the new models and hear about the new Mustang from Henry Ford II and Lee Iacocca, ride those cars on the Skyway, see the Disney show, and then drive the new Mustangs to their home cities in an over-the-road test of quality and performance. The press "test drivers" were besieged by car buffs and curious motorists everywhere as they drove coast to coast, stopping for gas, food, lodging, or any other purpose.

The Mustang was an immediate stunning success, and Henry Ford II gave the lion's share of the credit to Lee Iacocca, even though it was the end product of many minds and many hands. After all, Lee had sold the concept to the Ford board and obtained the funding to make the project possible. His product reputation was on the line. There were some, however, who felt the Ford chairman had been more than generous to stand aside for one of his young executives.

His late grandfather had been far less sharing, particularly as his company and its products became increasingly successful, and his own name became a symbol of worldwide achievement. At that point, the senior Ford was not inclined to share attention with anyone else.

It was part of the measure of the man — Henry Ford II — that he shared willingly if it was in his company's interest. For at that point in his business life he didn't have to prove anything to anyone. His name was on the building, and with the substantial help of Ernie Breech, he had turned potential disaster into unqualified success. He was in complete charge.

In a remarkable tribute to what Ernie Breech had accomplished for Ford Motor Company, Henry Ford II had made a personal appearance on a "This Is Your Life" television salute to Breech to publicly thank him for helping to save his company and return it to the top ranks of American industry. It was obvious then, and always, that he was ready at all times to give credit where it was due and not claim every accomplishment for himself.

Chapter XXIII

One Million More than '64

The first year of the New York World's Fair was a rocky experience. The fair had been launched with great hoopla and showmanship. Everyone had a shoulder to the publicity and promotion wheel, and P. T. Barnum himself couldn't have done better. The automotive giants and the other leading participants had all spent large amounts of money to create shows, exhibits, and entertainment offerings that were informative, entertaining, and even outstanding — and they were prepared to spend more.

Every exhibitor had had some form of behind-the-scenes advance preview, "look-see," or press event to garner attention for its show or exhibit, and many had retained outside public relations services to work with their own in-house PR staffs. Additionally, the fair had its own substantial press service headed by Bill Donoghue, Mayor O'Dwyer's former press secretary. It was staffed by people like Murray Davis, a Moses favorite, who had been a top writer for the *World Telegram*, and Peter McDonnell and Joyce Martin, two experienced PR professionals. Tom Deegan's public relations organization was also involved even though he was part of the management of the fair organization, working directly with Robert Moses. That, of course, was an obvious and blatant conflict of interest, though nothing was ever done about it. Debs Meyers, a Deegan partner, and another former mayoral press secretary, was the key account executive in the Deegan shop.

There was plenty of PR clout and a tremendous blitz of advance publicity, but not all of it was upbeat. There were the usual labor problems, slowdowns, and a surprising amount of political infighting before the fair ever got to opening day. Much work had to be done on the surrounding highways, road accesses to the fair, and parking. In addition, there were a myriad of other details involving site preparation and exhibitor squabbles. There had also been substantial tugs and pulls with the city owing to Bob Moses's petulance, occasional displays of arrogance, and heavy-handed way of doing things. It often brought him into conflict with Mayor Wagner, who felt at times that city interests were becoming secondary to fair interests, and Robert Moses was acting like he was the mayor.

The other side of the coin, however, was that a major postwar fair in New York City would have been out of the question without Robert Moses. In my opinion, he was the only person with the vision, experience, political and other connections, tenacity, clout, and personal capability to make it all come together as it did.

Despite the infighting and jockeying for influence and management control, some of it now spreading to Moses and Deegan (who seemed to be going in opposite directions), the fair opened on time in April 1964 and seemed to be off to a good start. But after a while it became apparent it was going to be undersupported, not only by tourists and other out-of-towners but even by the home crowd. It was easier to understand the lack of enthusiastic support by those from elsewhere in the country because New York always intimidated many outsiders. The city was too big, too expensive, and too insecure for many of them. The costs of hotels and motels, restaurants, and related expenditures turned off those who might otherwise have planned a trip.

But the hometowners? They simply were caught up in the process of living, working, and commuting to their jobs. They were unimpressed, if not blasé, and a single visit to the fair would suffice for many if not most of them. The fair, however, couldn't cover its expenses and turn a profit on single visits. Multiple visits were essential to the fair's financial health, and they didn't materialize in sufficient numbers that first year.

The fair closed on schedule in October, and everyone was concerned about the 1965 season. Few exhibitors were truly satisfied. The Ford Pavilion, while popular, had fallen short of attendance estimates. Ford attendance was respectable when measured against everyone else's and the disappointing gate overall. But poor results brought out all the I told-you-so-types, who either were antifair or felt that the cost of participating was exorbitant. And it was. For the two-season fair period, Ford would spend in the neighborhood of thirty-five million dollars, and General Motors, substantially more than that. Our financial people did not like what they were seeing at the end of 1964. It was costing dollars per visitor head, and not dimes as originally planned.

Following the first season, I was asked by management if I would take overall responsibility for the operation and devote virtually all of my time to a bail out attempt. Robert Moses felt our pavilion and others hadn't done enough to promote the fair, and there were some strained relations. Our dealers hadn't really been told how to use the fair to their advantage, and Restaurant Associates, our caterers, had to charge us for unconsumed food stocks that were either given away or thrown away. Our dining room and lounge were not fully utilized, for lack of attendance, and staff morale needed a boost.

I said I would do my best, though many friends and press contacts wondered what I was doing spending virtually all of my time in Flushing Meadow. I couldn't at the time tell them about the thirty-five-million-dollar investment, because it was privileged and potentially negative information. It was something we did not want to see or hear on radio and TV and it would have caused major problems at the Ford annual meeting of stockholders.

During the 1939-40 World's Fair Edsel Ford, himself, as company president had come to New York to take charge of the Ford fair project with Fred Black, Ford advertising manager, to assist him. So these major investments always received a lot of top management attention.

Between seasons, I set about making physical changes in the pavilion to allow us to handle more people even if they didn't elect to take the Magic Skyway ride. I visited all our dealer organizations in the northeast region within reasonable driving distance of the fair and told dealers in a slide presentation how they could utilize the pavilion and its attractions and services to their advantage with customers, VIPs and their employees. I was also successful in having top media people and columnists like Bob Considine visit the fair and the Ford, Vatican, and other pavilions between seasons and write upbeat articles. I also cultivated Robert Moses early on, and during the 1965 season, he regularly brought high level guests to our pavilion, where they always received red carpet treatment.

It's almost a dream as I look back on that experience now. I was "Mr. Ford" as I greeted Walter Reuther, Princess Grace and Princess Caroline of Monaco, Cardinal Spellman, Julie Andrews, Chung Park Hee, the president of South Korea, William Conrad, Elizabeth Montgomery, Andy Warhol, Marty Allen and Steve Rossi, Sammy Davis Jr., Dan "Hoss Carnwright" Blocker, and untold other familiar names and faces and hosted them in the chairman's private lounge or in our thirty-seat private dining room. The dining room featured a gold leaf suspended ceiling depicting the four seasons, and close by was a wine cellar that rivaled the best you would find anywhere. The food service was supervised by a Scot maitre d', and meals were prepared by a French chef and an Italian cook and served by four waiters from Switzerland and Germany. The arrangements and the service were "four star" in every respect.

The place was really jumping in the second year, which was a testimonial to a new management approach and an intensified public relations program. But despite those encouraging developments at our own pavilion, the fair overall was not without continuing problems.

The fractured relations between Robert Moses and Tom Deegan continued to worsen between seasons and finally reached a point of no return. We were all busy making press and public appearances to get the fair off to a good start for the 1965 year. Walter Engels, an old friend who was vice president for news and special events at WPIX-TV, featured me on an Easter Parade special with local TV anchor John Tillman, and I was asked to introduce Tom Deegan at a meeting of the Public Relations Society of America at the Waldorf-Astoria Hotel. Under the circumstances, I gave Tom a warm introduction, but he borrowed and copied my remarks and sent copies to every member of the fair's board of directors. Robert Moses was not happy about that until Murray Davis told him how it happened. Then he understood. I simply wasn't taking sides in that no-win internal political situation. I had no desire to get in the middle of their personal differences, and I hoped they could be resolved. Then Tom Deegan abruptly resigned, and Robert Moses was free to do things his own way, right or wrong. Unfortunately, the Moses way was often heavy-handed, and the exhibitors were powerless to do much about it.

Because the fair had become such an intramural political football, it got off to a wobbly start the second year. On preview day, we released thousands of balloons carrying offers of free tickets to anyone finding them. Arjay Miller, then Ford president, cut the line holding the net that released them. The cards came back from far and wide. Later, however, we learned that some of the cards had been pilfered by those inflating the balloons, ending up in the black market for fair tickets. It was impossible to beat a system where people thought honesty was not the best policy.

On opening day in 1965, the fair was under threat of a complete closedown by civil rights activists. We were open to the public for less than an hour when demonstrators sat at the bottom of the escalators that carried visitors from the lower rotunda, the International Gardens area, to the Magic Skyway ride. That resulted in immediate, effective shutdown of our show.

Stuart Constable, a Teddy Roosevelt-type character who had been former Parks commissioner and was a personal friend of Robert Moses, wanted all demonstrators thrown out bodily. Constable was in charge of security for the fair, and that was his quick and easy solution. He said it was necessary under the terms of our contract with the fair to keep the pavilion operating. All pavilions were required to take whatever actions were necessary to live up to the terms of their agreement with the New York World's Fair Corporation, he thundered, and "By God, no ragged army of troublemakers is going to stand in our way." He was prepared to bring in his security force to "throw them out."

We could see prominent headlines, stories, and pictures on front pages and television news shows as the demonstrators were carried bodily out of the building, with the Ford oval (not the World's Fair symbol) displayed prominently. Of course we were unalterably opposed. Ted Mecke, our vice president for public affairs, had come on from Dearborn for the opening, and Joe O'Relly, a company attorney, was also present. Stuart Constable hammered the table, flustered and blustered, with former New York City Police Commissioner Kennedy at his side. Kennedy was chief of security for the fair. We were adamant, however, and felt we had every legal right to decide to shut down our pavilion for that day to avoid a negative press and any further problems. Kennedy agreed privately, but not in front of Constable.

Henry Ford II was kept advised of all developments by telephone and concurred with our position. That was all we needed. In the end, we prevailed. Stuart Constable backed down and left in a huff, and we closed the pavilion for the remainder of the day. The demonstrators lost interest when they found no opposition and realized they would not get their names and faces in the papers or on the evening newscasts. They took off, and the situation was diffused without incident. There were only minor mentions in the press that demonstrations at the fair had closed "the Ford Pavilion and several others," and that was about it. We had won the battle with the fair management at a cost of most first-day visitors, but there would be other days.

During the balance of the season, the fair suffered from lower-than-expected attendance despite every effort to talk the fair up at every opportunity. I often appeared on television interview shows, in news features and columns, and on radio talk shows. My message was always the same: "This is a truly great World's Fair. Where can you go for the admission price of $2.50 and see the equivalent of a broadway theatrical production? Where can you dance to the live music of Guy Lombardo and his Royal Canadians in an open bandshell under the stars? Where can you sample the foods of the world in one convenient location at affordable prices? And where else can you see such an update of science and technology and product innovation from the world's leading corporations in one central location?"

Despite lower attendance at the fair and resulting lower attendance at most of the pavilions, including General Motors and Chrysler, our attendance was up for the entire 1965 season. When we exceeded 1964 attendance by one million visitors, we proudly passed out thousands of lapel buttons with the Ford oval and the line, "One Million More Than '64." They appeared all over the city. We thought it, was a noteworthy achievement, and it was. We were proud of it and Dearborn rated it "outstanding." So did the Public Relations Society of America, which presented the company with a silver anvil award based on the overall public relations success of the Ford Pavilion during the 1965 year.

We could attribute much of our success to the hard work between seasons and the enthusiasm we were able to generate on the part of our young hosts and hostesses who welcomed and looked after our visitors. Every time we set a new attendance and Magic Skyway ride record, I hosted a one-hour end-of-the-day champagne party for our hosts and hostesses in the pavilion lounge area. They loved the recognition of their efforts and began setting new records regularly, I quickly came to the conclusion that they loved champagne. More importantly, one of the dangers was that they were getting six people in cars on the Magic Skyway ride that were built to carry four in comfort. And we had to caution them about that. But they were doing an outstanding job, and it was important to recognize that.

Employee recognition and employee satisfaction, are always part of the bedrock of a sound internal public relations effort.

One interesting development of many during the 1965 season was the presentation of seventy-five-hundred dollars by the Ford Pavilion to UNICEF, Foster Parents Plan, and the United States Olympic Committee. The money came from coins thrown into the fountain and pool that were part of the International Gardens display in the pavilion rotunda. Pennies, nickels, dimes, quarters, and foreign coins from many countries were pitched into the pool every day as if it were the famous Trevi fountain in Rome. Donation of those funds to the three worthwhile causes was well covered by the media during a brief ceremony at the pavilion as we neared the end of the 1965 season.

While on assignment at the fair, I often looked longingly at the huge stainless steel sphere of the world next to the Grand Central Parkway at the fair site. It was the official World's Fair symbol, donated by United States Steel Corporation, and it will be there forever as a lasting remembrance. When the fair closed, I even talked to Jim Moran, a much publicized press agent, about the possibility of placing a smart looking Ford product atop that globe. We could both visualize the photo caption: "Ford covers the world" or "On top of the world with Ford." The idea was tempting, if fraught with risk. I figured if anyone could pull off that stunt, Moran could, because he had gained a lot of notoriety by "selling an ice box to an Eskimo," "taking a bull through a china shop," and "finding a needle in a haystack." Jim was an almost legendary stunt man in the nineteen forties and fifties with a wide following in the media.

I finally shelved the idea. Robert Moses would have had the two of us arrested, or worse!

The day before the official closing of the Ford pavilion and the fair, we hosted a special private luncheon in Mr. Ford's lounge for Cardinal Spellman, Bishop MacEntagert of Brooklyn, and a group of priests and monsignors. The only layperson present was the manager of day-to-day operations at the Vatican Pavilion.

When the Spellman party arrived, I met them at the door with Shirley Jamar, our guest relations supervisor. As we entered the private elevator to take us to the reception area on the second floor, Shirley's assistant pushed the wrong button and exclaimed in dismay, "Oh, my goodness, I've pressed the wrong button. We're going down instead of up!"

"Don't worry, Marie," the cardinal said, "Wherever we go, it's going to be good!"

Chapter XXIV

"We've Been Robbed!"

When the New York World's Fair closed, I again devoted full time and effort to my New York office activities. There was always more than enough to do, and new projects and programs were always on the way from the many and diverse areas of the company's or the Ford family's interests.

I hadn't been free of the fair for long when there was an assignment to work with the Italian Cultural Foundation on a scholarship program that interested Cristina Ford. Mrs. Ford had accepted chairperson responsibility for a fund-raising benefit dinner to be held in the St. Regis Maisonette, and Mr. Ford wanted us to see that her interests and participation were properly looked after. I got the distinct impression he was concerned about the people in charge of the project and what might happen to the money that was raised. I soon found myself working with Bob Boyce, our company security chief and an accountant, to make certain there was no potential embarrassment.

I had worked similarly with Anne Ford, the chairman's first wife, when she became involved with Southampton socialites who were launching a Nixon for President office on the eastern end of Long Island.

I can't say that working with Ford family members ever favorably affected my career, but it most assuredly called for large amounts of caution, awareness, protocol, and respect.

When Charlotte Ford and her husband, Stavros Niarchos, were expecting a baby, we were called from time to time by Phil Dougherty of the *New York Times* society department news staff for progress reports. Phil seemed to make the pregnancy part of his regular beat, so I was designated to keep up with developments right up to the time of the baby's birth.

That led to an interesting experience one afternoon as I was returning from lunch.

I was crossing Madison Avenue to enter our office at 477 Madison when staff assistant Ruth Koupal hailed me from the sidewalk. "Mr. Ford called from his apartment. He wants you to come up right away. I've been waiting out here for you. It seems urgent."

Cabs seemed to be non-existent, so I started "power walking" up Madison with my head half turned. After several blocks of no cabs, I headed over to Park Avenue thinking I might have better luck. The Ford apartment was then in the Regency Hotel. Previous apartments had been in the Pierre and the Carlyle. The Regency was located at Park Avenue and Sixty-second Street, a fair distance from Madison and Fifty-first Street.

Wherever the cabs were that day (and it wasn't raining), they were not on Madison or Park avenues, so I had to lope the entire distance.

When I reached the Regency, I went up to the penthouse level, where there were three neighboring apartments. One was leased by Dan Topping, owner of the New York Yankees; a second by Capt. Eddie Rickenbacker of Eastern Airlines, and the third by the Fords.

I pressed the doorbell, and there was a brief pause before the chairman appeared at the door in robe and slippers. I was out of breath and probably looked and sounded it as I said, "I got here as fast as I could. No cabs on the avenue."

"Come on in," Henry Ford II said, "We've been robbed!"

"Oh boy!" I responded. "I thought something might have happened to Charlotte."

The Ford chairman just stared at me as if he didn't understand what I was saying or what Charlotte had to do with what was going on. She was some months pregnant, however, and having gone through the experience in Miami Beach with Elinore, the thought of a miscarriage went through my mind, though I didn't mention it and dropped the entire subject right away.

"This hotel has lousy security," HFII said. "Those bastards got away with some of Cristina's jewelry and my studs." I could only guess at the value of the studs alone.

"Get the manager up here," he said. "I want to tell him what I think of this place." I called the manager's office and asked if he would please come to the Ford suite right away.

As we were waiting, the chairman of the board of one of the world's best known and most powerful corporations got down on his knees with a credit card in his hand, and said, "Here, let me show you how they did it." He caught me by surprise, and I had to stifle a laugh. As I did, I had a moment of déjà vu. Only a month earlier I had also stifled a laugh, following the Italian Cultural Foundation dinner at the St. Regis. As we were at the elevators waiting to leave, Rosetta Valente, organizer of the fundraiser, had rushed up, grabbed Henry Ford II around the neck, and planted a big kiss on him. He was taken by surprise and annoyed. I stood there chuckling, and he caught me.

"You're next, Buster," he said. And I was, as she headed in my direction.

My thoughts returned to the present at the sound of a knock at the Ford apartment door. Just then the door of the closet, which was being used as a safe, swung open by manipulation of the credit card. I let the manager in, and Henry Ford II told him what he thought of a number of things, including house security. The contrite manager, apologized. He would call the police.

When Mr. Ford became otherwise occupied, the manager took me aside and said, "What can I do? They loan these apartments out to friends, and we never know who some of the people are. A month ago Peter Lawford was up here, threw a party, and ended up in the lobby naked. The Fords weren't even here."

I sympathized and he left. Mr. Ford asked me to call J. Edgar Hoover's office and say Henry Ford was calling. I did, but the FBI director wasn't in, and we were referred to John Malone, then head of the New York office. I called Malone and reported what had happened.

I didn't think the crime was in the FBI's bailiwick, but Henry Ford II and Hoover were personal friends, so all bets were off. Then the phone rang, and it was William Federici, a top police reporter for the *New York Daily News*. It was obvious there was a close working relationship between the police and the press.

"We understand there's been a robbery at the Ford apartment. What can you tell me about it?" Federici asked. I told him very little, as Mr. Ford could not fully inventory the loss until his wife, Cristina, returned to the apartment.

"We understand it could be in the millions," Federici persisted. I didn't think it was that large from some things Mr. Ford had said, but I couldn't put a dollar figure on it.

And that's the way it went. I finally took leave of the chairman, taking all the information with me and relaying it to Jim Cumming, his administrative aide in Dearborn.

That night Henry Ford II, his daughter Charlotte, and Stavros Niarchos were at P. J. Clarke's saloon on Third Avenue when the first edition of the *Daily News* was brought in by Pat Doyle, a police reporter for the *News*. Doyle considered himself a close friend of Henry Ford II and his family. They were often together in Clarke's, and Doyle would entertain the chairman with streetside stories of what went on behind the scenes of the Big Town. Henry Ford II liked P. J. Clarke's hamburgers as much as he might have liked a porterhouse steak at "21." Maybe even better!

And there it was on the front page of the *News*. "Henry Ford Robbed." Pat Doyle told me later that Henry read it out loud to his daughter and her husband and they all laughed. Somehow it must have all seemed different in that setting. The story carried Bill Federici's byline.

I followed the case for a time, checking with the FBI periodically and with the New York police, but got involved in so many other things, I left it to Jim Cumming to handle with the insurance companies and others. The story never received any further attention in the press. If they caught the culprit(s), the papers never reported it, to my knowledge. I think the burglary was another one of life's unsolved mysteries.

One night some months later, I was staying at the New York Athletic Club. My wife called about 6 A.M. to say Charlotte Ford was on her way to the hospital to have her baby. The doctor who would make the delivery had just called our home at the request of Charlotte's mother, Anne to tell me what was happening.

I called the doctor immediately, and he verified everything. I was to advise Mr. Ford at the first opportunity, since I would be seeing him that morning at the New York Hilton Hotel, where he, Arjay Miller, Ford president; and Ed Lundy, Ford's top financial executive, had a meeting with the New York security analysts.

I showered, dressed, had breakfast, and headed for the Hilton. There I met Ted Mecke, who'd come from Michigan for the analysts' meeting, and filled him in. We waited for an opportunity to advise Mr. Ford, who was sitting on the speaker's platform. Finally we caught his eye and got a message up to him. A bit later I was able to report that a baby girl had been born to Charlotte, that her mother was with her, and that mother and child were just fine. I also advised Phil Dougherty and the *Times*, and a story ran the next day. We didn't regard it as much of a scoop.

After the meeting with the security analysts, we all went to the Ford Madison Avenue office. I had arranged a picture session and an interview with Henry Ford II and Arjay Miller for *Forbes* magazine. Jim Michaels, the editor, had scheduled a cover story on the new Ford management team, Ford growth and expansion and plans for the future. Arjay Miller had succeeded John Dykstra as president of the company in 1963, and Henry Ford II had retained his role as chairman. It was now 1966.

I liked Arjay Miller very much. He was a perfect gentleman and sat in my office reading the *Wall Street Journal* as another call came in for me from Mrs. Anne Ford. When Miller heard my secretary announce who was calling, he immediately excused himself to read the paper out in the reception area. He didn't have to do that, but he was exceptionally considerate in the circumstances.

"John, tell Henry that Charlotte and Stavros have decided to call the baby Elena," Mrs. Ford said. "Everything is fine here." I could only assume she was calling from the hospital and was with Charlotte and her husband. It was about noon or so, and Mr. Ford was due at the *New York Times* to lunch with Arthur Ochs Sulzberger, the publisher, and his key editors.

I wondered whose name he would be signing under in the private dining room guest book, and I thought of an earlier time and "Edward, Duke of Windsor," though I certainly never mentioned that to the chairman.

When I went into Henry Ford II's office, he was sitting with Ed Wergeles, the *Forbes* photographer; Arjay Miller; and a *Forbes* staff writer. When Mr. Ford asked if there was anything new, I told him about the latest call from his former wife and the baby's name. "That was quick," he said. "I didn't think they had a name." Arjay Miller suddenly realizing what had happened said, "Henry, you're a grandfather. Congratulations!" Mr. Ford smiled, accepted Arjay's good wishes and those of the two press people and got up to leave. There were no cigars from the new grandfather.

Twenty-five years later, in October 1991, Elinore and I sat in Sacred Heart of Jesus and Mary Roman Catholic Church, on Hill Street in Southampton, and watched Elena Niarchos marry Stanley Olander, a local landscaper and businessman.

Stavros Niarchos was not present at the wedding. He and Charlotte Ford had had a romantic interlude aboard the Greek shipping magnate's yacht in the Mediterranean Sea twenty-five years earlier, and it had led to marriage and parenthood, with Niarchos divorcing his first wife of many years. They were married in Mexico, arriving and departing on a Ford company plane. In the years that followed, they divorced, and Charlotte eventually married Edward L. Downe, a magazine publisher and private investor. They maintain homes in Manhattan and Southampton.

On Elena's wedding day it was her stepfather, Ed Downe, beaming as broadly as the bridegroom, who escorted Elena down the church's center aisle. I had had no occasion to meet Elena Niarchos during the years she was growing up, nor did I meet her that day. I was there simply to see a small piece of family history come full circle.

I could not help but feel that twenty-five years — and indeed fifty years — had a way of changing a lot of things. Henry Ford II had died just a few years earlier, in 1987, of legionnaire's disease, and I couldn't avoid thinking of him during his granddaughter's wedding. He and Elena's maternal grandmother, Anne Ford Johnson, who was present at the wedding, had walked down the center aisle of the same church when they were married in 1941, and his parents and grandparents, Eleanor and Edsel Ford and Clara and Henry Ford, Sr., had all been present on that happy occasion.

Now they were all gone, including "young Henry."

The passing of time is often a mixed blessing.

Chapter XXV

A Farm in Michigan

In March 1967, Elinore and I were on a vacation in California and had just returned to our motel one afternoon from Fisherman's Wharf. As was my custom, I called my office in New York to find out what was going on, because we had no planned itinerary, and they weren't able to reach me.

My secretary, Sally MacLaren, reported that Ted Mecke, our vice president for public affairs, was trying to reach me. Would I please call him right away. Ted told me that one of the key directors of the public relations operation was leaving, and he wanted to replace him immediately. Would I be interested in coming to headquarters after all the years in New York? He needed me immediately, he said, because the Ford annual report, the annual stockholder's meeting, and a world's fair in Texas were immediate and pressing priorities. It would be my decision, however.

It was a major challenge, but the other side of the coin was the long service in New York, the detachment from Dearborn, and the autonomy and freedom of running one's own operation with no one constantly looking on. Performance, of course, had always been the bottom line, and if our office hadn't performed well, there would have been plenty of looking over the shoulder, or worse.

Mecke said he would like an answer by the next day, and that meant a fairly quick decision. I fully understood the pressures and priorities.

I hung up, told Elinore what the conversation was about and her immediate reaction was, "Well, we have to go, of course. They need you for that fair and all those other things. How can you say no?" That was it. Elinore had a way of getting right to the heart of things, so I called Mecke back and told him we'd do it.

"Tell Elinore she won't regret it," he said.

Within two weeks, I checked into the Dearborn Inn and spent the day getting my bearings on the new assignment. That night as I went to bed at the Inn, I felt like some of the World War II inductees at Camp Upton who had left home for the first time and found themselves in unfamiliar surroundings. I had a strong feeling of claustrophobia and thought the walls were closing in on me. I didn't have to pull up roots in New York and go to Michigan, but I had, and I wasn't sure I was going to like it.

I stayed awake staring at the ceiling for a long time that night.

The next day on the twelfth floor of the World Headquarters building, I was walking down the corridor with Ted Mecke when Henry Ford II came out of a conference room. "Well, John, I see you've decided to come out here and see how the rest of us work," the chairman said. "How do you like it?" Before I could respond Mecke laughed and said, "He'll love it. He'll eat Kowalski frankfurters and go to the Red Wings hockey games every Sunday night." We all laughed, but my laugh was a bit hollow. Nobody had to tell me the toughest part of the job would be getting used to the place.

Thanks to Elinore, again, we soon found the right place to live, and that helped a great deal. She had checked available real estate in Ann Arbor, Grosse Pointe, and Bloomfield Hills and opted for an old but charming farmhouse in "the Hills." It had acreage, a barn, and utility buildings, and we soon settled in. In the end, it made all the difference. At one end of the new arrangement was the World Headquarters Building sitting virtually alone in landscaped but open fields that Ford owned, and at the other the daily and weekend escape hatch in Bloomfield Hills, called home. We also kept our property on eastern Long Island, as part of our long range planning. It proved to be a wise decision and a sound investment.

The job itself was fine. I was director of public relations programs and services, and I had a major portion of all public relations operations under my wing, — financial and stockholder relations, educational affairs, and all publications activities, including the *Ford Times* (with two million circulation and published since 1908). I was also responsible for special projects and events of all types. Later, I would acquire the worldwide Ford corporate identity program, responsible for signage of all company-owned facilities and dealerships and all usage of the famous Ford oval. Beyond that, there were innumerable special assignments, such as working with Michigan Governor George Romney on a major statewide public relations campaign to combat pollution and restore "clean water for Michigan." Michigan is a veritable water wonderland from one end to the other, surrounded by the Great Lakes, which contain twenty-five percent of all of the fresh water in the world. But the state faced the same problems of environmental damage and deterioration that have become a plague throughout the world. With the help of a task force headed by Len Barnes, a highly respected editor and Michigan booster, we put together a program that gained wide coverage, public attention, and support throughout the state, and helped reverse a serious negative trend.

The impending World's Fair in San Antonio, Texas, was almost a crisis assignment. It was now April 1967, and the fair — to be called HemisFair '68 — was scheduled to open twelve months down the road. Nothing had been planned because originally there had been a decision not to participate.

That decision had caused a major problem for the company and for Mr. Ford personally, and it had to be reversed at the eleventh hour. That was one of the reasons I was there.

Texas Governor John Connally was honorary chairman of the fair and his friend and political colleague, Lyndon Johnson, was sitting in the White House as president. They were both personally interested in the success of everything that happened in Texas — especially HemisFair. Henry Ford II was particularly friendly with LBJ and a frequent guest at the Johnson ranch. Nevertheless, the Ford chairman, on someone's advice, had signed a letter to John Connally saying Ford Motor Company had elected not to build a pavilion at HemisFair but would, instead, participate by providing an assortment of original *Ford Times* art to be exhibited in the Texas Pavilion.

John Connally, who was later invited to serve on the Ford board of directors, was more than taken back when he received Mr. Ford's letter. He was just short of enraged and picked up the phone to call Allen Merrell, Henry Ford II's longtime aide and then vice president for government affairs. Connally declared that it was unthinkable that Ford would not play a prominent role in HemisFair. What would Lyndon think? Merrell promised he would "get into it right away" and get back to Connally. "The fat," as they say, "was in the fire."

Henry Ford II, who had signed the letter on the advice of others, was embarrassed, and now all systems were go to participate.

Once again we started with a blank sheet of paper and began to dream and visualize. That was what I did on my second day in Michigan. I knew I could call on a range of talented people for help, both inside and outside Ford Motor Company, but we had only one million dollars to work with. That was the original budget, and then Arjay Miller, the company president, took one hundred thousand of that away. The finance people did not like what had happened in New

York a few years earlier, and they were "anti" any fair, no matter where it was being held. Arjay Miller had a finance background.

We brainstormed for a week or two and decided the simplest and least costly thing we could do was rent a geodesic dome as our main exhibit structure and put a show within it. The key feature of the show we decided would be a 360-degree-circular-motion picture developed around the general theme "Ford and its people." On the outside of our theater-in-the-round, we would display products in tasteful settings and at the entrance to the theater, entertain waiting visitors with an "automobile parts band" that had been a popular feature at the New York World's Fair in 1964-65. The parts band instruments had been created from car parts, and they swung and swayed like Sammy Kaye's band without musicians. Following the New York Fair, we had kept the parts band and some of the other elements of the New York show in storage for possible future use. Now it fit our needs perfectly.

Our HemisFair show proved to be one of the most popular on the fairgrounds. It was opened officially by Henry Ford II and Governor Connally. We also used the HemisFair exhibit to launch a new Lincoln car series. It opened with a press and VIP reception, with Henry Ford II and his wife, Cristina, as host and hostess.

Semon "Bunky" Knudsen, who had just succeeded Arjay Miller as president, also planned to attend the pavilion opening with his wife, Florence, but had to cancel plans when Martin Luther King was assassinated in Tennessee on the eve of the opening. Ford employed many African-Americans in plants and offices everywhere, and we wanted it understood our top people weren't attending a fair in Texas during a period of national mourning and possible unrest. Mr. Ford had a luncheon speech to make to the San Antonio Chamber of Commerce on opening day and then he, too, returned to Dearborn immediately.

After the fair was open and operating, we were challenged by the Disney organization for an alleged patent infringement. Disney held patents on a full-circle motion picture technique used in a Disneyland show sponsored by one of the telephone companies. The technique we used, however, was different, developed for us by Display and Exhibits Company of Michigan. While similar, it was not the same even though it produced the same visual effects. The Ford show employed multiple projectors that displayed a variety of scenes that came together on the screen. The Disney show, which was far more costly, could surround the viewer with a single scene. Disney's suit was deemed to be without merit and it was dropped for lack of substantiating evidence. I was somewhat surprised by the entire experience after our close working relationship during the New York World's Fair period. It reminded me of that old Jimmy Walker political campaign slogan, "Will you love me in December as you do in May?"

Several years later, under pressure from our Northwest-area dealers, we participated in still another world's fair in Spokane Washington. It was called Expo '74. The Spokane fair had a "Great Outdoors" theme, as befit that part of the country, and we planned our show accordingly. We decided on a storyline based on the environment, the settlement of the West, and camping through the ages from the time of the Indians to present-day family camping. It concluded with a look into the future, focusing on vehicles designed with outdoor living in mind. I was very proud of that show, which had its own private island setting in the Spokane River.

Once again we used a geodesic dome and constructed a small theater, where guests could see a ten-minute movie produced inhouse by John Holmstrom of our motion picture staff. "The joy of living" was the general theme, and our inspiration was the remarkable success of *To Be Alive*, the award-winning film produced by Robert Flaherty for the Johnson's Wax Pavilion at the New York fair.

After exiting our theater under the dome in Spokane, visitors saw an Indian tepee, a campfire and native equipment, a Conestoga wagon, a functioning waterfall and a stream, George Washington's personal camp cot and footlocker (on loan from the Henry Ford Museum), and a variety of modern and futuristic outdoor equipment often used with Ford products for recreational camping. It was somewhat commercial, but it was entertaining and interesting, and children and their parents enjoyed what they saw and experienced. Once again we felt we had put together a highly respectable show!

When Lee Iacocca and his wife, Mary, came to Spokane to officially launch the pavilion, he told the press and VIP guests assembled for a news conference, "I'm really proud of this exhibit. It's entirely in character with Ford Motor Company's product philosophy that cars and trucks should be fun to own and drive. It also reflects the late Henry Ford's love for the great outdoors."

Henry Ford, Sr., had been a pioneer camper and hosted many camping trips around the United States with guests who included Thomas Edison; John Burroughs, the naturalist; Harvey Firestone, the tiremaker; and President Warren Harding.

We lived in Bloomfield Hills for fourteen years during my time at World Headquarters, and the members of our family who were still at home were happy in Michigan. Grandchildren, who were beginning to arrive on the scene, came often for visits.

Of our three daughters, Sandra, Joan, and Lin, the first two were married, and Lin was in college when we moved to Michigan. John, Jr., was then fourteen, and Kevin, the youngest, was ten. Michigan represented a different lifestyle, and our children particularly liked its winter sports. Sandra and Kevin both married Michiganites, and they still live there with their families.

Elinore busied herself during the Michigan years as a breeder of champion Dachshunds and was often on the show circuit with her niece and cobreeder, Lynne Allen, while I commuted to Dearborn and elsewhere and looked after our farm.

We had a donkey called Birmingham, named after the neighboring town, as well as a ram and a ewe. The ram would butt our friendly Hills policemen on occasion, and the ewe, named Josephine after my mother, surprised us one day by having a little lamb, which Elinore found at the edge of the pasture. The newborn was so small she thought it was a little black poodle. As an animal lover it made her day — if not week!

There were also pigeons and chickens and a pony named Gidget, which Lin brought home from a horse farm. Gidget was so small Lin simply put her on the back seat of the Mustang she was driving. Fortunately, she made the short trip without incident, and Gidget got high marks for that.

Elinore also busied herself working on the fiftieth anniversary of Bloomfield Hills and as a member of the local elections committee.

Because the Grank Trunk and Western Railroad ran through the back of our pasture, the place had been called Whistlestop and we gave the same name to our property on Long Island.

Chapter XXVI

Men for Their Times

I never fully adjusted to working in Michigan and, more specifically, to working at Ford World Headquarters. After almost a full career of working in New York with its special ambiance, tempo, and vitality, anything else had to be a big adjustment or disappointment. In fact, it was both.

Working at World Headquarters was like working in the Pentagon every day. There were levels of responsibility and rank that were nonexistent in a field operation, and almost everything seemed to revolve around committee actions. There were meetings of one type or another at any hour of the day — and sometimes night — to the point that you wondered how people had time to get anything done. In addition, you could feel like a virtual prisoner in the clinical atmosphere of a building that sat by itself out in the country. It was a far cry from Madison Avenue, where you could walk along and see a variety of buildings, businesses, and people, even if they were all total strangers.

No wonder Henry Ford II liked to go to New York or England or almost anywhere — which is not to suggest he was a copout. In fact, he was just the opposite. He was dedicated to his company, and when he wasn't taking a break — which he certainly deserved from time to time — he was on the job every day in that building. I marveled at it myself, and thought I wouldn't have done it if I'd been he, but then, how does one know?

Bill Morrell, who'd been deputy PR chief to Charly Moore and loved to slip into New York as often as possible, had warned me. "John, if the subject ever comes up, take my advice and stay put. You've got the best job in the company. That damned headquarters is a prison."

While that was a somewhat harsh description, it didn't take long to realize the place was somewhat inbred. Ford people talked to Ford people all day long except for the phone calls, and one rarely left the building for lack of time or motivation. Besides, there were very few places to go. The food in the building was better than most local restaurants, but even that was organized. Management ate in its own dining rooms, and it was a pleasant break on occasion just to get in the cafeteria line. (Today, much of that has changed.)

But you can get used to almost anything in time.

Once I took a large contingent of my publications people to New York and Chicago so they could see what went on in the outside world of commercial publishing. They never forgot it. We had lunches, dinners, and shirt sleeve seminar meetings with top editors from *Look, Life,* the *New York Times Magazine, Playboy,* and the financial press as well as with some of the women's magazines. Patricia Carbine, Sheldon Wax and Frank Zachery, top magazine editors, were luncheon speakers, and all of the participants were of that caliber. The trips proved to be great morale boosters and creative shots in the arm.

I spent a total of fourteen years in Dearborn working in and out of World Headquarters, and aside from the venue, there was never a dull moment. No other industry touches the lives of people with the frequency of the automobile business. The industry was, and still is, constantly under review and scrutiny from everywhere — from government, overseas interests, customers, dealers, the media, stockholders, and the public at large. New models were always in the planning stage and were introduced each year, sometimes more often than that, and everybody got involved. There were always new facilities somewhere in the planning mix, such as in Valencia, Spain, where Ford entered an entirely new market with the biggest facilities and sparkling new products ever seen in that country.

There were performance tests at LeMans or Monaco or Watkins Glen or Daytona, and there were labor negotiations, strikes, walkouts, and disruptions on a grander scale than we had ever had to handle in New York. There was indeed never a dull moment, and that kept life interesting.

At one point in time during the late sixties, I made a presentation to the company executive committee on plans for the annual report and the annual meeting of stockholders. As part of it, I proposed that a condensed version of the annual report be distributed as a supplement with the *New York Sunday Times*. That had never been done before to the best of our knowledge and research, and I thought it would be an attention-getter.

Wright Tisdale, our legal vice president and Ed Lundy, the financial whiz, were opposed and their views dominated the discussion period, as Henry Ford II sat mute and others followed suit. Unfortunately, Lee Iacocca was out of town that day, and I had counted on his support. It was the type of innovative action that I felt would have appealed to him. But, no such luck. The supplement idea was "shotdown" despite our efforts to salvage it.

Wright Tisdale said it "smacked of touting the stock," and Ed Lundy was his usual conservative self. The idea surfaced successfully some years later at another company and it was a "tenstrike."

There are times when it is impossible to change entrenched attitudes — particularly when the lawyers and financial people join forces.

I saw much less of Mr. Ford in Dearborn than I had in New York. He seemed to have more meetings to go to than anyone else, and you could see him toting briefing books back and forth to the board and meeting rooms. But, I was able to detect changes in his moods, his temperament, and his physical appearance.

Of course, we were all getting older. I was forty-eight when I went to Michigan, and Henry Ford II was then fifty. I thought he had pushed himself very hard over the years sometimes to the point of self-punishment. He drove himself to the brink at times and on occasion drank himself to that point, as well. So did some of the rest of us. It seemed obvious that his personal life wasn't always happy or serene. And all of those daily pressures were beginning to take an emotional and physical toll. When I got him to read copy or check layouts for the quarterly or annual reports, I noticed that his hands shook. Also he had developed an obvious tick that caused his head to jerk. His face was sagging, and so was his waist; but he plugged away when he could have been doing virtually anything else that he chose to do. He was doing what he felt he had to do, and that was to run his company. To me it was the mark of the man.

When he became separated from his second wife, Cristina, the pressures seemed to intensify. I thought the strain could be felt throughout the building and the company itself.

Then his angina problem intensified, and he ended up first in Ford Hospital and then St. Joseph's Hospital in Ann Arbor. His brother Ben had been similarly struck down one time and had been rushed out of the building. So had several other top executives. The automobile business provided great rewards in terms of job satisfaction and remuneration, but it was not without its risks, penalties, and pressures. They all took their toll.

To add to the pressures and uncertainty of the times, there had been a series of management changes that brought Lee Iacocca to the top level of the company when Semon Knudsen was fired in 1969; and Henry Ford II was having second thoughts about Iacocca, who thought of himself as the most qualified to step into the chairman's shoes.

Lee Iacocca had nothing short of a meteoric rise from his early days as a sales trainee in the Philadelphia offices of the company. He was bright, ambitious, driven, and talented. And he seemed to have more self-esteem and chutzpah than anyone I had ever met. He had degrees from Lehigh and Princeton, and was a qualified engineer and quite possibly the most capable marketing executive in the industry. He was a natural with the media, was always good for a pithy comment, an interview that made news, a solid backgrounder, or a leak on an upcoming product development. He also had a natural instinct and talent for putting product and marketing plans together and had fronted for the team that created and launched the Mustang, one of the most successful car lines ever marketed.

He owed a great deal of thanks for his early rise through the corporate ranks to Robert S. McNamara, one of Ford's original "whiz kids," who brought Lee to Dearborn from Philadelphia and to the attention of Henry Ford II. Mr. Ford was impressed and, in turn, was more responsible than anyone for Lee Iacocca's rise through the Ford executive ranks. Without Henry Ford's approval and support, he would never have reached the topmost rungs of the Ford corporate ladder, though that was not apparent in his best-selling autobiography *Iacocca*, which he wrote with William Novak.

Both Lee Iacocca and Henry Ford II were men for their times. Henry Ford II had earned deserved recognition for ousting Harry Bennett and putting Ford Motor Company on a sound management and financial footing during a period of supreme peril. He became the most recognized spokesman in his industry. Lee Iacocca also represented a major success story, the son of immigrant parents who had become one of the most talked-about members of the new generation of young business leaders, and the potential heir to Ford management leadership.

But had Lee Iacocca pushed too hard? And what had he done to invite his benefactor's distrust?

Lee Iacocca had set early goals for himself, and he was determined that nothing would stand in his way — not even Henry Ford II, as it turned out. That may well have been the biggest personal mistake he ever made at Ford and perhaps during his entire career. But as few people can, he could and did turn adversity to advantage. With a lot of help, he landed on his feet and sprinted to success in an entirely different set of circumstances when Henry Ford II fired him.

At some point in the seventies Henry Ford II apparently became uncomfortable and concerned about some of Lee Iacocca's friendships and associations. It's possible the chairman might have thought of him as a reincarnation of Harry Bennett, standing in the wings and waiting to walk on stage for the final act at the right moment.

Their relationship had seriously deteriorated, and there came a time when Henry Ford II simply didn't trust the man he had brought to the pinnacle of power. He realized something had to be done about it. When Ford was in the hospital at Ann Arbor, he was on the phone daily, checking in various ways to find out what was going on.

"What's that son-of-a-bitch doing now," he would ask. "I'll bet he's screwing around with all the product lines." Ford was a "big car" man, believing that large cars were what the public really wanted, and he was often suspicious of the motives of

Hal Sperlich, a product designer associate of Lee Iacocca. Sperlich and Iacocca both favored smaller, sport-type products at that time.

There was something to be said for both viewpoints, but market timing and economics were the final determinants in most product actions, along with cost and pricing. It was a risky and complex business, at best.

During a meeting one day, there was a confrontation that involved all three. Sperlich challenged Henry Ford's product knowledge in a somewhat abrasive manner. That led to his abrupt dismissal — by Lee Iacocca, who was firmly told by Henry Ford II, "Get rid of him." It was a message to Lee from the chairman that was direct and meaningful, and it was unsettling, if not devastating, because Iacocca had high regard for Sperlich, and needed him.

At Ford, no one's job was sacrosanct except one.

Later, when Ford made his decision to do something about removing Lee Iacocca from his top-level position in the company, he did not fire him outright. He hoped Lee would "pick up his glove and get out of the game," but that didn't happen. Meanwhile, the Ford chairman neutralized him by promoting Philip Caldwell to vice chairman of the company and having Lee report to Caldwell. That infuriated Iacocca, of course, but he did not leave. I think he felt he could bide his time, ride it out, and win the game in the end. That did not happen either.

Interestingly enough, after he became the chairman of Chrysler Corporation, Lee Iacocca took an action identical to Henry Ford's. He brought a General Motors executive into Chrysler over Robert Lutz, a former Ford executive he had recruited, and a man who considered himself Iacocca's successor. It was an interesting irony of corporate history, and Bob Lutz had to be no less unhappy than Iacocca had been when he suddenly found himself reporting to former underling, Phil Caldwell.

Caldwell was a seasoned Ford executive, who had made numerous contributions to the success of the company. He had worked on countless major assignments, and for a number of years, he had worked directly under Iacocca. Now the reverse was true. It was a bitter pill to swallow, and it stuck in Iacocca's throat. Finally, perhaps in desperation, he decided to take his case to certain members of the Ford board of directors he felt were sympathetic to his situation, and he did it while Henry Ford II, then back at work, though on medication, was out of the country on business.

Apparently there was some sympathy for Lee's situation, and when everything surfaced during a board session, which Iacocca did not attend, Henry Ford II said to the board members, "Well, it's either him or me. Make up your minds," and stormed out of the room. Obviously, it could go only one way. The Ford family owned and controlled the bulk of the voting stock, notwithstanding public ownership of the Ford Motor Company. Lee Iacocca was finished, and all that remained was for Henry Ford II to tell him, as he had told Harry Bennett.

Firing anyone was not Henry Ford II's strong suit. He hated it and would avoid it to the greatest extent possible. He would have executives moved to different assignments, placed on early retirement, or fired by someone else, but he simply did not like to do it himself. Aware of the shock effects and the possible public relations implications of such actions, particularly at high levels of the organization, he would also make an effort to condition the individual in advance.

One night in New York when Ford; Arjay Miller; Ed Lundy, vice president for finance; and several of us from public relations were attending a Financial Follies dinner, sponsored by the New York Financial Writers Association, I introduced Mr. Ford to Jimmy Breslin, then writing for the *New York Herald Tribune*.

When Breslin left, Ford was still standing at our table. Sidney Fish, a financial writer for the *Journal of Commerce*, came over to say hello to him. Henry greeted him warmly and introduced Fish to Lundy. "Lundy's the best damn financial man in the business," he said. "He never has any fun, but he makes a totem pole full of money for us." I think he really intended to say a "piss-pot" full of money, but caught himself and changed it. Ed Lundy was nonprofane and one of the most reserved people in the Ford hierarchy. He managed a smile at the comment and waved a hello to Sid Fish.

The chairman then scanned the faces at our table, and said, "They're all great guys, but I don't like him," and he pointed at a colleague sitting next to me. We all laughed and thought it was a joke. The man was a confidante and speechwriter for Lee Iacocca. Some years later, after Ford fired Lee, he called that man at two o'clock in the morning and told him he was fired too. It underscored the potential perils of corporate politics and the unpredictability of Henry Ford II.

When he felt he had to make a move on Bunky Knudsen, the Ford president he had personally recruited from General Motors, Henry II sent someone to see Knudsen and tell him, "I understand you'll be leaving." It was during a Thanksgiving weekend, and Knudsen and his wife, Florence, didn't quite know what to make of it, but it did set them to thinking. It was a conditioning process. The dismissal action actually took place when Knudsen reached the office. The ice had been broken in advance, presumably reducing some of the anxiety and tension, and hopefully avoiding a coronary, or worse.

Virtually the same thing happened with Lee Iacocca. On the night before the final confrontation and firing in Henry Ford II's office, the publisher of *Automotive News*, Keith Crain, called Lee Iacocca to report he had heard it was "all over" for Lee. Crain had received his information from a good source, or he would not have made the call. Some said it was Edsel Ford II, a good friend of Keith's. Iacocca, who already knew he had major problems, then had the night to think about things, even though the action itself was unpleasant and bitter when it happened.

William Clay Ford, Henry's younger brother, who was present when Iacocca was called to the chairman's office and who was an Iacocca supporter, became emotional in the circumstances, but the die was cast, and it was all over for Lee.

Thereafter, with numerous outside offers to consider, Iacocca finally settled on the Chrysler Corporation and wrote automotive history with his turnaround of that company.

A number of Ford executives who were Iacocca supporters, followed Lee to Chrysler. Others came out of retirement to work with him on the Chrysler challenge. And many of them brought along knowledge and files that included Ford styling, product design and marketing plans for the future.

In fact, the concept for Chrysler's highly successful minivan came out of Ford. But to the new Chrysler management's credit, they did it first. It was another Ford "better idea" that got away, but it wasn't the first time that had happened.

In 1976 while doing research at the Ford archives to plan events for the Ford seventy-fifth anniversary program, I ran across photographs of early-to-mid-thirties product designs and show car models that were clearly the forerunners of the highly successful Volkswagen "Beetle." The car had been conceived and designed by John Tardja, a Ford design engineer and it was written about as a dream car Ford product in the automotive magazines of the time.

The car had been unveiled and first displayed in the Ford display area of the Chicago World's Fair, during 1934, as a "mini Lincoln Zephyr dream car."

All the design and engineering information on the Tardja show car concept was shared with Ford of Germany at the time in addition to the public display in 1934. Two years later, in 1936, Ferdinand Porsche, the German automobile magnet, brought forth the almost identical design as the volkswagen, and the rest is history.

The Volkswagen eventually became a postwar marketing success story, and volume ultimately exceeded total production and sales of Ford's famed Model T. To some that was like Hank Aaron or Mickey Mantle beating Babe Ruth's homerun record. It didn't seem possible it could ever happen.

Ironically too, during the early postwar years, Ford was offered the opportunity to purchase the Volkswagen works and merge it with Ford of Germany or operate it separately but turned down the offer. Ernie Breech and Henry Ford II decided it would be more than they could manage with the problems they already had in rebuilding a rundown Ford Motor Company.

That was like passing up IBM stock at ten dollars a share, before it went to a thousand dollars or more!

Henry Ford II with the author's 1903 Model A Ford, the 68th of 1,708 production cars built by Ford in 1903, it's first year in business.

As 1961 President, New York Chapter, Public Relations Society of America, the author presented distinguished service citations to singer Marian Anderson, and Caroline Hood, PR Vice President, Rockefeller Center.

Osmon Osmon, Egyptian minister for reconstruction, is shown explaining the reasons for Egypt's invasion of Israel during the Yom Kippur War in 1973, as the author listens in.

Sheep's eyes, pigeon eggs, and other middle eastern delicacies were served up during a tour of the arab countries in 1974.

Accepting coveted Silver Anvil Award for 1965 year at New York World's Fair. Bob Considine, Awards master of ceremonies, left, and Robert Walcott, PRSA President and presentor, right, in 1966 photo.

Wang Lien Yi, PR representative, Luxingshe, China International Tour Service, and the author, in conversation at the Forbidden City, Beijing, 1978.

Children are the world's best "PR Ambassadors" as the face of this little Chinese girl indicates.

Members of the Board of Management, International Public Relations Association, received by Spain's King Juan Carlos, at the Palace in Madrid. Counter clockwise, Rev. Carlos Tomas, Spain; John E. Sattler, United States; Michael Barzilay, Israel; and Sanat Lahiri, India.

With Arnold Hirsch, 75th Anniversary coordinator, examining gold and silver replica of 1903 Model A, two-cylinder Ford runabout, and other Ford Anniversary promotion items.

Welcoming barnstorming pilot of replica of Lindbergh's Spirit of St. Louis on visit to Ford Airport, Dearborn, Michigan, 1977, fifty years after the "Lone Eagle's" historic flight.

Detroit's Mayor, Coleman Young, at the 1979 World Energy Conference. Mayor Young delighted in referring to Henry Ford II, as "Hank the Deuce", much to the annoyance of family members and Ford executives, who considered the "street slanguage" demeaning.

Lee Iacocca casts a meaningful glance at Ford Board Chairman Henry Ford II, during a meeting that preceded his loss of presidential power and eventual departure from Ford Motor Company.

With the principals of Ariama Paneta Reka (Ariama PR), Indonesian PR firm established in Jakarta, Indonesia, in 1987. (L/R) Mustafa Jatim, Willy Sastranagara, the author, and Harris Thajeb.

Elinore and John Sattler accept Golden World Award for "Excellence in International Public Relations" from Professor Sam Black, Chairman, Board of Judges, International Public Relations Association, Toronto, Canada, 1991.

Accepting the 1991 John Wiley Hill Award for Public Relations Excellence, from Dale Evanson, Awards Chairperson, New York Chapter, Public Relations Society of America. The award was for leadership and significant contributions to public relations.

Thomas S. Carroll, President, International Executive Service Corps, presents IESC's "Service to Country" award to Elinore and John Sattler, for work in Indonesia in 1987, teaching and establishing a PR and communication activity.

iving the Good Life

Working for Ford Motor Company was an exciting, stimulating, and rewarding experience, and the financial and related benefits were substantial. The people who worked for Ford during the decades following World War II were all well compensated at all levels of the organization, from top to bottom. That included assembly-line workers and those who held what might be considered the more menial jobs.

Many members of management with sufficient years of service retired as millionaires. A longtime employee in public relations, a woman who had been an editor of the company's magazine, the *Ford Times*, retired after close to fifty years with the company with a nest egg of close to a million dollars, much of it from the company investment and retirement programs. Workers on the assembly line often had two homes, two or more cars, boats, and numerous other acquisitions for comfort and recreation. The work they did was hard and often confining, but the rewards were generous, and virtually everyone had an opportunity to participate if they chose to do so.

As in everything, of course, there were the daily hazards of life and work and the uncertainties — cyclical downturns in the car business or the economy, products that didn't come up to market expectations, corporate retrenchments, job or departmental contractions, plant relocations. But those were risks to be found anywhere in corporate life as circumstances changed.

On balance, though, Ford Motor Company was hard to match when it came to personal rewards. And no one benefited more than those at the very top of the pyramid, because the "perks" at that level were almost incomparable.

I never forgot my first company bonus. It came at Christmas in the late forties, and it was $2,400. That was the largest lump sum Elinore and I had ever seen. It was a total surprise, and it was tangible evidence of Henry Ford II's plan to share the fruits of his company's progress. Charlie Seyffer, my old regional boss, insisted that we all send Mr. Ford a note of thanks, and we did. I had no trouble expressing surprise and appreciation.

Thereafter there were many bonuses over the years but none with the impact of the first one. In fact, — human nature being what it is — we all expected them, looked forward to them, were disappointed when a poor year might deprive us of them, or as the old human trait of greed took hold, were disappointed if we felt they weren't large enough.

What that first bonus told all of us was that "young Henry" and "Uncle Ernie" were doing a remarkable job of turning the tired old company around, that instead of losing eight million dollars each month, we were beginning to show a tidy profit. This news, suggesting some job security, was just as good as the bonus itself.

While things were always on hold or worse during the bad years, like 1958 when we were out beating the bushes for business, the mood was just as apt to be a bit reckless during the upswing periods. The expenditure of thirty-five-million dollars for participation in the 1964-65 New York World's Fair was just one example of excess, and there were others as well. Some of the financial staff, for example, felt that diversification of the company into five divisions, one of them Edsel, during a period of financial buoyancy represented a high-water mark of bad judgment. Those actions ultimately led to the retirement of "Uncle Ernie" Breech and a number of other high-level executives.

A far more modest excess occurred in the early seventies when the company bought a 727 jet aircraft from Japan Airlines, ostensibly for corporate use. It was reported to be Lee Iacocca's brainchild, and the wags said he wanted as big a toy as Hugh Hefner's. The jet was turned over to the Ford styling staff to be completely refurbished at a cost of countless hours and millions of dollars in time, talent and materials. That project resembled the type of things that went on in the old Harry Bennett days when labor and materials were used for questionable projects, many of them personal, on or off company property.

If Henry Ford II approved of the idea initially, he quickly soured on it, and the jet was grounded almost before it became airborne. The chairman ordered it sold, and the buyer turned out to be none other than the shah of Iran, just before he was deposed by the revolution in Iran. Cristina Ford and her close friend Imelda Marcos had journeyed to Iran prior to the sale to attend a gaudy observance of the 2,500th anniversary of the founding of the shah's family dynasty the Persian (Iranian) "Peacock Throne." The price paid by the Persian potentate was in the range of five million dollars, and overall, Ford barely broke even.

The shah's departure for exile, followed one of the biggest and most ostentatious private parties the world has ever seen. Malcolm Forbes did somewhat the same thing on a more modest scale some years later in Morocco, where he maintained a Moorish castle. Forbes sat on his own corporate "throne," and his party, involving his birthday and an anniversary for *Forbes Magazine*, which permitted a business tax writeoff, attracted a wide range of jet-setters, celebrities, and paparazzi, including Elizabeth Taylor, who also likes publicity, and Lee Iacocca and Lee's companion.

I was aboard the converted Ford jet on only one occasion, in Spokane, Washington, during the World's Fair there in 1974. Lee and Mary Iacocca had flown to Spokane aboard it with guests from Michigan, to officially launch our pavilion at the Spokane Expo. The plane certainly didn't lack for extravagant comfort, and for a moment I thought I was on board Air Force One with another president.

Lee Iacocca was a regular corporate air traveler, as were the Fords. He was often enroute to New York to see his personal barber, according to our New York office transportation supervisor, who eventually became a personal aide and Man Friday to Iacocca. Lee would frequently bring another corporate vice president with him, and when work was out of the way, it was often playtime, with an overnight stay in the Waldorf Towers Suite, which my guest relations staff kept well stocked for the "happy hours" and the good life.

Ed Lundy, the highly-respected company financial wizard, strongly questioned the need for the Waldorf quarters, but Henry Ford II consented to the arrangement for a long time, even though he might never have thought well of the idea. When his relationship with his president soured sufficiently, however, he summarily closed it down. It was another straw in the wind and a message of major changes to come. Lee Iacocca, who aspired to live and operate the way Henry Ford II did, was not going to get "his name on the building" during Henry's lifetime, and he was beginning to see the first of much handwriting on the wall.

But the Ford president wasn't the only one in the executive suite who enjoyed all the perks and benefits at the top of the pyramid. Philip Caldwell, who leap-frogged over Iacocca to become vice chairman and second in command, redid his new office in early American with furniture to match. The cost was said to have reached seven figures and the project had to have had Henry Ford II's approval.

Those were only some of the ways money was spent in the automobile business during the "golden years," before the invasion of the imports on an alarming scale. The Japanese, who swarmed all over Ford and the other companies with armies of camera- and tape-recorder-equipped technicians, finally had to be shown the door by Henry Ford II when it became obvious we were giving the store away. Up to that time, Ford had been fully cooperative in every possible way, until it became obvious we were cutting our own throats to help Japan get back on its feet. And with those actions, the excesses also began to disappear.

Henry Ford II, of course, had grown up surrounded by luxury. Grandfather Ford had indulged his grandchildren with all manner and means of playthings. You could begin with the Rouge plant, where there were engines, trains, and private railroad cars and one hundred miles of track. There were boats named after the children for trips on the Great Lakes to the iron mines of Minnesota, hand-built miniature automobiles to be driven all over the estate grounds, log cabins, and a Santa Claus house in the woods of Fair Lane that was filled to overflowing every year at Christmas time.

Personally, I never thought the indulgences of childhood and youth seriously affected the judgment of Henry Ford II and his brothers. During an interview on "Good Morning America" one time, Henry II was asked what it was like to have his name and his money. He laughed and said, "Well, you have to remember, you can only wear one suit at a time, and we all put our pants on the same way." He went on to say that if people thought he ate steak every night, they were wrong. The truth of the matter, he said, was that he preferred hamburgers. What he didn't say, of course, was that the filet mignon used for the purpose wasn't exactly hamburger meat.

Not surprisingly, he had the tastes his money could afford. His valet would lay out his clothes from a closet full of J. Press custom tailored suits, and his wine cellar was stocked with Dom Perignon and the best wines from the vineyards of his good friend Baron Ilse de Rothschild, in France.

I had a taste of that life when I virtually took up residence in our pavilion at the New York World's Fair. Our food-and-beverage service was catered by Restaurant Associates, then headed by the venerable restaurateur Joseph Baum, who recently redid the Rainbow Room at Rockefeller Center.

I often used Mr. Ford's private quarters in the pavilion to entertain people like Walter Reuther and his wife, Princess Grace, and Cardinal Spellman. The pavilion planners had spared little on the chairman's suite, which featured pumpkin mouton carpeting several inches thick, a concealed ebony bar, custom drapes and furniture, an oval ebony dining table with custom chairs to match, and Philco TV sets suspended from the ceiling. It was fit for royalty, and Henry Ford II used it no more than a half-dozen times over two seasons. It was at my disposal the rest of the time, and we kept it busy during the 1965 season with a constant flow of VIPs.

If anything could be attributed to Henry Ford II's, "royal" upbringing, it was his excellent taste in virtually everything except some of his private affairs. His greatest failing, in my opinion, was when he forgot his good taste and his good manners during periods of overindulgence and overpartying. Having been there myself, I know the best or the worst in us can surface under the influence of John Barleycorn. It was Henry Ford II's greatest weakness and our worst fear as members of his public relations staff. He wanted to be what he could never be, just another person at the party, and it gave us nightmares.

"Never complain, never explain" became part of Ford public relations lore when he used the expression to fend off questions after he was ticketed in California. He had been driving down a one way street with his future wife, Kathy Duross, following a salubrious dinner. At the time, he was still married to

Cristina. It might have been a routine happening if it had involved anyone but a man with one of the world's most familiar names. He felt chagrined, contrite, awkward, and embarrassed. Several days later upon his return to Detroit, he attended a dinner of the Society of Automotive Engineers, and was given a standing ovation when he entered the room to sit on the dais. He was back home again with friends, and with that particular audience, it was "human to err."

During a ball game at Tiger Stadium in Detroit, he was involved in one incident that I'll never forget. It was harmless and funny, but it made the front pages in Michigan and was widely reported elsewhere. He had to go to the men's room halfway through the game, after consuming an assortment of ball park franks and beer. Bob Irvin, a reporter for the *Detroit News* followed him and stood next to him as they leaned against the urinals. After brief greetings, Irvin asked Henry II how he stood on "Soapy" Williams, who was campaigning for governor of the state. "Soapy" was G. Mennen Williams, an heir to the shaving cream fortune, and he lived near Ford in Grosse Pointe.

Henry Ford II's reply was a "shot from the lip." "Soapy?" he said, "I wouldn't vote for Soapy as dog catcher for Grosse Pointe." Bob Irvin took his little exclusive to the nearest telephone, and it was on its way to the front page of the *News* as HFII headed for his box seat at the game.

But that was the nature of politics. Soapy Williams, a Democratic candidate, carried a union label and could be expected to come down on the opposite side of any confrontational issue that involved the management interests of the automobile companies. I doubt it ever had any serious effect on the relationship of the two men, and Williams, who went on to be elected without Henry Ford II's support, turned out to be a pretty good governor.

Chapter XXVIII

"The Only Good Thing That Happened Last Year"

One of the most rewarding assignments I ever had during my thirty-four year career with Ford Motor Company was responsibility for the company's seventh-fifth anniversary. Ford had been founded, officially, on June 16, 1903 in a coal yard office along the banks of the Detroit River, in what is now downtown Detroit. The same date in 1978 would mark the company's Diamond Jubilee.

In a blue paper to management on August 12, 1976, Henry Ford II gave responsibility for planning and carrying out a "suitable observance" to the Office of Public Affairs, of which public relations was the major function, along with government and civic affairs. Mr. Ford said: "The company has had a long and distinguished role in the history of the worldwide automotive industry. In our seventy-fifth year we should be prepared to demonstrate how this lengthy experience benefits our customers, our dealers, and the people in the countries in which we operate." That announcement was followed by another that named me to head the Seventy-fifth Anniversary Program.

We had begun thinking about the seventy-fifth anniversary in a preliminary way as early as 1974, with a series of informal staff meetings to brainstorm and put ideas in the hopper. Preliminary program outlines stretched from a modest, no-budget, "take-advantage-of-everything-that-will-be-going-on" approach to an estimated five-million-dollar extravaganza. We could "cut the cloth to fit the suit," so to speak.

Once Mr. Ford approved the idea of an anniversary program and I was named to head it, planning began in earnest on a daily basis. We immediately formed a working task force from all areas of the company (including overseas), appointed a small staff, and developed an organization chart. There would be an advisory steering committee made up of twelve people with responsibility for specified areas of action, such as community events, advertising and promotion, and international and employee events. A fifty-five-member task force was organized, representing every possible area of company interest and activity, such as product divisions, finance staff, engineering and research, and export operations.

We planned to take advantage of all ongoing actions of the company that would lend themselves to a Diamond Jubilee theme during the year-long program, but we also came up with fourteen specially created projects that had to be funded individually. Those would cost $1,834,000. They included old-car rallies, tours and special events, production of the company's 150-millionth vehicle, press previews and special media actions, publication of anniversary books and related literature, and the biggest ticket item of all, a major motion picture, *The World of Ford*.

The company policy committee held a special meeting in May 1977 to review our plans, and it approved all major projects and the budget. The proposal was then reviewed and approved by the Office of the Chief Executive, which then included Henry Ford II as chairman; Philip Caldwell, vice chairman; and Lee Iacocca, president. The approval actions were just prior to Lee Iacocca's departure.

Members of the Ford family were to provide a basic link with the past, since a number of them were still active in the company. Young Edsel Ford II, for example, joined with New York City Mayor Abraham Beame in a parade and City Hall ceremony. Similar events took place all over the country on June 16, 1977, the kickoff date for the celebration.

Later, Benson Ford, in his last official act before he died one month later, met with Michigan Governor William Milliken and Mayor Coleman Young of Detroit to unveil a state historical marker on the downtown site of Malcolmson's Coal Yard, where the Ford Motor Company had been incorporated seventy-five years earlier. The site is now part of the Renaissance Center area along the Detroit river front, near Ford Auditorium. Ren Center itself had been made possible by Henry Ford's grandson (and namesake) to be a lasting testimonial to the site, the city, its people, and the modest beginning of the Ford Motor Company.

Henry Ford II, William Clay Ford, and Philip Caldwell were on hand when the company's 150-millionth worldwide product, a 1979 Mustang, came off the line at the Dearborn assembly plant.

William Clay Ford was joined by Frank Caddy, president of Greenfield Village, in driving a "newly assembled" 1903 Model-A Ford out of a replica of the original two-story wood-structure Mack Avenue plant, one of the vintage attractions in Greenfield Village. The 1903 Model-A car had been taken apart earlier to enable a group of vintage-Ford car buffs to recreate a scene from the past. They donned period clothing and reenacted the simple assembly operations of the beginning of the century. Testimonial to the success of that stunt were the black-and-white and color photographs that accompanied major news stories about the company's early history and its first commercial product.

Perhaps our greatest success, however, was the motion picture, produced for us by Universal Pictures. It won ten film festival awards. Arnold Hirsch, my seventy-fifth anniversary staff deputy, and I had to do a crash eleventh-hour rewrite of the script, but finally it all hung together. The film told the story of a company that was a reflection of a man and his dream for a universal product that would serve people's needs at a price everyone could afford.

The most lasting contribution of the anniversary however, was the flags that fly today in front of the Ford Motor Company's World Headquarters on The American Road in Dearborn. Putting them there wasn't an entirely original idea. I'd seen similar flags flying in front of the United Nations Building in New York. The flags now in place on The American Road represent every country worldwide where Ford Motor Company has plants and facilities, and they serve as a symbol of friendship and global cooperation.

Because this book deals with some of the fundamentals and elements of public relations, I have included in this chapter a summary of the anniversary program. Overall, it was recognized by the public relations media as a "classic how-to-do-it case study."

The bottom line as far as our "bean counters" and members of the Ford financial staff were concerned was the fact that we not only completed the entire project within budget, but actually saved and gave back $280,000 of the $1,834,000 budgeted. That's the part of public relations every CEO, treasurer, and finance person can understand and appreciate.

In 1979, during a Ford worldwide management meeting in Michigan, Henry Ford II referred to the Diamond Jubilee observance as "the only good thing that happened around here last year," and he meant it. At that point in time, the chairman's personal life was in chaos.

Ford Seventy-fifth Anniversary Program —
A Summary

In 1974, professionals from various Ford public affairs/public
relations functions began meeting from time to time to develop
ways of observing the seventy-fifth anniversary of the company's
founding, which would occur on June 16, 1978. Their proposals
stretched from a modest, no-budget program all the way to a
five-million-dollar extravaganza.

As the anniversary date drew nearer, the planning pace
accelerated. The mass of ideas was tightened into a basic
program proposal to management, supplemented by a list of
possible additions or alternatives. From these, the Policy
Committee in May, 1977 approved a program consisting. of
fourteen budgeted and fifty no-added-cost elements, with a
total cost of $1,834,000. Later that month, the Office of the
Chief Executive gave its endorsement — and the Seventy-fifth
Anniversary Program became a fact of Ford Motor Company
life. Its influence would be felt throughout the company for
the next year and a half.

The program was to be launched with a series of special
events across the country on June 16, 1977, and would peak
— but not conclude — 365 days later. Four employees were
assigned to staff the program office: a public relations
coordinator, Arnold S. Hirsch; an administrative coordinator,
Sharon H. Stepp; a staff assistant, Shirley Przywara; and a
secretary, Barbara A. Hawkins. General direction was provided
by John E. Sattler who in addition to his regular duties as
director of the Public Relations Programs and Services Office,
served as chairman of the seventy-fifth anniversary committee.
John B. Warren was executive assistant to Mr. Sattler for the
first six months of the program.

To ensure companywide involvement, top management of virtually every component had been asked to name a coordinator to serve on a seventy-fifth anniversary Task Force. Some sixty components were represented on the Task Force. In addition, a twelve-person Steering Committee was named, with each member chairing a subcommittee responsible for a special area (e.g., media, advertising, special events, audiovisual, publications). The Task Force served as a sounding board and a communications link to company components. The Steering Committee was more of a working group. The news sub-committee, for example, developed ideas for two dozen news releases, then assigned staff members to research and draft them. These two bodies helped prepare the final program proposals that were presented to management.

The no-added-cost elements of the approved program included use of the seventy-fifth anniversary symbol on all company print and television advertising, outgoing mail, and publications. In addition, several advanced-concept vehicles under development at the Design Center were to be identified as anniversary show cars, and the annual meeting of stockholders and the annual report were to have Diamond Jubilee themes.

Budgeted items included a "Flags of the World of Ford" display at World Headquarters plus a number of exhibits, including one showing the development of Ford advertising through the years and another demonstrating the company's leadership in global communication and weather satellite technology. There would also be special media events to mark production of Ford's 100-millionth domestically built vehicle in the fall of 1977 and production of the 150-millionth vehicle (tallied on a worldwide basis) in 1978.

During the course of the program, virtually every public relations technique was used. There was at least one general news release — usually accompanied by one or more photographs — each month, with special material provided upon request from news media. Leading up to the anniversary date, five press kits were mailed at two-week intervals to four hundred key news-media representatives. Each packet contained two or three stories and a number of related photographs, many of them researched out of the Ford archives.

In addition, a twenty-minute slide presentation on the history of the company was prepared for showing to both employees and general audiences, and three videotape presentations were developed. Two carried anniversary status reports to management across the country and another conveyed a special message to employees from Henry Ford II. A twenty-eight-minute film, *The World of Ford*, produced by the commercial-industrial unit of Universal City Studios, provided a global overview of the company, with the narrative soundtrack available in more than a dozen languages and dialects for showing around the world.

Also utilized were parades, special events, limited-edition books (three published by Ford, two by outside firms), anniversary issues of Company and noncompany periodicals, plus employee, dealer, and community events.

Employees enjoyed anniversary-theme lunch menus throughout the year and attended open-house celebrations on or around the anniversary date. In August of 1977, North American dealers attended special Diamond Jubilee introduction meetings in Detroit and Dearborn, where they got their first look at the 1978 cars and trucks, all of which were designated as seventy-fifth-anniversary products. Many dealers subsequently staged their own anniversary-related sales promotions and/or community events.

On or around the anniversary date more than seventy company-sponsored luncheons were held for civic leaders and VIPs across the country. In addition, special events, such as parades of antique and current-model Ford and Lincoln-Mercury cars, were held in major cities, including New York City, Boston, Chicago, and St. Louis. In Dearborn, history came to life at Greenfield Village, where a group of old-car experts wearing turn-of-the-century clothing assembled one of the remaining 1903 Model-A Ford cars, which had been disassembled for the occasion. Television, cameramen, and newspaper and wire-service photographers recorded every careful move. The car was cranked up and driven off by William Clay Ford, chairman of the Executive Committee and vice president of product design. It then headed an unprecedented motorcade of seventy-five vehicles, one from each year of the company's existence.

News-media coverage of the program, from beginning to end, was exceptional. Four thick clipping reports, produced quarterly, reflect the worldwide attention the seventy-fifth anniversary Program generated. Radio and television coverage, although more difficult to document fully, also was extensive. It is estimated that coverage of anniversary events totaled some six hours of viewing time, on a national and local basis.

The observance also generated substantial showroom traffic at dealerships. Sales of the limited-edition Lincoln Continental Diamond Jubilee Mark V exceeded projections, and additional production was needed to fill demand. All company car lines benefited from the anniversary. The company's sales and profit levels set records in 1977, particularly in the last quarter. And 1978, from a sales and financial standpoint, was one of the most successful years Ford has ever known.

Dealers were pleased, too. "All in all, I think it was a great year," said a dealer in Naples, Florida. "A lot of effort was spent, and quite frankly a lot of cars and trucks were sold." A Texas dealer wrote: "My business actually exceeded my objectives for the year, and for all the assistance I had I would like every Ford Motor Company employee to know that I am grateful." A dealer in Wisconsin commented: "The seventy-fifth anniversary gave me as a Ford dealer a feeling of pride. I believe all the anniversary activities enhanced the image of Ford dealers and Ford products across America."

The anniversary had another effect, less tangible but in a way more meaningful. The observance struck a responsive chord in the hearts of people in all walks of life. Thousands of letters, postcards, greeting cards, wires, and cables flowed into company offices from people all over the world, including some from behind the Iron Curtain.

Within the company itself, commendation for the seventy-fifth anniversary Program came from many levels, starting at the top. Henry Ford II, chairman of the board, noted: "Our seventy-fifth anniversary celebration met with an outpouring of goodwill and good wishes in many countries, and the media gave us a far bigger and more favorable play than many of us had expected." And Philip Caldwell, vice chairman of the board and president, observed, "It was an excellent program — excellently conceived and executed."

Chapter XXIX

An Oasis in Southampton

I retired from Ford Motor Company in early 1980 at about the same time that many others who had joined Ford after World War II were getting ready to leave. I was sixty years old, and felt fulfilled. It was time to do other things. Henry Ford II had announced his own plans to retire and relinquish control to his new management team. He wanted to stay involved in less demanding ways and said he would remain chairman of the finance committee. He intended to devote time to visiting overseas Ford locations as an expression of his appreciation and as a farewell to active participation in the affairs of the company.

I also wanted to do more traveling, but first there was the challenge of completing what had been one of the major undertakings of my life — a family "compound" in the town of Southampton, Long Island. We had bought the original property at Red Cedar Point, on Great Peconic Bay, after the Blue Bird experience.

It was in early 1961 on a Saturday morning when I drove to a real estate office in Westhampton Beach, which I had passed many times on the Montauk Highway. I was looking for a "fixer-upper" and found one through Herbert Bellringer, the agent I met there. Bellringer had a friend he'd worked with at General Motors Acceptance Corporation who was the Chevrolet dealer in Southampton, Arthur B. Hull. Art Hull had just bought part of Clairdale, an estate in Red Cedar

Point, and Herb was the broker. Herb was now looking for a suitable neighbor for Hull, and as a Ford man, I must have qualified. The property was being shown on a limited basis.

The Red Cedar Point property had once been the Penny family estate, but Penny had died, and his widow, Claire, married again and became Claire Dixon. Her neighbors at one time had been Marjorie Merryweather Post and her husband, E. F. Hutton, who had owned the adjoining "Black Duck" Lodge. Claire Dixon raised and showed pure bred whippets and airedales and had a substantial kennel on her property, along with various other estate buildings.

As it turned out, it was the time to be buying property in Southampton or almost any place on the water.

Bellringer showed me the property, which had become somewhat run down owing to Mr. Dixon's death and Claire Dixon's poor health. I had Elinore ride out from Garden City and look it over. She always had vision and "better ideas," and she immediately approved of what she saw. The place had endless possibilities, but it would need a lot of attention.

We settled on what had been the "kennel house" property, a colonial structure used for a number of things — living quarters, dog infirmary, office, and storage. With it came a three-car garage, a dog hospital, dog runs, an estate laundry, and a commercial-size potting shed. Seedling beds ran for a hundred feet behind the potting shed, which was still equipped with workbenches for transplanting and cutting flowers. The huge glass greenhouse that had been part of it, however, was gone. That was a plus, since we didn't need a full-size greenhouse and planned to eventually expand the potting shed.

Several years later we acquired some adjoining property, which had a small English-style cottage and a meadow. The place had great potential for a growing family, and it soon became a thirty-year project. We kept it all the years we were in Michigan and traveled back and forth for holidays and vacations whenever time would permit. That meant many plans could not be carried out for a number of years.

Today, Whistlestop as we call it, consists of four adjoining single and separate properties, each with distinct and individual character. The first and original kennel property we call the Carriage House. It had a huge patio and a carriage shed behind it. The former adjacent potting shed has been expanded to create a barn home, of a type much sought after on eastern Long Island. To build it we bought a 100-year old barn in Michigan and trucked the barnboard and timbers to Long Island, along with brick for the fireplace The brick came from the famous Mission Church in downtown Detroit, which had been located along the waterfront area.

The weathered barn board with its silver grey patina was used for inside paneling.

The English cottage is almost unchanged, but a sizable family room was added to provide more space and comfort.

On the fourth and final parcel, which had been a small meadow, we built a railroad station home to go with a caboose we installed on the property some years ago after obtaining a permit from the town of Southampton. The station home is identical to what was once a working railroad station in the hills of Pennsylvania near Tunkhannock. It features high ceilings, wainscotting, finished yellow pine floors, a station platform at ground level, and baggage carts. Behind the station house is the vintage caboose purchased from the Southern Railroad in 1975 and brought over the rails from Spartanburg, South Carolina, to Hampton Bays. My two sons and I laid the forty feet of track it sits on. The rails, spikes, and ties were provided by the Long Island Railroad, and Bob Kennelly, a professional Southampton house mover, moved the caboose over back roads to the site and installed it with a building crane. Surprisingly, our rail bed wasn't a half inch out of the way, and although the caboose weighs twenty-five tons, in twenty years it hasn't settled more than an inch on its sand base.

Our children, now living in places like Rochester and Kalamazoo, Michigan; Palos Verdes Estates, California; Mansfield, Pennsylvania; and Aquebogue, Long Island, all love the place, as do our grandchildren. It has always been theirs to enjoy.

The area we live in on Long Island is surrounded by parklands, wetlands, and water. Not surprisingly, it was originally an Indian campground, and artifacts turn up periodically. Major excavation in the area frequently reveals piles of oyster and clam shells, and occasionally, old shelters and forts at former Indian campsites.

Red Cedar Point was settled shortly after the village of Southampton itself in the early 1600s. The place once had a small fish "factory," an inn, iron works, a small shipyard, and a one-room schoolhouse, now located at the Southampton Historical Museum.

Whaling ships, records tell us, used the deep water on the western side of the point to unload their cargos. The place is steeped in history, but Red Cedar Point is so secluded, you could drive by and never know it is there.

At some point, the early settlers moved on, and so did all of their Colonial-period enterprises.

Down the road from Red Cedar Point are the oldest cemetery in the area and the oldest homestead. They were owned until recently by an old friend and media contact, Walter Engels, former vice president for news of WPIX-TV. The property is still called Fournier House, as is the cemetery on Red Creek Road in front of it. Both were named for two brothers who built the house during the Revolutionary period. They had been prisoners aboard a British ship in the East River, and escaped by jumping overboard. They apparently then found a small boat and eventually worked their way up the East River, through Hell's Gate, and along the northern shore of Long Island to the Hamptons. There they hid out in the dense woods and built their house near Red Cedar Point. When they died, they were buried, as were their descendants, in what became known as the Fournier Cemetery on the homestead property.

Not far up the road from Fournier House is what remains of Berns's Bluff, the former home of the late Charles Berns, a partner with Jack Kriendler in a speakeasy that eventually became the famous Jack and Charlie's "21" Club. Jack, who predeceased Charlie, was also an early local resident. His former home on Newtown Road, near the Shinnecock Canal, features a "21" Club jockey at the entrance, and part of the original Jack and Charlie's speakeasy bar is still a feature of the home, now owned by Douglas Penny. Penny is a local attorney and Southampton town board member. I am told that Charlie Berns's old home on Berns's Bluff features the other half of the original bar, so Charlie and Jack apparently were partners in everything, and though now both are gone, their colorful contributions to local folklore live on!

If you look across from Jack Kriendler's former home, you see structures that haven't changed since the turn of the century. They are the farm buildings of the Hubbard family, where locals say more than farming went on at one time or another. The Hubbard property, still in the family, is located on the Shinnecock Canal, close to the canal's entrance to Peconic Bay. It was there the rum runners did their unloading during prohibition. Where the prize cargos were taken is a matter of local gossip, for no one kept records for posterity. Earl Pike, a former Southampton town building inspector, who was a Coast Guard chief petty officer during that period, told me he and his boys picked up ten dollars apiece and a personal bottle every time they helped offload the stuff from the rum runners. He was off duty and moonlighting, of course.

Did some of the "amber gold" go across the street and up the street to Jack and Charlie's places? After all, they had those special bars and no one knew the business better.

Walter Engels used to like to show visitors the cistern in the center of a back room of the Fournier house. You'd never notice it, because the cover blends in with the wide plank floorboards. "They used to use this during and after the Revolutionary period in the event there was ever trouble with the Indians," he would say, explaining, "You always had to have access to water." Then he would add, "During prohibition, this is where they hid the stuff before it was trucked to New York." Walt was never sure whether it was Dutch Schultz or Owney Madden, or "Legs" who did the trucking, but as an early *New York Daily News* photographer, he could point out more than a few places in Manhattan where the stuff was served up to celebrities, VIPs, businessmen, politicians, law enforcement officers and any others who had money and who could be trusted.

One day the two of us were walking west on Fifty-second Street, past the "21" Club, and a site where a groundbreaking for a Toots Shor restaurant was underway. Jackie Gleason was on hand, sitting on a steam shovel, and mugging for the press photographers. Walt loved it and felt right at home.

"If I dig much deeper, I may find Judge Crater," Gleason wisecracked, and everybody laughed. The site was where Leon and Eddie's, another noted prohibition-era speakeasy had been located. Leon Enken and Eddie Davis retired, intact. One of their customers, Judge Joseph Force Crater, a man-about-town of the jazz era, disappeared one night, and was never seen again. His fate was the subject of endless speculation. It was generally agreed that he was a victim of foul play, but nothing was ever proved, nor was his body ever found. Like Jimmy Hoffa, of a later day, he simply disappeared without a trace.

The "21" Club, by the way, had its own colorful history, almost unequaled anywhere else. I was in the air force with Maxwell "Mac" Kriendler, a member of the clan, and through him got to know his brothers, Bob and Peter, and uncles, Charlie and Jerry Berns. Mac liked to take friends into the basement of "21" and show them how the family had outwitted the Feds during prohibition by dumping the bar contents from no. 21 down a chute that carried everything into no. 19 West Fifty-second Street, next door. The only way into the basement of no. 19, was through a one-ton steel, concrete, and brick door, eighteen inches thick, that operated by a secret spring latch. The door had ball bearing hinges.

The unpainted red brick basement wall that separated No. 21 from No. 19 was thoroughly pockmarked with holes. Only one of those small holes would accommodate the slender steel wire that could trip the sensitive spring latch so the wall door could be swung open. The revenue agents never found that hole, according to Mac. True or not, it was a great story, especially after a cold martini and before you got your "21" dinner check.

Jack Kriendler enjoyed his home in the Hamptons, according to the late Burton Koons, a former bootlegger who owned a liquor store in Hampton Bays. So did Charlie Berns. Burt Koons and his wife said Jack and Charlie were regulars at the Canoe Place Inn. The inn was a hangout for the landed gentry of the time and was a watering hole, gathering place, and gambling mecca for the Tammany crowd. Al Smith was one of the regulars, and years earlier John L. Sullivan had trained there for his heavyweight fight with James J. Corbett — a slugging match that Corbett won.

According to Robert Keene, historian for the town of Southampton, the owners of the Canoe Place Inn always claimed that Smith, who occupied one of the inn's "cottages," never paid for anything and ran up big bills. When I heard that, it reminded me of a trip to Saratoga, New York, to meet Monty

Woolley, the actor, who was doing some work for us. Woolley invited me to join him at a local bar, one of his favorite hangouts. When he left, he didn't pay his bill. The bartender told me Monty never paid for anything in Saratoga. It was his hometown, and he felt the town "owed him" for giving it celebrity status. Al Smith might have had a similar outlook when it came to the Canoe Place Inn and other haunts of the time.

The Canoe Place Inn is still on the corner of Montauk Highway, Newtown Road, and the Shinnecock Canal, and Jack Kriendler could walk from there to his house across from the Hubbard farm. It was about half a mile up Newtown Road. Charlie Berns was halfway between there and where I live, and that was a good "buggy ride." Today the Canoe Place Inn is a weekend discotheque known as the CPI, which to some old-timers is a sad commentary on the passing of time.

The east end of Long Island has always had its share of colorful characters, from the upperworld, the underworld, and all worlds in between. A couple of years ago, the reputed head of the Genovese mob was gunned down in a Brooklyn restaurant. His name was Carmine Galante, and he lived with a daughter in Hampton Bays.

And then one summer, the FBI and State Police descended on Red Cedar Point. They apprehended a member of the Columbo crime family, who had rented a local cottage in the woods and hidden on the grounds a dozen cement trucks he'd "requisitioned" from a construction site. Subsequent intelligence indicated the authorities then "turned" him, and he testified in a case that sent Carmine Persico and other Columbo family members to prison on tax evasion charges. Victor Puglisi hasn't been seen since and is presumed to be in the witness protection program, or like Jimmy Hoffa, in somebody's foundation.

But those are only a few, if colorful aberrations. The area abounds in celebrities, second-home owners, entertainers, financial wheelers and dealers, members of the old 400 of a bygone social era and international jet setters. Sprinkled among them you will find the bedrock of eastern Long Island, families that settled the area a hundred or more years ago. Their descendants are still here — names like Terry, Penny, Corwin, Hildreth, and Halsey.

On the outskirts of the village of Southampton is the Shinnecock Indian Reservation, where the descendants of the first settlers still live, and a portion of their reservation land is also located down the road from our family compound. Much of the land between the current local Indian property and the main reservation property was bartered to early colonists on December 13, 1640. The transaction was recorded in a deed now in the archives of the town of Southampton. As recorded, the deed states the following:

"Indian Deed of Dec. 13, 1640."

"This Indenture made the 13th day of December Anno Dom. 1640, between Pomatuck, Mandush, Mocomanto, Pathemanto, Wybennett, Wainmenowog, Heden, Watemexoted, Checkepuchat, the native Inhabitants and true owners of the eastern part of the Long Island on the one part, and Mr. John Gosmer, Edward Howell, Daniell How, Edward Needham, Thomas Halsey, John Cooper, Thomas Sayre, Edward Ffarrington, Johnb Sayre, George Welbe, Allen Bread, William Harker, Henry Walton on the other part, witnesseth, that the sayd Indians for due Consideration of sixteen coats already received, and also three score bushells of Indian corn to be paid vpon lawfull demand the last of September which shall be in the yeare 1641, and further in consideration that the above named English shall defend vs the sayd Indians from the unjust violence of whatever Indians shall illegally assaile vs, doe absolutely and forever give and grant and by these presents doe acknowledge ourselves to have given & granted to the partyes above mencioned without any fraude, guile, mentall Reservation or equivocation to them their heirs and successors forever all the lands, woods, waters, water courses, easemts, profits & emoluments, thence arising whatsoever, from the place commonly known by the name of the place where the Indians hayle over their canoes out of the North bay to the south side of the Island, from thence to possess all the lands lying eastward betweene the foresaid boundes by water, to wit all the land pertaining to the parteyes aforsaid, as also all the old ground formerly planted lying eastward from the first creek at ye westermore end of Shinecock plaine. To have & to hold forever without any claime or challenge of the least title, interest, or propriety whatsoever of vs the sayd Indians or our heyres or successors or any others by our leave, appointment, license, counsel or authority whatsoever, all the land bounded as is abovesaid. In full testimonie of this our absolute bargaine contract and grant indented and in full and complete ratification and establishment of this our act and deed of passing over all our title & interest in the premises with all emoluments & profits thereto appertaining, or in any wise belonging, from sea or land within our Limits above specified without all guile wee have sett to our hands the day and yeare above sayd.

"Memorand. Before the subscribing of this present writing it is agreed that ye Indians above named shall have liberty to breake up ground for their vse to the westward of the creek aforementioned on the west side of Shinnecock plain.

"Witnesses of the deliverie & subscribing of this writing.

"Abraham Pierson,"Manatacut, his x mark,

"Edward Stephenson,"Mandush, his x marke,

"Robart Terry,"Wybenet, his x mark,

"Joseph Howe,"Howes, his x mark,

"Thomas Whitehome,"Setommecoke, his x mark,

"Joseph Griffeths,"Mocomanto, his x mark,

"William Howe,"these in the name of all the rest.

"Recorded in ye office at New York Oct 3, 1665, by Matthias Nicolls, Sec."

There is no explanation as to why it took twenty-five years to record a presumably legally constituted deed, even though the native Americans had to use an "X" and could not write their tribal names. They had agreed to an arrangement allowing them to retain the lands that make up the Shinnecock Indian Reservation, adjacent to what would become the Village of Southampton, and the right to use the lands west of their canoe portage trail, which was dredged to become the Shinnecock Canal. Beyond that, the Indians gave up all control over the lands described in the 1640 deed.

Almost three-hundred-and-fifty years later in November, 1992, one of their descendants, Roberta Hunter, a lawyer and resident of the Shinnecock Indian Reservation, was elected to the Southampton town board as a town council member. She had won a narrow victory over entrenched political interests and scored a stunning victory with a successful personal public relations campaign that rallied public support and crossed political party lines. It would go down in "east end" political and town history, and restore dignity and recognition to Long Island's earliest settlers.

If the Dutch struck a bargain when they bought Manhattan Island from the natives for about twenty-four dollars worth of trinkets, the settlers on eastern Long Island struck a pretty hard bargain themselves. The land described in the 1640 deed represents prime real estate. It begins on the eastern side of Shinnecock Canal and runs all the way to the Shinnecock Reservation on the western border of the village of Southampton. Now known as Shinnecock Hills the area, which includes the campus of Long Island University's Southampton College, has hundreds of six- and seven-figure private homes.

During 1991 a developer clearing land for additional home sites there uncovered the remains of the oldest known Indian fortifications and settlement on eastern Long Island. All development on the site was stopped, and what remains will be preserved as a permanent historical site for future generations.

The roots of Southampton town are deep in the sands of time and history, and although changed forever, the area is still one of the most appealing I've found anywhere in forty years of world travel.

Chapter XXX

or Service To Country

I've visited many different countries during the forty years since our first trip to Ireland and Europe in 1952. Elinore has been able to accompany me on many of the trips and feels that Norway may be her all-time favorite. I happen to like East Africa, and Kenya in particular. But we are both agreed that none of the places we've visited can compare overall with what we have in the United States.

One has to travel to appreciate in every possible way what we have at home — the freedom, comfort, food and water, accommodations, taxes, living costs, medical and health protection, and above all the full range of scenic wonders.

The United States has everything — oceans, mountains, fertile plains, water wonderlands, and even desert. Many nations have virtually none of those things, and a good many have only some of what we have. No wonder so many of the world's population would like to live in the good old U.S.A. and are willing to risk life, limb, savings, and almost anything else to do so.

By and large, too many Americans do not appreciate how blessed we are compared to most of the rest of the globe. And somewhat surprisingly, you can travel around a good part of the world and think at times that you never left home. Parts of Germany, Australia, Israel, and a good many other places will remind you of Pennsylvania, Virginia, Florida, Arizona or California; but other areas and nations as a whole are almost totally unique geographically, topographically, architecturally, and culturally.

For example, there is no other place on earth quite like China, in my opinion.

We were privileged to visit China in 1978 after the Nixon-Kissinger visits and spent an absolutely fascinating couple of weeks touring with a group of doctors from various parts of the United States.

Reaching China at that time was an experience in itself, as it sits almost opposite us, on the other side of the world, and flights were rarer, and contact far less frequent than now. We flew to China from New York by way of Romania, where we also spent time, and then to Beijing by way of Karachi, Pakistan, flying over the Himalayas and part of the Gobi Desert. With clear weather most of the way, the sights were incredible, and so was the plane we were on, a Russian Illyushin owned by Romania's Tarom Airlines. It had canvas seats and cargo bays that we used for beds. The Romanian crew spent most of the time taking care of itself and not the passengers, but the views of Mount Everest, Annapurna, and the rest of that snow-covered range, from a height of what seemed only a few thousand feet was something few mortals ever get to see. And while flying over the Gobi Desert can't compare with a flight over the Sahara, it seems just as endless until you get to the outer reaches of civilization again.

And then you're coming in for your first glimpse of the Great Wall of China as you prepare for landing at Beijing International Airport. The Great Wall, said by our astronauts to be the world's most recognizable landmark from outer space, is worth the trip just by itself. It is nothing short of incredible, and we were absolutely fascinated by the "Chinese experience."

Our group of twenty was billeted in the Hotel of Nationalities, an old, *Death of a Salesman*-type hotel on the widest street in

Beijing. A mile to our left was Forbidden City, Tienanmin Square, the Mao Mausoleum, Communist party headquarters and the railroad station. Not far away, in another direction, was the famous Temple of Heaven, the Summer Palace, and other antiquities of that remarkably resilient country — a country that at times seems to have one foot still in the Ming Dynasty and the other somewhere in the twentieth century.

We also were privileged to see and walk along the Great Wall and watch the Siberian Express on its way to Beijing after its trip across Siberia and Mongolia from Moscow. The Chinese have an excellent rail system, widely used but greatly overcrowded. When we left Beijing, we used the rail system to visit a number of provinces, including Nanjing and Shanghai. Four to a compartment was tight, but we made do, and the sights out of the train windows were like a trip through a time machine to another world.

Since part of our mission was to study medicine and medical capability in the cities and countryside, we visited both major hospitals and village paramedic facilities. Several of our doctors ended up donating their own personal equipment, such as stethoscopes, blood pressure devices, and similar items, to some of the "country doctors" who had none and were working under the most primitive conditions.

Those familiar black bags of the medical profession were ever-present in our group, and that was comforting knowledge for the rest of us.

China was a land of contrasts. In a single field we could see an overworked farm tractor, a "walking tractor" not unlike our rototiller, horse-drawn equipment, primitive plows pulled by oxen, and men and women in countless numbers moving dirt stone or lumber on their backs, just as they had for centuries. While all of this was going on, there was an incessant background sound of martial music and high-pitched female voices delivering lectures and propaganda on the merits of the

Communist system. It was a terrible assault on unaccustomed ears. And we wondered how the captive population could take it, day in and day out.

Among the more unforgettable experiences were tours through hospitals that lacked heat. With many forests eliminated or denuded (since the Chinese do their cooking with vast amounts of coke), the country had a major energy problem. All hospital patients were fully clothed in bed, wearing Mao jackets under the blankets. The wards were dormitory style, with no private rooms and no heat. It was March and still very much winter there as well as at home.

The acupuncture operations we witnessed were also not to be forgotten, with the patients smiling and waving to us from the operating tables while long, slender needles were stuck through their arms, shoulders, necks, or legs. We never saw them inserted, but they were the only anesthetic or pain killer used we were told, as Chinese doctors carried on all manner of surgery, including an operation we witnessed to remove a neck goiter. We were fascinated as the patient (a woman) smiled and waved to us while under the knife.

Managing the daily lifestyles and needs of one-billion-plus people is mind boggling, and the Chinese are proud of what they feel they have accomplished, notwithstanding criticism of their system. I believe they will undoubtedly be the last bastion for communism, despite a number of steps already taken in the direction of capitalism. Feeding and clothing all those bodies daily is a tremendous challenge all by itself, and no piece of land is too small to cultivate, including the rights-of-way along the railroad tracks. The Chinese are born farmers, who seem to be able to grow anything anywhere and make it look fresh and appetizing.

Public relations was just beginning to make its appearance in a modest way in China in 1978, and even our guide and host from Luxingshe, the Chinese government tour agency, knew and used the term "PR." I spoke on the subject to students of English and communication at Nanjing University, and there was genuine interest and enthusiasm.

Since then I've made additional trips to China, and it is amazing how the subject and even the practice of public relations have expanded and grown during the past decade. Recent conferences there sponsored by the newly created Public Relations Society of China indicate that there are now thousands of qualified Chinese engaged in various forms of public relations activity in all key areas of China. Even if the numbers are overblown (and they certainly appear to be), progress from now on should be steady as more and more qualified Chinese are attracted to this new field of study. I have also found this same trend in most other developing areas of the world.

The growth of the public relations and communication field may present growing problems for the Chinese government, since an educated and informed public is much more difficult to manage and control than one that is uninformed. Witness the student upheaval in Tienanmin Square two years ago and the increased jailing of so-called dissidents — political prisoners, who receive no trials. The winds of change are blowing all over China, as indeed they are over Asia as a whole, and television is behind much of the change, as people see and hear for the first time what is happening in the rest of the world.

The continuing spread of knowledge and information can no longer be contained and controlled by the Chinese government as TV satellite "dishes"spring up throughout the cities and rural areas of the country.

In the years since 1978, I have made many work and professionally related trips to all of the continents, including a four-day trip down the Nile River with Rosalyn and Jimmy Carter when they visited Egypt in 1983; a visit to the Nobel Peace headquarters and an audience with Crown Prince Bertil, honorary chairman of the Nobel Awards Committee; an audience and meeting in Madrid with King Juan Carlos of Spain; participation in the historic east-west public relations seminars in Vienna, and Budapest in 1988 that brought public relations practitioners from both sides of the old iron curtain together for the first time in a strictly professional way; and trips to Africa, Australia, Southeast Asia, and the Middle East. In all of these areas public relations was showing signs of healthy, if not dynamic, growth and increasing maturity and professionalism.

During 1987, after retiring from Ford, I was doing a considerable amount of pro bono work and I was on a trip to Zimbabwe in southcentral Africa when I received a call from Ted Okie, a recruiter for the International Executive Service Corps in Stamford, Connecticut. He asked me if I would go to Indonesia for several months to help some nationals there establish a public relations and communication business. I said I would after I completed my work in Africa.

The IESC was founded in 1964 by Frank Pace, David Rockefeller, and others who had served our government from time to time. They saw the need for American expertise overseas to help small businesses, particularly in the developing nations. IESC is nonprofit and receives funding from the Agency for International Development as well as from corporations and individuals with an interest in its work.

Volunteers who take on IESC assignments are generally retired or semiretired former executives. Their travel and living expenses are provided while they are out of the country working on projects. Additionally, their spouses are encouraged to accompany them and participate.

I was pleased to take on the Indonesian project, since Elinore could accompany me, and it was a part of Asia we hadn't previously visited. We were quartered in the Mandarin Hotel in Jakarta during our stay.

I went to work in July 1987. As it turned out, my tour would require twelve-hour days, seven days a week to accomplish what I knew was needed to get my "clients" in the public relations business during the three-month period I was there.

I was to work with four highly placed Indonesian nationals. The principal was Sharif Sutardjo, who headed an "umbrella" business known as P. T. Ariobimo Perkasa. Under that umbrella, Sharif had at least a dozen businesses, including some that dealt with shrimp farming, palm oil refining, and shipping, and oil brokering. The public relations counseling service was to be an entirely new venture, started from scratch and would be managed by Mustafa Jatim, Harris Thajeb, and Willy Sastranegara.

Harris and Willy had diplomatic backgrounds and Mustafa was a banker. Harris's father and uncles had represented Indonesia in it's diplomatic service all over the world, including Washington, D. C. Willy Sastranegara had also served in Indonesia's diplomatic service and had just retired as a member of President Soeharto's palace staff where, curiously enough, his duties included food tasting for the president. It was a special assignment later taken on by Joop Ave, who eventually was to head up Indonesia's Office of Tourism and Travel. It was hard to make the connection, but it was obvious that those who survived food tasting went on to better things.

Mustafa Jatim served as president of our fledgling PR service, which they named P. T. Ariama Panata Reka. I abbreviated that to Ariama PR as one of my first recommendations.

It was another of those assignments where you start with a blank sheet of paper and let the creative juices flow. This time, however, although virtually nothing existed prior to my arrival, I had a game plan based on my experience in launching Ford's first public relations office in New York, all those years earlier, plus the experience of a full career.

Nevertheless, we still had to arrange office facilities, hire preliminary staff, establish office procedures, and cost controls, and get the business launched in the short space of ninety days. It was a difficult challenge in a totally new environment, particularly when I learned that my executive team, while experienced diplomats and chamber-of-commerce types, were unfamiliar with most of the basics of day-to-day public relations. I soon found out they preferred to leave the nitty-gritty of the business to me and concentrate on executive management. And that became something of a major problem for me.

The bottom line was that I had to give all four principals a short course in elementary public relations while I was recruiting people, getting the office started, creating in-house and client literature, planning VIP and press introduction programs, and putting out feelers for business.

It did not hurt, of course, that the principal of the group, Sharif Sutardjo, was a close friend and business associate of "Bang Bang" Soeharto. They both had shares in an Indonesian oil business known as Mindo Oil and were tied into the state-owned oil monopoly, Pertamina.

The Soeharto family, it soon became apparent, had a veritable hammerlock on many of the best businesses in Indonesia. While I was there, the country was being referred to by some locals as the next Philippines, with obvious comparisons to what had happened to Ferdinand Marcos when he strapped his country financially during his presidency. There wasn't any question the Soeharto family had taken good care of all family members. They held interests in, and control or ownership of, numerous enterprises, including some that were government regulated.

To his credit, however, and unlike President Marcos, President Soeharto was doing an excellent job of transforming Indonesia from a tribal-feudal society into a more democratic, industrially developed society, even though he ruled like a dictator. Indonesia, with its 13,000 islands that stretch from

Australia to mainland Asia, has 180 million people and is the fourth largest nation in the world, after China, India and the United States. Its potential for growth and economic success is substantial and hopefully will be shared with its growing population.

Prior to my departure for home in September 1987, Ariama PR was launched with a VIP reception and press conference at the Mandarin Hotel. Coverage in the Indonesian and English-language press was extensive, including an article in the *Fortune* magazine of Indonesia, *Swasembada.*

As "bread-and-butter accounts," the new firm had the subsidiary businesses of the parent company, Ariobimo Perkasa, and we made a presentation to Joop Ave for the contract to handle Indonesia's participation in the World's Fair in Brisbane, Australia, to be held the following year, 1988. Ariama PR won the account, and when I went to Australia in 1988 to attend the World Congress of Public Relations at Melbourne, I visited Brisbane to see the fair and critique the Indonesian pavilion show.

It was an excellent exhibit, and Ariama PR handled all public relations activities, from opening day press conference to closing-day ceremonies.

Elinore and I enjoyed Indonesia and its people. She taught english to students at a local school and to the staff at the Mandarin Hotel while I was otherwise occupied, which was most of the time. Before we left for home we did manage some sightseeing and a side trip to Bali, a beautiful and mystical island with its Hindu temples, melodious bells, and daily religious observances.

When we returned home, we were invited to IESC Headquarters in Stamford, Connecticut, where Tom Carroll, the president of the International Executive Service Corps, presented us with its Service to Country Award and a gold medallion in recognition of our contributions to the IESC program. Our work in Indonesia was also recognized by the International Public Relations Association, which gave us its coveted Golden World Award for the uniqueness and success of the project.

Chapter XXXI

Closing One Door and Opening Another

It was late 1979 that I decided to retire from Ford Motor Company, after almost thirty-five years of service. I had handled my various assignments to the best of my ability and thoroughly enjoyed the work. I had also had a lot of fun doing it, and that was important to me. My efforts and the results achieved were always rated excellent or outstanding during annual management performance reviews, and as a person I felt fulfilled and blessed. It isn't everyone who finds the right niche in life.

Henry Ford II had said I could stay on with Ford Motor Company for as long as I wanted, in view of the job I'd done, and especially during the trying period of the seventy-fifth anniversary year, when everything but our celebration efforts seemed to be going wrong. But things were changing, as they always do. Old friends and colleagues were leaving, including the chairman himself, and it simply wasn't going to be the same anymore. Besides, at sixty years of age, there was still time to do other things — perhaps another challenge elsewhere, the chance to spend more time with Elinore, to travel to distant parts of the world. She'd been the patient partner for all those years at Ford and had to raise the family and look after things at home so often while I was elsewhere.

I decided I would become a selective consultant on public relations matters, doing only what I wanted to do as a sole proprietor, and call myself Sattler International, and that's what I did. Under the terms of my executive retirement, I was available to Ford Motor Company as a consultant for a period of years, as needed. I also decided to devote a good part of my time to community service and to volunteer activities, something I had always done over the years because I felt, and still do, that we all have an obligation to give something back during our lifetimes, particularly to our fields of interest and our communities.

Before I left Ford at the end of March 1980, I sent personal notes to Henry Ford II, Philip Caldwell, and Don Petersen, who had been named president following Lee Iacocca's departure. I also sent a note to Lee, with a piece of Ford seventy-fifth anniversary etched glass. The glass was a small oval of original rear window glass from the Model-T era and it carried the anniversary logo. We had sent them to VIPs and members of the press as mementos. They were highly prized by all who received them and have since become collector's items. In his note to me from his home in Bloomfield Hills, Lee Iacocca wished me well and thanked me for remembering to include him.

In my note to Henry Ford II, I told him what a rewarding and memorable experience my service with Ford represented and that I would always feel I was a part of that great organization. I also told him I was proud to have been part of a unique experience during his years of company leadership. In his reply, he thanked me for my "many contributions to the company's progress" and went on to say that "applying the same dedication you displayed here, I'm sure your new ventures will be a big success."

I have spent the decade since traveling, lecturing, writing, and doing pro bono service, along with selective consulting assignments. Because of the years at Ford, nothing has caught my interest any more than a project at the University of Michigan to write the definitive history of Ford Motor Company, covering the period when I was there. An earlier history covered the period from Henry Ford's birth through his death in 1947.

It was written by Dr. David L. Lewis of the university's Graduate School of Business Administration, and Dr. Lewis is leading the team on the present assignment.

I have had the pleasure of working with Dave Lewis on the current project, providing some of the research and oral history tapes. As part of his research, he has traveled the world during the past several years, visiting overseas Ford locations and taping interviews with current and retired Ford employees and executives. More than seven hundred interviews have been conducted, including thirty hours of taping with Henry Ford II, prior to Mr. Ford's death in 1987, Mr. Ford destroyed virtually all of his personal papers on the premise that his life was his own personal business and should not be subject to the scrutiny given the private affairs of his father and his grandfather. Henry, Sr., of course, almost never threw anything away, and his personal papers became part of the Ford Archives following his death. It has been said the collection contained both "treasure and trash."

It was during the private taping sessions with Dr. Lewis that Henry Ford II discussed in some detail the final few years of his life and the much publicized events leading up to the confrontation with Lee Iacocca and the latter's dismissal. Ford's version of those events has never been told. The tapes were to be put under lock and key for the balance of his lifetime and not revealed in any way until five years following his death. Five years have now passed, and whatever new information Mr. Ford chose to provide will find its way into the manuscript of the university's scholarly reference work, scheduled for publication during 1994.

Lee Iacocca contends that Henry Ford II "left no stone unturned," to try to get something on him that would justify the events that took place at Ford Motor Company in the late seventies and his eventual dismissal in 1978. Did he?, beyond the fact that there was a highly visible worsening of personal and operating relationships between the two men? What happens in 1994 may hold the answer to that question.

Meanwhile, having passed over Robert Lutz, the president of the Chrysler Corporation, to bring in a General Motors executive, Robert Eaton, as he prepared for his own retirement at the end of 1992, Lee Iacocca seemed to cast himself more and more in the image of the man he criticized in his autobiography — Henry Ford II. Robert Eaton headed GM's overseas operations until the Chrysler chairman named him vice chairman and heir apparent, much to Bob Lutz's disappointment. Lutz has said he will accept the arrangement and remain on the Chrysler team just as Lee Iacocca did when Henry Ford II named Philip Caldwell vice chairman and passed over Lee. Will Ford history repeat itself at Chrysler? That remains to be seen.

One thing is certain, during the years at Ford, Lee Iacocca was often prone to emulating Henry Ford II. As he rose through the ranks to become Ford president, his custom-tailored suits increasingly reflected the expensive tastes and style of the Ford chairman, and he also expected the same degree of recognition, respect, staff support and corporate "perks" enjoyed by Mr. Ford.

Doron Levin, Detroit Bureau Chief of the *New York Times* summed it up in the lead paragraph of a feature story about the Chrysler chairman's desire to prolong his stay at that corporation even as he was presumably making plans to retire. "Lee Iacocca has been many things in his storied automotive career," the *Times* story pointed out, "but one important goal has eluded him. For what he wants most is to be like Henry Ford II, who ruled the Ford Motor Company as if it were a fief, whether he was in the executive suite or in retirement."

There is little doubt Lee regarded himself as having full entitlement to the topmost job at Ford and did everything possible to achieve that goal. It was the only part of a carefully thought-out career game plan that didn't work out — at least at Ford. To his credit, however, he found another way to get to the top of the pyramid at a different time and in a different place.

The hardest thing of all, sometimes, is to face up to the fact that the game is almost over.

Chapter XXXII

Changing The Map of the World with PR

When I entered public relations in 1940, it was a vastly different field of work than it is today. The changes have been almost as substantial and surprising as those that have occurred in the world as a whole.

Publicity was the name of the game in the early days, and in the case of nations, propaganda, which was essentially the same thing but often sinister, controlled, and contrived.

The techniques and methods of public relations were simple and direct. Everyone tried to get something said or printed that was upbeat, informative and that would result in favorable impressions. That applied to corporations, labor unions, community and philanthropic groups, individuals, and even to entire nations.

In some respects, the goal hasn't changed that much, but the game plan and the techniques most assuredly have. To paraphrase George Bush, public relations used to be a simpler, kinder business than it is today.

In 1971, I spoke to a group of students about career opportunities in public relations and some of the changes that had taken place since I entered the field in 1940. Among other things I said: "It wasn't too many years ago that some of us went to lunch with a reporter with just a news release in our pockets and not much more on our minds. Today, we have to do considerably more homework, because our work has become increasingly complex and our media contacts so much smarter, better educated, and more informed. We start by studying a thick, sectional binder containing briefs on subjects such as environment, consumerism, emissions controls, air bags, alternate power sources, race relations, low income housing, and similar subjects that touch the ongoing interests or concerns of Ford Motor Company or the transportation industry."I also said: "And when we meet the press, which is often, the reporters and editors are a different breed from those we worked with two and three decades ago. They are younger, sharper, and better informed, and their research is more thorough, wide ranging, and penetrating. They want facts, unvarnished, unembellished, and straight." Two additional decades later, in 1993, I wouldn't say it any differently. The old days of quid pro quo are gone forever.

The press has become increasingly demanding, and its members are under greater pressure to get the story, whatever it is, and condense it into a shrinking amount of space and air time. And as the media have diminished — particularly newspapers — there is less and less opportunity for public relations practitioners to offer up what was once derisively referred to as puffery or even what might be regarded as legitimate "soft" news. Those are the kinds of stories, of course, that bring a warm feeling to the heart and mind of every chief executive officer as he or she reads the newspapers and magazines or watches TV. In contrast, the "downer" subjects too often surface, concerning sinking profit margins, product failures, service problems, employee unrest, walkouts, contract losses, or a major crisis of one type or another.

It's a meaner, leaner world out there today, and media people know it as well as anyone as they fight to stay competitive, financially solvent, and ahead of the competition in readership, viewing audience and ratings.

My remarks in 1971 were about the situation in the United States rather than the world at large. Public relations had its deepest roots here, though the British also lay some claim to a pioneering role in the field.

Public relations is now practiced to varying degrees almost everywhere in the world — but particularly in the sixty-two countries with eighty-three organized PR associations and groups. The level of professionalism and expertise, however, varies greatly. And so do the working relationships between PR people and journalists. In some countries, particularly those in the Third World, public relations today is about where it was in the United States shortly after World War II — just beginning to emerge in terms of concept, growth, and understanding. And although, to my knowledge, it was rarely, if ever, the case in the United States, in many parts of the world it is still necessary to buy your way into the media. This is known as the "no pay, no play" concept.

In southeast Asia, for example, where there are close to three billion people, who speak four hundred languages and dialects, getting any message across represents a major challenge. And the area is growing and changing so rapidly that the problem can only be intensified with the passing of time. But the potential is equal to the challenge, for Asia's economy is said to be expanding at a rate of close to three billion dollars each week.

Complicating the problem even further is the fact that in many areas of the world, ignorance, suspicion, and lack of education on the part of the public and lack of professionalism on the part of too many PR people have made the purpose and the role of public relations suspect. Frequently the lines between public relations, publicity, promotion, marketing and propaganda become so blurred, there is hardly any distinction among them.

The International Public Relations Association, with close to one thousand professional members in seventy countries, is attempting to bring order, understanding, and increased knowledge to the still emerging field. It meets twice each year in different worldwide locations and conducts briefings and seminars to further knowledge and acceptance of the field. IPRA was founded in 1954 and is attempting to do on a global basis what the Public Relations Society of America, with its fifteen thousand members, has done through its 100 chapters in the United States since 1948. Both organizations, through their highly professional annual conferences and seminars, are attracting an increasing number of members and guests who want to learn more about the field and sharpen their skills in an increasingly sophisticated and complex world society.

Two recent examples of the dramatics of modern public relations that wouldn't have happened quite the way they did without the far-reaching effects of radio and television are the Ross Perot experience and the fall of worldwide communism.

Ross Perot, although he had been a prominent business personality for many years, appeared to come from out of nowhere in a challenge for the presidency of the United States. A simple though widely watched appearance he made on a TV talk show led to an almost overnight meteoric rise in his public recognition and popularity. His timing, if accidental, was almost perfect, as people everywhere appeared to be fed up with "politics as usual." People were ready for a change and thought Ross Perot could provide the answer. And remarkably, in a very short time, public opinion polls rated him as high or higher than President George Bush and the Democratic candidate, Bill Clinton, who was then in the lead.

Overnight, however, Ross Perot's popularity, as reflected in the polls, plummeted when he declared suddenly that he was not a candidate and appeared to walk away from his volunteer organization of supporters. Many of his supporters were shocked and incensed. The reaction represented a rapid and major change in the way a large segment of the public perceived Ross Perot, and while he said at the time he wasn't concerned about his image, his former advisors said otherwise. "Ross quit," the *New York Times* quoted one advisor as saying, "because his image was beginning to come under attack in the media and he hadn't expected that to happen." When he finally did quit, it worsened matters. He was referred to by many as a quitter and "the yellow rose of Texas."

The bottom line was that Ross Perot's personal public relations hit a new high and a new low within a matter of just a few weeks first because of statements he made and then because of the withdrawal which did not register well with the general public.

What happened not only took Ross Perot by surprise — which it shouldn't have — it angered and unsettled him. He could not and would not let the press and public reaction permanently mar his reputation. He had acted in haste, exercising questionable judgment when he abruptly terminated his candidacy, and he soon resolved to return to the campaign to clear his name, but it would be on his own terms and by his own methods. He did return in early October 1992, just weeks before the election.

Many of Ross Perot's former supporters and most professional political observers were skeptical when he returned as a serious candidate. Most gave him little chance of recovering lost momentum and his former standing in the polls, and they were right. Remarkably, however, he did recoup a great deal of the support he had lost and made a respectable showing in the November election. And while he never fully recovered from his abrupt departure, he regained a remarkable degree of respect and support, because the public in general liked what he was saying, was disenchanted by the other candidates or the political system as a whole, and wanted a change. If anything, Ross Perot epitomized that change.

And while he didn't carry a single state, candidate Perot did wind up with substantial voter support, almost twenty percent of the more than six million votes that were cast.

It still remains to be seen to what degree he will be a political factor in the future, but it now appears obvious his image and reputation have rebounded to a substantial degree from the lows of the post-June 1992, "no-longer-a-candidate" period.

Such are the ups and downs and sometimes volatility of changes in public perception, public opinion, and public relations.

The cave-in of communism throughout eastern Europe and elsewhere in the USSR, after four decades of the cold war, is another dramatic example of the impact of worldwide public relations and public opinion.

Vaclav Havel, a political prisoner of Czechoslovakia before he went on to become its president, said in early 1990 while addressing a meeting of the Voice of America, "You informed us truthfully of events around the world and in our own country as well. In this way, you helped to bring about the peaceful revolution which has taken place." The truth, served on a regular basis, had a tremendous impact on the people of Czechoslovakia as well as all the other nations in the Soviet orbit, including the USSR itself. Information presented regularly and honestly is a powerful force for molding and reinforcing public opinion. And it is only a matter of time before we see more of these positive developments as what remains of communism falls apart.

Some years after his retirement from the British intelligence services, Sir William Stephenson, the man called Intrepid, said: "Totalitarian powers don't have to answer to their people for their actions. They don't have newspaper and television outlets probing and watching their actions constantly. Our primary defense against them, therefore is, more than ever, *information*."

And more recently, in a speech to students and faculty at the American University, Washington, D. C., in February 1993, the newly elected President of the United States, William Jefferson

Clinton, said essentially the same thing in discussing world political and economic changes. "Products and services have become global," President Clinton said, "and most important of all, *information* has become global and has become king of the global economy. In earlier history, wealth was measured in land, in gold, in oil, in machines. Today, the principal measure of our wealth is information: its quality, its quantity, and the speed with which we acquire it and adapt to it."

Focusing directly on the fragility of the moves toward democracy and greater freedom behind what was formerly the "Iron Curtain," the President concluded: "If we were willing to spend trillions of dollars to insure communism's defeat in the cold war, surely we should be willing to invest a tiny fraction of that to support democracy's success where communism has failed."

Vladimir Pozner, a prominent and respected Russian journalist, stated recently that United States "propaganda" was "more sophisticated and effective" than that of the Soviet Union. In his book *Eyewitness*, published by Random House, he says the United States did a more effective job of public relations for its policies and positions than did its USSR counterparts. He also says that people in the United States accepted the premise that communism was bad even though they didn't know enough about it to make a serious judgment, and he credits United States "public relations interests" with successfully creating a "bad image" of communism.

Pozner also takes the position that the achievements and benefits of the Soviet system were never well reported in the United States, owing to failure on the part of those in the USSR who were responsible for projecting a better image. At the same time, he believes, the Soviets failed to instill the idea of the "ugly American" in the minds of its own people, because sixty million of them were tuned in daily to the Voice of America and the BBC and believed what they heard. (The same thing is happening in communist China, today.)

Pozner also looks on the fall of Michail Gorbachev and the rise of Boris Yeltsin as resulting from world stage "public relations developments, actions, and pronouncements." He warns, however, that the jury is still out on whether or not Russia and its satellites will continue along the present path toward capitalism or return to a form of socialism/communism because of disillusionment, economic pressures or inability to change.

During the World Congress of Public Relations in Toronto, Canada, in 1991 and the annual conference of the Public Relations Society of America in Phoenix, Arizona, the same year, I had several conversations with Alexander Borisov, the founding president of the newly formed Soviet Public Relations Society. During those conversations, he told me he feels public relations is helping to transform his country from a totalitarian society to a democratic society. The reason the coup involving Michail Gorbachev failed, Borisov says, is that the old-guard Soviet hardliners ignored the power of public opinion, while Boris Yeltsin seized the moment to support Gorbachev, cause uncertainty in the ranks of the coup conspirators, and take control. He contends that the old leadership of a society molded by propaganda underestimated the role and significance of communication as an agent of change, and that it was a major blunder.

As this book goes to press, Boris Yeltsin is under fire for his economic policies and authoritarian control, and the strong public support he once had is being severely tested. The weeks and months ahead will provide a major test of his popularity, and his survival for the ebb and flow of public opinion and support is relentless and ever-changing.

As Vladimir Pozner said, the jury is indeed still out regarding the final outcome of change in the eastern European and Soviet area. It is also out on many other things that are happening in the world-at-large today as well as on the future of public relations itself.

From rather modest beginnings, public relations has grown to a point where it is a major consideration and a factor in our daily lives, whether most of us realize it or not. It has become and will continue to be a major factor in world affairs. When I began my career, half a century ago, I thought I knew virtually everyone in the field, it was that small. Today, there are said to be half a million people working in public relations throughout the United States and at least that many, or more, elsewhere in the world. In just a few short years the number of public relations practitioners in China alone is said to have grown to nearly 100,000, and many times that number are studying various aspects of the field. The source of this information is Chai Zemin, the former Chinese ambassador to the United States, who is currently the president of the recently formed China International Public Relations Association.

Where the future will take the public relations field is anybody's guess, but no one can question its usefulness and its need as the world enters a new millennium, with a range of shared problems that include religious and tribal wars, "ethnic purification" drives, toxic waste control, trade wars, Aids and other health problems, air and water pollution, global warming, wildlife destruction, famine, drought, garbage problems, erosion, deforestation, rain forest destruction, and an almost staggering number of other plagues that simply don't go away and often seem to defy solution.

It seems to me there is hardly another field where the need for experience, talent, and dedication is greater, and I am proud to have had some part in the development of the field during my lifetime.

Epilogue

During the period this book was planned, researched, written, edited, and printed, the world continued to change for better and for worse, as it always has and always will. The ebb and flow of public attitudes and opinions continued to rise and fall with as much certainty as the tides of the world's oceans.

Some individuals, groups, corporations, and nations were the beneficiaries of the changing times and circumstances. Others were not. Some experienced unexpected impacts and crises that temporarily or permanently marred or seriously damaged their reputations. Others, through good performance and positive actions, enhanced their reputations. Those who experienced setbacks will, hopefully, recover in time. Some, however, may not.

One company that experienced unexpected negative notoriety was Denny's Restaurants, when a group of African-American United States Secret Service agents claimed discrimination by one of the chain's restaurants. The group said it received no service while a group of colleagues at a nearby table received prompt attention and service. The second group was made up of white agents, with one exception.

Denny's attributed the incident to inexcusably poor service and apologized for what happened. The public at large, however, undoubtedly had mixed reactions. By most, the incident will probably soon be forgotten, but not by all.

The Pepsi Cola Company also found itself the sudden target of major media attention when syringes and hypodermic needles began to turn up in freshly opened cans of its product. Virtually all of the incidents, which occurred across the country, were attributed to consumer tampering or malicious efforts to embarrass the company. None were taken lightly, however, and the net immediate effect was a crisis situation for the worldwide company and its products.

No organization needs an experience like that, no matter how minor, isolated, or even quickly resolved. In both instances, Denny's and Pepsi Cola received widespread media attention over an extended period.

Also, on the world stage, the United Nations, and the United States and its European allies came under fire for what appeared to many to be a lack of clear-cut policy and action concerning the ethnic problems and bloodshed in Bosnia-Herzagovina and indecisiveness in Somalia.

And at the topmost levels of the United States government, President Clinton experienced major media, congressional and public pressure following a series of highly publicized gaffes and policy waffles. Some key administration appointments boomeranged, causing consternation and embarrassment; some Presidential personal actions seemed totally out of step with public needs and interests; and more than a few of the administration's public statements seemed ill-timed and misunderstood. The net result was a series of "fire-alarm" actions, including a major overhaul of staff personnel and procedures in the White House communication operation.

The American public voted for change in leadership and policies when Bill Clinton won the 1992 Presidential election. What has happened since then and during Mr. Clinton's first six months in office proved to be a major disappointment to many Americans, including many who voted for him. His approval rating was at the lowest level of any President since Harry S. Truman held the office more than forty years ago.

Can President Clinton recover? It most assuredly will take more than a change in White House communication policy, management and operating procedures to bring it about. Those changes can and should help, however, for public perception and approval — public relations — will certainly be a factor in his future. As another President, Abraham Lincoln, once said: "You can fool all of the people some of the time, and some of the people all of the time, but you can't fool all of the people all of the time."

During the past year, the term "public relations" became increasingly familiar to millions as it appeared more and more on the front pages of respected newspapers and on nightly radio and TV newscasts. The media are more understanding and accepting of the term and what it represents, and leaders of business, government and countless other interests have become increasingly familiar with what public relations is all about and how it can serve their needs.

Much still remains to be done, however, to advance broad understanding and acceptance of public relations as a valid field of specialized activity. That also applies to those who labor in the "vineyards" of the field. Good personal conduct and solid job performance are the yardsticks by which we are all measured.

The ball, as they often say in the sports world, is still on the playing field and the goal posts, while in sight and attainable, are yet to be reached. Nevertheless, it was a vintage period in many respects.